CRIMINAL LAW IN NIGERIA

A MODERN APPROACH

CRIMINAL LAW IN NIGERIA

A MODERN APPROACH

LAWRENCE ATSEGBUA
LL.B. (East Anglia), LL.M. (London), LL.M. (Alberta), B.L.
Professor of Law and Dean, Faculty of Law, University of Benin, Nigeria

VIOLET OMON OKOSUN AIGBOKHAEVBO
BA (Lagos), LL.B, LL.M (Benin), BL; Ph.D (Benin),
Senior Lecturer, Faculty of Law,
University of Benin, Benin City, Nigeria.

SUNDAY OMOKHUDU DAUDU
LL.B (Benin), B.L., Faculty of Law,
University of Benin, Benin City, Nigeria.

malthouse MP

Malthouse Press Limited
Lagos, Benin, Ibadan, Jos, Port-Harcourt, Zaria

First Published 2012
Revised 2021
ISBN: 978-978-58979 -9-9

Malthouse Press Limited
43 Onitana Street, Off Stadium Hotel Road,
Off Western Avenue, Lagos Mainland
E-mail: malthouselagos@gmail.com
Facebook:@malthouselagos
Twitter:@malthouselagos
Istagram:@malthouselagos
Tel: 0802 600 3203

International Distributors:
African Books Collective, Oxford, UK
Email: abc@africanbookscollective.com
Website: http://www.africanbookscollective.com

ACKNOWLEDGEMENTS

This book would not have seen the light of day without the assistance of friends and colleagues. We are grateful for the support of our colleagues at the Faculty of Law, University of Benin. We are also grateful to our families for their support and encouragement.

We thank Mrs. Christie Ohiokhai who typed the manuscript for her patience in ploughing through our difficulty hand writing.

In all things, we give God the Glory.

PREFACE

William Paley, the eighteenth-century English theologian and moral philosopher, once said that an apology is called for whenever the public is presented with a new book in an area previously traversed by others.

This book is however justified for several reasons. First, no comprehensive work on Criminal Law has been published since the text by Okonkwo and Naish, now in its second edition 1980. Secondly, this book is the product of an analytical research work which took three years to complete. It also has the advantage of being up-to-date, with recent Nigerian and English cases.

This book is made up of fifteen chapters. In chapter one, we examined the nature, definition and function of the criminal law, while in chapter two, the elements of criminal liability is examined. Chapters three and four deals with strict liability and corporate criminal liability respectively.

In chapter five, the issue of vicarious liability is x-rayed, while chapter six deals with sedition. Inchoate offences are the subject of chapter seven and participation in crime is discussed in chapter eight.

Homicide, which covers murder and manslaughter is extensively discussed in chapter nine. Chapters ten and eleven examines offences related to property. Sexual offences which have assumed a wide proportion is examined in chapter twelve and in chapter thirteen, corruption is discussed. In chapter Fourteen, the topic of terrorism which has now found inroad into our country is examined.

Finally, the defences to criminal liability are examined in chapter fifteen.

We have also made extensive references to the penal code, which is applicable in the northern part of Nigeria. Also, were applicable, references were made to relevant English statutes.

It is our sincere hope that this book will be of immense assistance to students and researchers on criminal law.

We have stated the law on the basis of materials available to us as at 29th February, 2012.

Professor Lawrence Atsegbua
Professor Violet Omon Okosun Aigbokhaevbo
Dr. Sunday Omokhudu Daudu
Faculty of Law, University of Benin
5th April, 2021.

ABBREVIATIONS AND ACRONYMS

CA	Court of Appeal
CC	Criminal Code
CJ	Chief Justice
COP	Commissioner of Police
CPA	Criminal Procedure Act
CPS	Crown Prosecution Service (UK)
DoD	Department of Defence (USA)
EFCC	Economic and Financial Crimes Commission
FATF	Financial Action Task Force
ICPC	Independent Corrupt Practices and Other Related Offence Commission
J.	Justice
JCA	Justice of Court of Appeal
JSC	Justice of the Supreme Court
LGBT	Lesbian, Gay, Bisexual and Transgender
NPF	Nigeria Police Force
OAPA	Offences Against the Person Act
PC	Penal Code
PW	Prosecution Witness
SC	Supreme Court
SCN	Supreme Court of Nigeria
VAPPA	Violence Against Persons (Prohibition) Act
WACA	West African Court of Appeal

TABLE OF CASES

TABLE OF STATUTES

NATIONAL

STATE/REGION

Eastern Region

Anambra

Bendel State

Imo State

Lagos State

FOREIGN

CONTENTS

CHAPTER 3: STRICT LIABILITY OFFENCES

CHAPTER 4: CORPORATE CRIMINAL LIABILITY

CHAPTER 5: VICARIOUS LIABILITY

CHAPTER 6: THE OFFENCE OF SEDITION

CHAPTER 7: INCHOATE OFFENCES

CHAPTER 8 - PARTICIPATION IN CRIME

CHAPTER 9 - HOMICIDE

CHAPTER 10 - PROPERTY OFFENCES

CHAPTER 11: OTHER PROPERTY OFFENCES

CHAPTER 12: SEXUAL OFFENCES RAPE

CHAPTER 13: CORRUPTION

CHAPTER 14: TERRORISM

CHAPTER 15: DEFENCES

Chapter 1

NATURE, DEFINITION AND FUNCTION OF CRIMINAL LAW

INTRODUCTION

According to Smith and Hogan,[1] "it is now rather unfashionable to begin law books with definitions." The authors however concede that a law book must be concerned with the legal meaning of crime; and the reader is entitled to know what it is, and how it functions. Whatever difficulties may arise concerning the definition of crime and its exact nature and function are surmountable. In this chapter, the nature, definition and function of the criminal law are examined. No definition of crime can be exhaustive. The reader is presented with a plethora of views on the subject of crime. These views encompass the definition, nature and function of criminal law.

Criminal sanctions, necessity for criminal sanctions, utility of punishment and defences to criminal responsibility are also examined.

NATURE, DEFINITION AND FUNCTION OF CRIMINAL LAW

The nature, definition and function of criminal law are interrelated. A good definition must encompass both the nature and function of the criminal law. According to Black's law Dictionary,[2] a crime is an act or omission that the law makes punishable; the breach of a legal duty treated as the subject

---

[1] *Criminal Law*, 5th Edn (London: Butterworth, 1983) p. 17. Smith, Hogan and Ormerod's *Criminal Law*, Sixteenth Edition (Oxford: Oxford University Press 2021).

[2] 11th Edition.

matter of a criminal proceeding. Glanville Williams[3] is also of the view that a crime is an act capable of being followed by criminal proceedings having a criminal outcome. Henry S. Maine provides a further explanation. By stating:

> understanding that the conception of crime, as distinguished from that of wrong or tort and from that of sin, involves the idea of injury to the state of collective community, we first find that the commonwealth, in literal conformity with the conception, itself interposed directly, and by isolated acts, to avenge itself on the author of the evil which it had suffered.[4]

In Nigeria, the Criminal and Penal Codes use the word offence and not crime. However, the word criminal appears in the Codes and also in the Constitution. In this chapter, both the words "crime" and "offence" are used interchangeably.[5]

Offence is defined in section 2 of the Criminal Code as "acts or omissions which render the person doing the act or making the omission liable to punishment under this code."

The difficulty in defining crime is further compounded because of the dynamic nature of law. The law is not static. It changes overtime, thus making it difficult to give a definition of what constitutes a crime.[6] What is not a crime today may be a crime tomorrow; for example, driving without wearing a seat belt, is now unlawful.[7] Similarly, what is a crime today may not be a crime tomorrow. A good example, according to Smith and Hogan,[8] is suicide. Suicide was a crime in England until August 3, 1961, when, by the Suicide Act 1961, it became perfectly

---

[3] "The Definition of Crime (1955) 8 C.L.P. 107

[4] *Ancient Law* 320 (17th Edit. 1901)

[5] See also Okonkwo & Naish, *Criminal Law in Nigeria,* (Lagos, Spectrum, 1980) at p. 18-20

[6] Christian McAlhone & Rebecca Huxley-Binns, *Criminal Law - The Fundamentals*, 2nd Edit. (London Thomson- Sweet & Maxwell, 2010) at p. 2 See also Hon. Justice M. Nasir, "*Criminal Justice: Restitution, Compensation and Victims of Crime in Nigeria" in Compensation and Remedies for Victims of Crime in Nigeria,* Bola Ajibola Ed. (Lagos: Federal Ministry of Justice, 1990) 13 at 15

[7] McAlhone & Huxley-Binns, ibid.

[8] *Supra,* note 1 at p. 17

lawful to kill oneself. Smith & Hogan will prefer to give characteristics of a crime rather than attempt a definition. They, therefore, give the following characteristics of a crime:[9]

i. **A Public Wrong**- Crimes are generally acts which have particularly harmful effect on the public. Sir Carleton opines that:[10]

> Crime is crime because it consists of wrong doing which directly and in serious degree threatens the security or wellbeing of society...

The public nature of crimes is evidenced by comparing crime with civil procedure. The basic distinction between crime and civil law lies in the nature of the appropriate remedy provided by each. Civil law is basically aimed at compensating the person whose rights has been infringed by the award of damages. According to Stanton,[11] the criminal law exists to express the state's condemnation of particular forms of misconduct by means of punishment.

ii. **A Moral Wrong** - Crimes are acts which are morally wrong. Whether an act ought to be a crime simply on the ground of its immoral nature, according to Smith and Hogan,[12] has been the subject of vigorous debate in recent years.

The *Wolfenden Committee on Homosexual offences and Prostitution*[13] in England was of the view that the enforcement of morality is not a proper object of the criminal law. This view has been challenged by Devlin,[14] who opined that:

---

[9] Ibid. at p. 17

[10] *Legal Duties*, at p. 233 -234, referred to in Smith & Hogan, ibid. at 18.

Modern Law of Tort (London: Sweet & Maxwell, 1994) at 8.

[12] *Supra*, note 1 at 19.

[13](1957) CMND 247.

[14] Morals and the Criminal law (reprinted in the Enforcement of Morals) (1965), pp. 7-8, 14-17.

I think it is clear that the criminal law as we know it is based upon moral principle. In a number of crimes, its function is simply to enforce a moral principle nothing else. [15]

Similar views have also been expressed by other writers. For Hyman Gross,[16] it seems obvious that those crimes of violence, theft and destruction that stand as paradigms of crime and comprise the core of any penal code are also moral wrongs.

In the case of *Shaw* v. *Director of Public Prosecutions,*[17] the House of Lords expressed the view that the courts will conserve not only the safety and order but also the moral welfare of the state. *Shaw's* case still remains unclear with regard to conspiracy to corrupt public morals. Lord Simmonds, in *Shaw's* case seems to be of the view that the courts have a residual power to create new criminal offences to deal with new situations. However, in *Knuller (publishing printing and promotions)* v. *Director of Public Prosecutions*[18] the House of Lords relegated the suggestion that it has the power to extend the criminal law to enforce good morals.

Smith & Hogan[19] conclude that, the enforcement of morality, as such by the criminal law, is losing ground.

No doubt, some moral wrongs may constitute criminal conducts; however, not all moral wrongs are criminal conducts. The criminality of an act or conduct is determined by the legislature at any given time. Also, not all criminal acts or conducts are morally wrong. Public nuisance, driving without a seat belt, is a crime, but it lacks any element of moral wrongdoing. The last may not have been heard on this matter.

Having examined the various definitions of crime, it is now much easier to state the function of the criminal law.

---

[15] Ibid.

[16] *A Theory of Criminal Justice* (New York: Oxford University Press, 1979) pp. 13.

[17] (1962) A.C. 220 (1961) 2 All E.R. 446.

[18] (1973) A.C. 435.

[19] *Supra*, note 1 at p. 20.

According to Clarkson and Keating,[20] "the function of the criminal law is to lay down a set of standards of what is permissible or not. It is a method of social control, a framework specifying the parameters of acceptable behaviour."

The criminal law is not simply a series of moral commandments. It is a series of moral commandments backed up with the treat of punishment. The protection of society by the imposition of sanction or punishment is meant to deter potential offenders or reform the individual offender.

In *Proprietary Articles Trade Association* v. *Attorney General of Canada,*[21] Lord Atkin opined that the criminal quality of an act cannot be discerned by intuition, nor can it be discovered by reference to any standard but one, namely, is the act prohibited with penal consequence? This is, I think, the true test of criminality.[22]

The function of criminal law is to exert societal abhorrence of the conduct, which is in question, through the imposition of punishment or sanction on the person who has deviated from the societal standard. Punishment is a conventional device for the expression of attitudes of resentment and indignation, and of judgments of disapproval and reprobation, on the part either of the punishing authority himself or of those in whose names the punishment is inflicted.[23]

There are four main theories of punishment, namely:[24]

1. retribution;
2. deterrence;
3. incapacitation;
4. rehabilitation.

---

[20] 7th Edn, *Criminal Law* (London: Thomson-Sweet & Maxwell, 2010) p. 1.

[21] (1931) A.C. 310.

[22] Ibid., at 324.

[23] Joel Feinberg, "The Expressive Function of Punishment," (1965) Vol. 49, No. 3, *The Monist*, 397 - 423.

[24] Clarkson & Keating, *supra*, note 20 at p. 23.

According to Clarkson & Keating,[25] retributive theory looks back to the crime, and punishes because of the crime. The remaining three theories are aimed at crime reduction. The infliction of punishment by law gives definite expression and a solemn ratification and justification to the hatred which is excited by the commission of the offence, and which constitutes the moral or popular as distinguished from the conscientious sanction of that part of morality, which is also sanctioned by the criminal law.[26]

The American Law Institute's Model Penal Code is incisive on the proper objectives of the law of crime:

a) forbid and prevent conduct that unjustifiably and inexcusably inflicts or threatens substantial harm to individual or public interests;
b) subject to public control persons whose conduct indicates that they are disposed to commit crimes;
c) safeguard conduct that is without fault from condemnation as criminal;
d) give fair warning of the nature of the conduct declared to be an offence;
e) differentiate on reasonable grounds between serious and minor offences.

While it is not the intention to examine the theories of punishment, suffice it to say that the imposition of punishment on an offender may serve more than one purpose. It may, on the one hand, be for the purpose of deterrence of future conduct. It may also serve the purpose of showing societal abhorrence for the conduct of the offender (retribution).

The imposition of punishment also serves the purpose of justice; which is to ensure that those who violate the law are made to pay for it.

---

[25] Ibid., at p. 23-24.

[26] Stephen, *A History Criminal Law in England*, (1883) at 81 - 82. See also R.A. Duff, Theories and policies Underlying Guidelines Systems (2005) 105 *Columbia Law Review* 1162 at 1182 - 1183

The recent call for compensation to the victims of crime further expands the function of criminal law to victims' compensation. Compensation has originally been thought of as being within the ambit of civil law, but this is no longer so. *Hari Singh* v. *Sukhbir Singh*, the Supreme Court of India held that the power to reassure victims that they are not forgotten by the criminal justice system, create an avenue for victim - offender reconciliation and negate the necessity for civil litigation for the desired compensation.[27]

Justice Karibi-Whyte,[28] opines that the repression of anti-social conduct by means of punishment is the paramount objective of the criminal law. Hall Jerome[29] further observes that the ultimate aim of the criminal law is the maintenance of order, survival security and the conditions which facilitate progress in the society. Again, Sir Fitzjames Stephen stated:[30]

> The criminal law regulates, sanctions, and provides a legitimate satisfaction for the passion of revenge; the criminal law stands to the passion of revenge in much the same relation as marriage to the sexual appetite.

Finally, it is the function of the criminal law to prevent crime by means of appropriate punishment of the guilty, or the prevention of the commission of crimes.[31] Crime is an antisocial act. It is a deviant behaviour. No society can exist in which deviant behaviour is not punished by imprisonment or fine.

---

[27] (1988) 4 SCC, 551.

[28] *Ground work of Nigerian Criminal Law*, p. 93

[29] "Studies in Jurisprudence Criminal theory" (1958), p. 253, referred to in Karibi-Whyte," National Policy on Compensation to victims of Crime? How Desirable?" P. 252 in *Compensation and Remedies for Victims of Crime in Nigeria*, Ajibola, Ed., *supra* note 6, 252 at 255

[30] General views of the criminal law in England p. 99, referred to in Karibi-Whyte, ibid. at 255.

[31] Karibi-Whyte, ibid. at 257

CRIMINAL POLICY

Justice Karibi-Whyte observed, commenting on criminal policy:[32]

> This has proved a mission impossible for Governments, of all ages and levels of civilisation. It seems to me that three approaches have been adopted. First, by dealing with causes of crime, their removal or neutralisation. Secondly by dealing with prospective delinquent, his education or deterrent. Thirdly, by the punishment imposed on the guilty. The total measures formulated to attain these objectives is regarded in criminal science as criminal policy.

A thorough understanding of the nature and function of the criminal law in Nigeria would not be possible without an understanding of the rationale of criminal law and criminal policy. The aim of the policy is to guide the State as to what its criminal law should contain.

Criminal policy is concerned with the formulation of the offence, the indices for liability, the concepts to be applied and the formulation of rules for determining appropriate sanctions for those who have been adjudged to have breached penal rules.[33]

Criminal policy is discoverable from an examination of penal statutes, judicial decisions, and the pronouncements and actions of the executive. Consequently, the criminal policy of a country is usually influenced by officials of the legislative, executive and judiciary who originate, influence and implement criminal policy.

Criminal policy derives its materials from criminology and uses these materials to formulate the principles and doctrines of the criminal law and rules of procedure.[34]

---

[32] Ibid at 259

[33] Karibi-Whyte, *Criminal Policy: Traditional and Modern Trends* (Lagos: Nigerian Law Publications, Ltd, 1988) at p. 3

[34] Ibid.

Gema Verona has identified the scope of criminal policy as follows:[35]

i. Criminal Policy must be founded on the known or assumed causes of crime. This will enable it formulate "preventive system which would include elimination or neutralisation of causes";
ii. Criminal Policy involves the study of existing legislations necessary to meet the demands of the situation in both substantive law and as to procedure. In other words, it is the function of criminal policy to determine the content of conduct to be regarded as criminal, and the entire procedure for the administration of justice;
iii. It is the function of criminal policy to determine the classification of criminals in accordance with the nature of crimes and their effect on society. Criminal policy also decides the appropriate punishment or other measures to be imposed on conviction. It is thus guided by the statistics of the efficiency of punishment as a deterrent or corrective instrument. Accordingly, it may be postulated that criminal policy is that branch of criminal science which has as its immediate aim the study and systemisation of all measures to be taken against crime in the sphere of prevention, of legislation and punitive treatment and as its ultimate aim, the coordination of the whole into an organized system of state activity;
iv. Criminal policy cannot stand in isolation. It has to act through the Criminal law and Constitutional Law. This is because it is in these laws that the rules prescribed by criminal policy for determining anti-social conduct, the rules of procedure governing determination of guilt and the

[35] See O. Aigbovo, Criminal Policy: An Appraisal of Modern Theory in Nigeria (2010), unpublished.

sanctions on conviction for the commission of an offence can be found.

The Nigerian criminal policy dates back to the advent of the civilian regime in 1999. According to Karibi-Whyte,[36] the Nigerian criminal policy could be found in the Nigerian Constitution and also case law. The sources of criminal policy in Nigeria include the Constitution, the legislature the executive and the judiciary. The exercise of discretion is also important in determining criminal policy. The Nigerian criminal policy covers the causes of crime, existing criminal legislation, the rules of criminal law and procedure. Criminal policy, therefore, encompasses the length and breadth of the science of crime (Criminology), and law. It also includes Sociology and Behavioural Science as they apply to the study of the criminal mind.

To facilitate speedy dispensation of justice, the Administration of Criminal Justice Act 2015, was enacted. It is the most comprehensive attempt at reforming the system. It aims at promoting efficient management of criminal justice institutions, speedy dispensation of justice, balanced protection for plaintiffs and defendants and decongestion of collection facilities through the incorporation of plea bargaining and non-custodial sentencing. Most states in Nigeria, including Lagos, Edo, Delta, Kano, Nasarawa, have domesticated the ACJL.

CONCLUSION

Determining the nature, definition and function of the criminal law is as complex as searching for the lost grail. Just when you think it is eureka it turns out to be a false alarm. We have however, provided a skeletal framework on the definition, nature and function of the criminal law. We have also examined the criminal policy of our criminal laws. In the final analysis, we

---

[36] *Supra*, note 31 at p. 3-5

posit here that criminal law analysis must now be seen from an interdisciplinary perspective. The whole gamut of our criminal laws cannot be fully comprehended without this approach.

Chapter 2

ELEMENTS OF CRIMINAL LIABILITY

INTRODUCTION

It is a fundamental requirement of received English law that before an accused person is convicted for an offence his guilt must be proved. There must be coincidence of the physical and mental element. These are the *actus reus* and the *mens rea.*

It must, however, be pointed out that both terms are absent in the Criminal and Penal codes.[1]

In *R.* v. *Miller*,[2] Lord Diplock expressed his disapproval of the use of the terms *actus reus* and *mens rea* thus:[3]

> My Lords, it would I think be conducive to clarity of analysis of the ingredients of a crime that is created by statute, as are the greater majority of criminal offences today, if we were to avoid bad Latin and instead to think and speak about the conduct of the accused and his state of mind at the time of that conduct, instead of speaking of *actus reus* and *mens rea.*

Despite the above reservations by his Lordship, both terms are still being used in England and also in Nigeria. In justification of their continual use, Clarkson and Keating submit that:[4]

> We shall analyse crimes in terms of *actus reus, mens rea*...We do this for the simple reason that as long as one appreciates

---

[1] See Okonkwo & Naish, *Criminal Law in Nigeria*, 2nd Edit (Lagos: Spectrum, 1980) at p. 43

[2] (1983) AC 161

[3] Ibid., at p. 175

[4] *Criminal Law* 7th Edit (London: Thomson, Sweet & Maxwell, 2010) at p. 70-71. See also McAlhone & Huxley Binns, *Criminal Law: The Fundamentals*, 2nd Edit (London: Thomson, Sweet & Maxwell, 2010) at p. 12

> that these terms are no more than tools, they are tools that can usefully aid the clear exposition of the rules of criminal law. Further, they have been so much part of the criminal law vocabulary for hundreds of years, and still are, that many of the cases to be discussed...would be highly confusing, if not totally meaningless, without some understanding of the orthodox meaning of these terms.

We fully agree with the view expressed by the authors and we need add that the continued usage of the terms *actus reus* and *mens rea* does not impact negatively on our criminal law. Indeed, it does have some positive impact. It makes for clarity of understanding, particularly concerning the decided cases.

ACTUS REUS

In simplistic terms, an *actus reus* refers to the physical act or omission of an accused person which is prohibited. In descriptive terms, *actus reus* is:[5]

i. an act;
ii. committed in legally relevant circumstance; and
iii. causing the prohibited result.

Each of these, whether it is an act or omission, circumstances and/or a consequence, is a part of the *actus reus* and of the crime.[6] There must always be an *actus reus* for liability to arise. However, all three elements need not necessarily occur at the same time for a particular crime. An *actus reus* may arise in terms of an act, or in terms of a result.

The importance of an *actus reus* as a prerequisite for an offence is succinctly described by Lord Mansfield when he said:[7]

> So long as an act rests in bare intention, it is not punishable by our laws.

---

[5] Clarkson & Keating, ibid. at p. 73
[6] McAlhone & Huxley -Binns, *supra*, note 4 at p. 13
[7] Referred to in Glanville Williams, *Criminal Law: The General Part (1961)* at p.1

Again, Clarkson and Keating opined that:[8]

> The law, however, is not concerned with punishing people for thinking evil thoughts or having evil intentions. The law will not interfere unless there has been some conduct, some physical manifestation of the evil intention.

The requirement for an *actus reus* as an ingredient of an offence is also well recognised in the United States of America.

In *Powell* v. *State of Texas*,[9] Justice Black of the Supreme Court of the United States said:[10]

> The reasons for this refusal to permit conviction without proof of an act are difficult to spell out, but they are nonetheless perceived and universally expressed in our criminal law.

Again, writing in the *Yale Law Journal* in 1959, Goldstein observed that:[11]

> The notion of not punishing evil intentions alone expressed today, as it did three centuries ago, the feeling that the individual thinking evil thoughts must be protected from a state which may class him as a threat to its security...the act requirement serves a number of closely related objectives: it seeks to assure that the evil intent of the man branded a criminal has been expressed in a manner signifying harm to society; that there is no longer any substantial likelihood that he will be deterred by the threat of sanction; and that there has been an identifiable occurrence so that multiple prosecution and punishment may be minimized.

An *actus reus* can present itself either as an act or an omission. Let us examine these in turn.

---

[8] *Supra*, note 4 at p. 7

[9] 392 US 514 (1968)

[10] Ibid.

[11] (1959) 68 Yale L.J. 405 at 405-406

THE ACT

The *actus reus* differs from one crime to the other. For example, an agreement to commit a crime is sufficient to constitute the *actus reus* of conspiracy. As Okonkwo and Naish,[12] rightly observe, a small gesture could be the *actus reus* of an assault and a slight movement of property can constitute the *actus reus of* stealing.

The actus reus of rape is the penetration of the vagina, anus or mouth of another person who does not consent to the penetration.

Crimes can be divided into two categories and the essential elements of an *actus reus* depend on which of these two species of crime is in question.[13] The first are crimes known as conduct crimes, where the only external element required is the prohibited conduct itself. For example, the *actus reus* of the offence of unlicensed driving is simply driving a motor vehicle on a road without a licence. Secondly, there are crimes known as result crimes. Here, the external elements of the offence require proof that the conduct causes a prohibited result or consequences.[14] For example, causing death by unlicenced driving.

The *actus reus* is causing the death of a person by driving a vehicle on a road while unlicensed. It is clears that both conduct and result crimes have two elements in common, i.e. (i) both require an act or conduct, i.e., driving, and both require that the act be carried out in legally relevant circumstances.[15]

AN OMISSION

An *actus reus* is not confined a positive act alone. It includes an omission. Consequently, the failure to do an act (omission)

---

[12] *Supra*, note 1 at p. 45

[13] Clarkson & Keating, *supra*, note 4 at p. 72

[14] *Ibid.* See also McAlhone & Huxley-Binns, *supra*, note 4 at p. 13

[15] Clarkson & Keating, ibid. at p. 73

could present itself as the *actus reus* of an offence. Although crimes are more often expressed in terms of acts than omissions, criminal liability may arise for a failure to act (omission).

Criminal liability in cases of omission is dependent upon the existence of a duty to act. Under English law, there is no liability to watch a child drown unless the observer owes the child a duty to save it, e.g., being the child's father.

The underlying reason is stated by Macaulay, when he said:[16]

> It is indeed, most highly desirable that men should not merely abstain from doing harm to their neighbours, but should render active services to their neighbours. In general, however, the penal law must content itself with keeping men from doing positive harm...It is evident that to attempt to punish men by law for not rendering to others all the services which it is their duty to render to others would be preposterous. We must grant immunity to the vast majority of those omissions which a benevolent morality would pronounce reprehensible, and must content ourselves with punishing such omissions only when they are distinguished from the rest by some circumstances which makes them out as peculiarly fit objects of penal legislation.

Omission has been defined by Glanville Wiliams[17] as something that the accused could have done if he had been minded to do so and had prepared himself in time, or at least something that another in his place could have done.

The common law recognises several situations where a failure to act, (where a duty to act exists) as giving rise to criminal liability. For example, parents owe a duty to their children.[18]

---

[16] *Works*, ed. Lady Trevelyan, vii (1866) 497 (Notes on the Indian Penal Code, 1837), referred to in Glanville Williams, *Criminal Law, supra*, note 7 at p. 34

[17] *Ibid* at p. 3

[18] Smith & Hogan, *Criminal Law*, 5th Edn (London: Butterworths, 1983) at p. 43

In *Gibbins & Proctor,*[19] where a father deliberately failed to feed his child; his life partner was also convicted as she had assumed *de facto* parental responsibility. Also in *Hood,*[20] the husband was convicted of manslaughter of his wife because he delayed calling for medical assistance for her.

A public office holder may be liable for failure to take care of others in his custody. In *Curtis* case, a local authority officer was held liable for manslaughter by neglecting to provide medical assistance to a destitute.

In English law, criminal liabilities which may arise from omission are mostly created by the Common Law. This has led one writer to conclude that:[22]

> the time is ripe for Anglo American systems to translate into legislative fact the modern consciousness of interdependence. Surely it is not in socialist countries alone that the duty of a citizen to help his fellows in these situations of extreme peril can be recognised.

In Nigeria, the Criminal Code is replete with instances of criminal omissions. For example, under sections 346-348 of the Criminal Code, duties are imposed on those in charges of railway, trains or of ships and on ships engineers, to ensure the safety of passengers.[23] The Criminal Code also provides that it is an offence for anyone to omit, without lawful excuse, to perform any duty which he is bound to perform by the provisions of any legislative enactment.[24]

Omissions form an important part of our criminal law, just as "acts".

Although majority of conducts that form the *actus reus* of an offence are acts, omission remains central to criminal liability.

---

[19] (1918) 13 CR App. R. 134

[20] (2004) 1 Cr. App. R. (s.) 73

[22] Graham Hughes, "Criminal Omissions" (1958) 67 Yale L.J. 590 at 626, 634. See also Andrew Ashworth, "The Scope of Liability for Omissions" (1989) 105 L.Q.R. 424 at 430 - 432.

[23] See Okonkwo & Naish *supra*, note 1 at p. 46

[24] Section 202 of the Criminal Code

We can therefore conclude authoritatively that liability for omissions may arise if two conditions are satisfied. These are:

i. the offence is capable of being committed by omission;
ii. the accused was under a duty to act either at common law or under statute.

MENS REA

The truth is that the maxim about *mens rea* means no more than that the definition of all or nearly all crimes contain not only an outward and visible element, but a mental element, varying according to the different nature of different crimes. Thus, in reference to murder, the *mens rea* is any state of mind which comes within the description of malice aforethought. Hence the only means of arriving at a full comprehension of the expression *mens rea* is by a detailed examination of the definitions of particular crimes, and therefore the expression itself is unmeaning.[25]

Mens rea is the term generally used to indicate the mental element requited by the definition of the crime.[26] It is a technical term.[27] It differs from one crime to another. In determining the *mens rea* of a crime, one has to look at the definition of that crime, and an example will suffice. For murder, it is intention to kill or cause grievous bodily harm. *Mens rea* as used commonly in criminal offences means; intention, recklessness, and negligence. Let us examine these terms.

INTENTION

There is no statutory definition of intention in English or Nigerian law. Controversy has therefore arisen as to the

---

[25] Stephen, *History of the Criminal Law of England*, vol. 11 (1883), p. 94-95
[26] Clarkson & Keating, *supra* note 4 at p. 132
[27] Smith & Hogan, *supra*, note 18 at 47

meaning of the word. Two views have been expressed. They are:[28]

i. a consequence is intended when it is the aim or objective of the actor (Direct Intention);
ii. a consequence is intended when it is the aim or objective of the actor, or is foreseen as a virtual, practical or moral certainty (Oblique intention);
iii. a consequence is intended when it was foreseen as a probable or likely result of the defendant's action.

Let us examine some English cases. In *Hyam* v. *Director of Public* Prosecution,[29] Mrs Hyam poured petrol through the letterbox of the house of her lover's new mistress and then ignited it knowing persons were sleeping inside the house. She contended that she had not meant to kill but had foreseen death or grievous bodily harm as a highly probable result of her actions. Ackner J. directed a jury that, in the law of murder, the accused intended death or serious bodily harm if she knew, when she did the act, that it was highly probable that it would cause death or serious bodily harm. Her conviction for murder was upheld by the Court of Appeal and the House of Lords

Smith and Hogan[30] conclude that two possible interpretations are possible from this case:

i. the *mens rea* of murder is an intention to kill or to cause serious bodily harm; and a person who foresees that death or serious bodily harm as a highly probable consequence of his act, intends that consequence;
ii. the *mens rea* of murder is either:

---

[28] See Clarkson & Keating, supra, note 4 at p. 136 and also McAlhone & Huxley-Binns, *supra*, note 4 at p. 47-49

[29] (1975) A.C. 55

[30] *Supra*, note 18 at p. 48-49. However, for a contrary view that intention cannot be inferred from foresight, see M. Cathleen Kaveny, "Inferring intention from Foresight" (2004) 120 L.Q.R. 81, where the writer said, "There is a conceptual distinction between intention and all degrees of foresight...no degree of foresight can, by itself, be the basis of a reliable inference of intention."

i. an intention to kill or cause serious bodily harm; or
ii. foresight that death or serious bodily harm is a highly probable consequence of one's act.

Hyam's case stands for the proposition that foresight was sufficient *mens rea* for murder.

In *R.* v. *Moloney*,[31] the appellant and his stepfather, both of whom had been drinking heavily, engaged in a contest to ascertain who was quicker on the draw with a shot gun. The appellant shot and killed his stepfather. He contended that he did not realise that the gun was pointing at him. He was convicted of murder and his appeal was dismissed by the Court of Appeal. On a final appeal to the House of Lord, his appeal was allowed.

Lord Bridge said:

> Looking on their facts at the decided cases where a crime of specific intent was under consideration, they suggest to me that the probability of the consequence taken to have been foreseen must be little short of overwhelming before it will suffice to establish the necessary intent. The golden rule should be that, when directing a jury on the mental element necessary in a crime of specific intent, the judge should avoid any elaboration or paraphrase of what is meant by intent, and leave it to the jury's good sense to decide whether the accused acted with the necessary intent, unless the judge is convinced that, on the facts and having regard to the way the case has been presented to the jury in evidence and argument, some further explanation or elaboration is strictly necessary to avoid misunderstanding. In trials for murder or wounding with intent, I find it very difficult to visualize a case where any such explanation or elaboration could be required, if the offence consisted of a direct attack on the victim with a weapon.... Even where the death results indirectly from the act of the accused. I believe the cases that call for a direction by

[31] (1985) A.C. 905 (House of Lords)

> reference to foresight of consequences will be of extremely rare occurrence...
>
> In the rare cases in which it is necessary to direct a jury by reference to foresight of consequences, I do not believe it is necessary for the judge to do more than invite the jury to consider two questions. First, was death or really serious injury in a murder case (or whatever relevant consequence must be proved to have been intended in any other case) a natural consequence of the defendant's voluntary act? Secondly, did the defendant foresee that consequence as being a natural consequence of his act? The jury should then be told that if they answer yes to both questions. It is a proper inference for them to draw that he intended that consequence.

In *R.* v. *Hancock and Shankland,* the defendants, two striking miners, pushed a large lump of concrete from a bridge on to convoy of cars below carrying a miner to work. The concrete struck a taxi's windscreen and killed the driver. The defendants claimed they had not meant to kill or cause serious injury. Their plan was to drop the concrete in the middle lane of the carriageway while the convoy was in the nearside lane. Their aim was to frighten the miner or block the road in order to prevent him from getting to work. The defendants were convicted of murder. The Court of Appeal allowed their appeals and substituted verdicts of manslaughter. The crown appealed to the House of Lords.

Lord Scarman opined as follows:

> The cases to which the guidance was expressly limited by the House in *Moloney*, i.e., the 'rare cases' in which it is necessary to direct a jury by reference to foresight of consequences, are unlikely to be so rare or so exceptional as the House believed. As the House then recognised, the guidelines as formulated are applicable to cases of any crime of specific intent, and not merely murder. But further and disturbingly crimes of violence where the purpose is by open violence to protest, demonstrate, obstruct, or frighten are on the increase. Violence is used by some as a means of public communication.

> Inevitably there will be casualties: and inevitably death will on occasions result. If death results, is the perpetrator of the violent act guilty of murder? It will depend on his intent. The question for the House is, therefore, whether the *Moloney* guidelines are sound Lord Bridge of Harwich in *Moloney* omitted any reference in his guidelines to probability. I agree with the Court of Appeal that the probability of a consequence is a factor of sufficient importance to be drawn specifically to the attention of the jury and to be explained. In **a** murder case where it **is** necessary to direct a jury on the issue of intent by reference to foresight of consequences the probability of death or serious injury resulting from the act done may be critically important. Its importance will depend on the degree of probability: if the likelihood that death or serious injury will result is high, the probability of that result may be seen as overwhelming evidence of the existence of the intent to kill or injure. Failure to explain the relevance of probability may, therefore mislead a jury into thinking that it is of little or no importance. In my judgment therefore the *Moloney* guidelines as they stand are unsafe and misleading. They require a reference to probability. They also require an explanation that the greater the probability of a consequence the more likely it is that the consequence was foreseen and that if that consequence was foreseen the greater the probability is that that consequence was also intended. But juries also require to be reminded that the decision is theirs to be reached upon a consideration of all the evidence...

The decision of the Court of Appeal *R.* v. *Nedrick* summarises the decisions in *Moloney* and *Hancock* cases. In *Nedrick*, the appellant poured paraffin through the letterbox of a house and set light to it. The house caught fire and a child died. The appellant claimed that he did not want anyone to die. He was convicted of murder and appealed.

Lord Lane, C.J. said:

> What then does a jury have to decide so far as the mental element in murder is concerned? It simply has to decide whether the defendant intended to kill or do serious bodily

harm. In order to reach that decision, the jury must pay regard to all the relevant circumstances, including what the defendant himself said and did. In the great majority of cases a direction to that effect will be enough, particularly where the defendant's actions amounted to a direct attack upon his victim, because in such cases the evidence relating to the defendant's desire or motive will be clear and his intent will have been the same as his desire or motive. But in some cases, of which this is one, the defendant does an act which is manifestly dangerous and as a result someone dies. The primary desire or motive of the defendant may not have been to harm that person, or indeed anyone in that situation what further directions should a jury be given as to the mental state which they must find to exist in the defendant it murder is to be proved?

We have endeavoured to crystallise the effect of their Lordships' speeches in *R.* v. *Moloney* and *R.* v. *Hancock* in a way which we hope may be helpful to judges who have to handle this type of case.

It may be advisable first of all to explain to the jury that a man may intend to achieve a certain result whilst at the same time not desiring it to come about....

When determining whether the defendant had the necessary intent, it may therefore be helpful for a jury to ask themselves two questions. (1) How probable was the consequence which resulted from the defendant's voluntary act? (2) Did he foresee that consequence? if he did not appreciate that death or serious harm was likely to result from his act, he cannot have intended to bring it about if he did, but thought that the risk to which he was exposing the person killed was only slight, then it may be easy for the jury to conclude that he did not intend to bring about that result. On the other hand, if the jury are satisfied that at the material time the defendant recognised that death or serious harm would be virtually certain (barring some unforeseen intervention) to result from his voluntary act, then that is a fact from which they may find it easy to infer that he intended to kilt or do serious bodily harm, even though he may not have had any desire to achieve that result. As Lord Bridge of Harwich said in *R.* v. *Maloney* [1985] A.C.905,925: 'the probability of the consequences taken to have been foreseen must be little short of overwhelming before it will suffice to establish the necessary intent.' At p.926 he uses the expression 'moral certainty'; he said, at p.929 'will lead to a certain consequence unless something unexpected supervenes to prevent it.' Where the charge is murder and in the rare cases where the simple direction is not enough, the jury should be directed that they are not entitled to infer the necessary intention, unless they feel sure that death or serious bodily harm was a virtual certainty (barring some unforeseen intervention) as a result of the defendant's actions and that the defendant appreciated that such was the case. Where a man realizes that it is for all practical purposes inevitable that his actions will result in death or serious harm, the inference may be irresistible that he intended that result, however little he may have desired or wished it to happen. The decision s one for the jury to be reached upon a consideration of all the evidence.

Also in *R.* v. *Woolin,*[34] the appellant lost his temper with his three-month-old son and threw him with great force causing the child to hit his head on something hard and die. In an interview the appellant admitted that he had realized there was a risk of serious injury. The trial judge directed the jury that they might infer intention if they were satisfied that the appellant appreciated that there was a substantial risk that he would cause serious harm. The appellant was convicted of murder and appealed on the ground that the judge should not have used the phrase "substantial risk", which is a test of recklessness, but should have used the phrase "virtual certainty".

Lord Steyn in a robust judgment said:

It may be appropriate to give a direction in accordance with *Nedrick* in any case in which the defendant may not have desired the result of his act. But I accept the trial judge is best placed to decide what direction is required by the circumstances of the case...

---

[34] (1999) 1 A.C. 82 (House of Lords)

> It follows that the judge should not have departed from the *Nedrick* direction. By using the phrase "substantial risk" the judge blurred the line between intention and recklessness, and hence between murder and manslaughter. The misdirection enlarged the scope of the mental element required for murder. It was a material misdirection...The conviction of murder must be quashed.
>
> In my view Lord Lane C.J.'s judgment in *Nedrick* provided valuable assistance to trail judges...
>
> ...{b} Where the charge is murder and in the rare cases where the simple direction is not enough, the jury should be directed that they are not entitled to infer the necessary intention, unless they feel sure that death of serious bodily harm was a virtual certainty (barring some unforeseen intervention) as a result of the defendant's actions and that the defendant appreciated that such was the case where a man realizes that it is for all practical purposes inevitable that his actions will result in death or serious harm, the interference may be irresistible that he intended that result, however little he may have desired or wished it to happen. The decision is one for the jury to be reached upon a consideration of all the evidence.

The prevailing view in England is that intention should extend beyond its core meaning to include foresight of a consequence as a virtual, practical or moral certainty (oblique intent). A similar view was expressed by Glanville Williams when he said:[35]

> Clearly, a person can be taken to intend a consequence that follows under his nose from what he continues to do, and the law should be the same where he is aware that a consequence. In the future is the certain or practically certain result of what he does. As Lord Hailsham said in *Hyam*; "intention includes the means as well as the end and the inseparable consequence of the end as well as the means."

[35] *Textbook of Criminal Law*, 2nd Edit (1983) at pp. 84-85

In Nigeria, under section 316 of the Criminal Code, a person who unlawfully kills another under any of the following circumstances, that is to say:

(1) If the offender intends to cause the death of the person killed, or that of some other person;
(2) If the offender intends to do the person killed or to some other person some grievous harm;
(3) If death is caused by means of an act done in the prosecution of an unlawful purpose, which act is of such nature as to be likely to endanger human life;
(4) If the offender intends to do grievous harm to some person for the purpose of facilitating the commission of an offence which is such that the offender may be arrested without warrant, or for the purpose of facilitating the flight of an offender who has committed or attempted to commit any such offence;
(5) If death is caused by administering any stupefying or overpowering things for either of the purposes last aforesaid;
(6) If death is cause by wilfully stopping the breath of any person for either o such purposes; is guilty of murder.

In the second case it is immaterial that the offender did not intend to hurt the particular person who is killed.

In the third case it is immaterial that the offender did not intend to hurt any person.

In the last three cases it is immaterial that the offender did not intend to cause death or did not know that death was likely to result.

In the Nigerian case of *Ubani* v. *The State*[36] the accused persons and the appellants armed with guns, matchets and clubs, beat the deceased until he fell down and discharged excreta through his anus. The deceased died as a consequence

---

[36] (2003) 18 NWLR, Part 851, P. 224. See also *Idowu* v. *The State* (2000) 12 NWLR, Part 680 , 48

of the assault on him. The trial court convicted the appellants and the other accused persons for the offence of murder. Their appeal to the Court of Appeal was dismissed. On appeal to the Supreme Court, it was held, *inter alia,* that the act or omission of the accused which caused the death of the deceased was intentional with knowledge that death or grievous bodily harm was its probable consequence. This was a case of direct intention, since the accused persons and the appellant intended death or grievous bodily harm to the deceased when they assaulted him.

Also in *Idiok* v. *The State,*[37] the Court of Appeal, held, *inter alia*, that for the prosecution to succeed in a charge of murder it must prove that the accused intend to cause the death of the accused.

The Nigerian Criminal Code is silent on the issue of foresight of consequences as an ingredient of murder (oblique intention). The above Nigerian cases only deal with the issue of direct intention. Section 316(1) and 316(2) of the Criminal Code are cases of direct intention. In these cases, the accused intended death or grievous bodily harm. It appears therefore that foresight of consequence will not be sufficient as *mens rea* for murder in Nigeria.[1]

RECKLESSNESS

According to Clarkson & Keating,[39] the concept of recklessness has had a chequered and uncertain history with judges vacillating as to its meaning. For many criminal acts, intention or recklessness (in England) is sufficient to impose liability. To establish recklessness, it is necessary to show that the accused took an unjustifiable risk. A person acts recklessly with respect to a result if he is aware of a risk that it will occur and it is unreasonable to take the risk having regard to the

---

[1] See Okonkwo & Naish, *supra*, note 18 at p.

[39] *Supra*, note 4 at p. 158

circumstances as he knows or believes them to be[40]. Recklessness entailed the conscious running of an unjustifiable risk. This is a subjective meaning.

In *R.* v. *Stephenson,*[41] the appellant, who had crept into a hollow in the side of a large straw stack to sleep, felt cold and lit a fire of twigs and straw inside the hollow. The stack caught fire and was damaged. He was charged with arson contrary to s.1(1) of the Criminal Damage Act 1971. Evidence on his behalf was given by a consultant psychiatrist that the appellant suffered from schizophrenia that could have the effect of depriving him of the ability of a normal person to foresee or appreciate the risk of damage from the act of lighting the fire. The judge directed the jury that a person was "reckless as to whether any such property would be destroyed or damaged," within S.1(1) of the 1971 Act, if he closed his mind to the obvious fact of risk. The jury returned a verdict of guilty and the appellant was convicted. He appealed against the conviction on the ground, *inter alia,* of a misdirection by the judge on what constitute recklessness.

Geoffrey Lane, L.J. said:

> Does the word 'reckless' require that the defendant must be proved actually to have foreseen the risk of some damage resulting from his actions and nevertheless to have run the risk (the subjective test), or is it sufficient to prove that the risk of damage resulting would have been obvious to any reasonable person in the defendant's position (the objective test)? In our view it is the subjective test which is correct.
>
> ...a man is reckless when he carries out the deliberate act appreciating that there is a risk that damage to property may result from his act. It is however not the taking of every risk

[40] English Law Com. No. 218, *Legislating the Criminal Code: Offences against the person and General Principles (1993).* For further readings on recklessness, see John Gardner & Heike Jung, "Making sense of Mens Rea" Anthony Duff's Account" (1991) 11 O.J.L.S. 559, A. Duff, "Recklessness" (1980) Crim. L.R. 282 and Alan Norrie, "*Subjectivism, Objectivism and the Limit of Criminal Recklessness*" (1992) 12 O.J.L.S. 45

[41] (1979) Q.B 695

> which could properly be classed as reckless. The risk must be one which is it is in all the circumstance unreasonable for him to take.

Under this "subjective" approach, the definition of recklessness, both as to consequences and circumstances, imposes a double test.

(1) whether the defendant foresaw the possibility of the consequence occurring; and

(2) whether it was unjustifiable or unreasonable to take the risk.

Whether a risk is justifiable or not depends on the social importance of the acts and on the chances of the forbidden consequence occurring.

In 1981 there was a radical change of direction when the House of Lords handed down two judgments on the same day, both concerned with the meaning of recklessness. It should be stressed that this change only affected the first limb of the test cited above, namely, whether the defendant must foresee the possibility of harm occurring. It did not affect the second requirement that it must be unjustifiable to take the risk.[42]

In *R.* v. *Caldwell*,[43] the respondent had done some work for the owner of a hotel as the result of which he had a quarrel with the owner, got drunk and set fire to the hotel in revenge. The fire was discovered and put out before any serious damage was caused and none of the 10 guests in the hotel at the time were injured. The respondent was indicted on two counts of arson under s.1(1) and (2) of the Criminal Damage Act 1971. At his trial he pleaded not guilty to the more serious charge under s. 1(2) of damaging property with intent to endanger life or being reckless whether life would be endangered. He claimed that he was so drunk at the time that the thought that he might be endangering the lives of the people in the hotel had never

---

[42] Clarkson & Keating, *supra*, note 4 at p. 160. See also McAlhone & Huxlay Binns, *supra* note 4 at pp. 60-64

crossed his mind. The trial judge directed the jury that drunkenness was not a defence to a charge under s. 1(2) and he was convicted.

The Court of Appeal allowed his appeal. The Crown appealed to the House of Lords, where in order to decide whether drunkenness was a defence to a charge under s.1(2), the House ruled that it was necessary to decide upon the precise meaning of the term recklessness as employed in s. 1(2).

Lord Diplock said:

> In my opinion, a person charged with an offence under section 1(1) of the Criminal Damage Act 1971 is reckless as to whether any such property would be destroyed or damaged, if (1) he does an act which in fact creates an obvious risk that property will be destroyed or damaged and (2) when he does the act he either has not given any thought to the possibility of there being any such risk or has recognised that there was some risk involved and has nonetheless gone on to do it. That would be a proper direction to the jury, cases in the Court of Appeal which held otherwise should be regarded as overruled. (His Lordship then went on to consider the defence of drunkenness.

What Lord Diplock is saying here is that an accused person need not be aware that there is any risk of the consequence in question. This case is in variance with the subjective test land down in *Stephenson*, where it was held that the accused must have foresight of the possibility of the risk occurring.

Lord Edmund-Davies (with whom Lord Wilberforce concurred) dissenting:

> It is well known that the Criminal Damage Act 1971 was in the main the work of the Law Commission, who in their working paper no. 31 codification of the Criminal Law, General Principles, the Mental Element in Crime (issued in June, 1970) defined recklessness by saying, at p. 52.
>
> A person is reckless if (a) knowing that there is a risk that an event may result from his conduct or that a circumstance

may exist, he takes the risk, and (b) it is unreasonable for him to take it, having regard to the degree and nature of the risk which he knows to be present.

It was surely with this contemporaneous definition and the much-respected decision of *R.* v. *Cunningham* in mind that the draftsman proceeded to his task of drafting the Criminal Damage Act 1971. It has therefore to be said that, unlike negligence, which has to be judged objectively, recklessness involves foresight of consequences, combined with an objective judgment of the reasonableness of the risk taken. And recklessness *in vacuo* is an incomprehensible notion. It must relate to foresight of risk of the particular kind relevant to the charge preferred, which, for the purpose of section 1(2), is the risk of endangering life and nothing other than that.

So if a defendant says of a particular risk, "it never crossed my mind', a jury could not on those words alone properly convict him of recklessness simply because they considered that the risk ought to have crossed his mind though his words might well lead to a finding of negligence. But a defendant's admission that he closed his mind to a particular risk could prove fatal, for: "a person cannot, in any intelligible meaning of the words, close his mind to a risk unless he first realises that there is a risk, and if he realises that there is a risk, that is the end of the matter"- See Glanville Williams, *Textbook of Criminal Law* (1978), p. 79

In the absence of exculpatory factors, the defendant's state of mind is therefore all important where recklessness is an element in the offence charged and section 8 of the Criminal Justice Act 1967 has laid down that: "A court or jury, in determining whether a person has committed an offence (a) shall not be bound by law to infer that he intended or foresaw a result of his actions by reason only of its being a natural and probable consequence of those actions; but (b) shall decide whether he did intend or foresee that result by reference to all the evidence, drawing such inference from the evidence as appear proper in the circumstances."

My Lords, it is unnecessary to examine at length the proposition that ascertainment of the state of mind known as "recklessness" is a subjective exercise...(His Lordship then went on to consider the defence of "drunkenness").

In *R.* v. *Lawrence*,[44] the appellant was riding his motorcycle at any excessive speed along an urban road and ran into and killed a pedestrian who was crossing the road. The appellant was convicted of causing death by reckless driving, contrary to s, 1 of the Road Traffic Act 1972 and appealed against his conviction.

Lord Diplock (with whom Lord Freser, Lord Roskill and Lord Bridge agreed), said:

> I turn now to the *mens rea*...Recklessness on the part of the doer of an act does pre-suppose that there is something in the circumstances that would have drawn the attention of an ordinary prudent individual to the possibility that his act was capable of causing the kind of serious harmful consequences that the section which creates the offence was intended to prevent, and that the risk of those harmful consequences occurring was not so slight that an ordinary prudent individual would feel justified in treating them as negligible. It is only when this is so that the doer of the act is acting 'recklessly' if before doing the act, he either fails to give any thought to the possibility of there being any such risk or, having recognized that there was such risk, he nevertheless goes on to do it.... in my view, an appropriate instruction to the jury on what is meant by driving recklessly would be that they must be satisfied of two things:
> (i) that the defendant was driving the vehicle in such a manner as to create an obvious and serious risk...;
> (ii) the defendant did so without giving any thought of the possibility of there being any such..."

According to Smith and Hogan,[45] after Caldwell, the inadvertent taking of risk (mere negligence), can now be regarded as reckless.

In *R.* v. *G and another*,[46] two boys aged 11 and 12 respectively, set fire to newspapers and threw them under a wheetie-bin.

---

[44] (1982) A.C. 510 (House of Lords)

[45] *Supra*, note 18 at p.57

[46] (2004) 1 A.C. 1034 (House of Lords)

The bin was set alight and adjoining buildings caught fire causing some £1 million damage. They claimed they thought the lit newspapers would burn themselves out on the concrete floor and that it never crossed their minds that there was a risk of the fire spreading. They were convicted of arson with the trial judge ruling that whether there was an obvious risk of the property being damaged was to be assessed by reference to the reasonable man and not a person endowed with the characteristics of the defendants: "the ordinary reasonable bystander is an adult." The defendants were convicted. Their appeal to the Court of Appeal was dismissed and they appealed to the House of Lords.

Their conviction was based on Caldwell. In quashing their convictions, the House of Lord reviewed the development of Caldwell recklessness and chose unanimously to overrule Caldwell which they described as "neither just nor moral."

Thus, the test for recklessness in criminal damage offences was brought into line with that of other offences, subjective recklessness.[47]

In Nigeria, recklessness is not a basis for liability for murder.

NEGLIGENCE

In England, for serious crimes, intention or recklessness would suffice as a basis of criminal liability. Negligence as a basis of criminal liability was in exceptional cases. The reason for this is not farfetched. According to Clarkson & Keating:[48]

> For much of the last century the law was strongly committed to subjectivism in the form of cognitive *mens rea*. Negligence was regarded as imposing an objective test which could not be accommodated within such an approach.

---

[47] McAlhone & Huxley-Binns, *supra*, note 4 at p. 64

[48] *Supra*, note 4 at p. 179. See also H.L.A. Hart, "Negligence, *Mens Rea* and the Elimination of Responsibility" in *Punishment and Responsibility* (Essays in Philosophy of Law (1968), pp. 152-157, Hart, *Oxford Essays in Jurisprudence*, at p. 42

The question now is, should negligence be a basis for criminal liability?[49]

By negligence we mean failure to exercise due care, skill or foresight as a reasonable man in his situation would exercise.

Hall[50] opines that there is no basis for negligence in criminal liability. He said:

> The incorporation of negligence into the penal law imposes an impossible function on judges, namely, to determine whether a person, about whom little is known, had the competence and sensitivity to appreciate certain dangers in a particular situation when the facts plainly indicate that he did not exhibit that competence.

Also, Robert Fine, *et al.*[51] expressed a similar view when they said:

> There appears to be no reasonable justification for punishing negligence as a criminal act under any of these four theories. It does not further the purposes of deterrence, retribution, rehabilitation or incapacitation; hence, there is no rational basis for the imposition of criminal liability on negligent conduct.

We need to posit here that there are different decreases of negligence. For serious crimes, like murder, rape, criminal liability could arise on the basis of negligence. However, for lesser crimes negligence should not be a basis for criminal liability. The above distinction will instil some sanity into this contentious area of the law.

---

[49] Sed Clariskon & Keating, *supra*, note 4 at p. 182

[50] "Negligent Behaviour should be Excluded from Penal Liability", (1963) 36 Colum. L.R.

[51] "Is Criminal Negligence a Defensible Basis for Penal Liability" (1967) 16 Buffalo L.R. 749. For a contrary view. See, George Fletcher, "The Theory of Criminal Negligence: A Comparative Analysis (1971) 119 U.Pa.L. Rev. 401, where the writer said: "from the view point of culpability as a standard of moral forfeiture, it seems fair and consistent to regard negligence as culpable and to subject the negligent offender to criminal sanctions." Glanville Williams, said that only in exceptional cases should negligence be a basis of liability, see *Criminal Law, supra*, note 7 at p. 123

In Nigeria, under section 24 of the Criminal Code, there is no criminal liability for negligent acts.

COINCIDENCE OF *ACTUS REUS* AND *MENS REA*

For a crime to be properly constituted, the *mens rea* must coincide in point of time with the act which causes the *actus reus*.

In the case of *Shorty*,[52] the defendant violently assaulted the deceased with intent to kill him. Believing that the victim was dead, he attempted to dispose of the body by putting it down a sewer. The deceased was in fact still alive at the time but died of drowning. The court held that became the *actus reus* of murder did not coincide with the *mens rea*, the defendant was not convicted of murder but manslaughter.

Also, in the case of *Thabo Meli* v. *R*[53] the appellant took the deceased to a hut, gave him bear to drink so that he was intoxicated and then struck him over the head. Believing him to be dead, they pushed his body over a cliff. In fact, the man was not dead, but died as a result of exposure to the elements. The Privy Council held that it was impossible to divide up what was really one series of acts in this way. Although the *actus reus* and *mens rea* did not coincide, the court held the accused guilty of murder.

Lord Reid said:

> It appears to their Lordships impossible to divide up what was really one series of acts in this way. There is no doubt that the accused set out to do all these acts in order to achieve their plan.... Their crime is not reduced from murder to manslaughter a lesser crime merely because the accused were under some misapprehension for a time during the completion of their criminal plot.

---

[53] (1954) 1 All E.R. 373

This case is to be preferred to the case of *Shorty*. *Shorty's* case makes a mockery of our law.

In *Church,*[54] the court applied *Thabo Meli*. The court said: "If they (Jury) regarded the appellant's behaviour from the moment he struck her to the moment when he threw her into the river as a series of acts designed to cause death or grievous bodily harm, they could convict for murder." Church was also applied in *R.* v. *Le Brun,*[55] Lord Lane said:

> It seems to us that unlawful application of force to the eventual act causing death are part of the same transaction, the fact that there is an appreciable interval of time between the two does not serve to exonerate the defendant from liability.

We agree with the submission of Lord Lane. We see no reason why an accused person should be found guilty of manslaughter instead of murder just because of the interval between the *actus reus* and *mens rea.* The mistake by the accused as to the method and time of death should not affect his liability.

CONCLUSION

For any society wishing to punish criminal conduct, the elements of criminal liability must be clearly defined. Lack of certainty in any area of criminal law will call into question the seriousness and resolve of the state to punish criminality.

It is our view that the time is ripe for a comprehensive review of our criminal laws, particularly on the issues *actus reus* and *mens rea*.

Such a review should encompass the ambit, and content of *actus reus* and *mens rea.* The present state of the law leaves much to be desired.

---

[55] (1992) 94 Cr. App. R. 101

Chapter 3

STRICT LIABILITY OFFENCES

INTRODUCTION

An offence is said to be a strict liability offence where the prosecution is not required to prove the requisite *mens rea* to bring about the commission of the offence alleged. What is only required of the prosecution is to prove that it is the accused person who committed the *actus reus* of the offence, i.e., the physical injury or harm suffered by the victim.

In strict liability offences the prosecution is relieved of the duty of proving *mens rea* in relation to any element of the *actus reus* and it may be that access to general defences is denied. The modern approach to offences of strictly liability was succinctly put by Lord Reid in the case of *Sweet* v. *Parsely*,[1] when he said:

> our first duty is to consider the words of the Act: if they show a clear intention to create an absolute offence that is the end of the matter. But such cases are very rare. Sometimes the words of the section which creates the particular offence make it clear that *mens rea* is required in one form or another. Such cases are quite frequent. But in a very large number of cases there is no clear indication either way...

However, strict liability offences may well require *mens rea* as to some elements of the *actus reus*, and that is why strict liability means that there is *mens rea* as to one (or more)

---

[1] (1970) AC 132 at 148

elements of the *actus reus*. Although, it has been opined that it does not mean that the prosecution is totally released from the duty of proving *mens rea*.[2] Many strict offences are concerned with regulating behaviour, and for this reason strict offences are often known as "regulatory offences". Strict liability offences are however, not restricted to minor offences.

In the past, strict liability was often called absolute liability. Absolute liability means that the accused person is guilty without any mental element at all and that he has no defence either at common law or under statute.

Strict liability is not restricted to statutory offences. There is a limited recognition in certain areas of the common law. In the area of criminal contempt of court, the strict liability rule which applied to the common law was given statutory recognition by section 1 of the Contempt of Court Act 1981. This section provides that someone may be guilty of contempt regardless of intent where the publication in question creates a substantial risk of serious prejudice or impediment to particular proceedings and those proceedings are active.

In *R* v. *Champ*[3] the Court of Appeal held that the crime of cultivating cannabis was a strict liability offence despite the fact that it is punishable by up to 14 years imprisonment.

Again, the House of Lords had no difficulty in *Pharmaceutical Society* v. *Stortwain Ltd,*[4] in concluding that section 58(2) (a) of the Medicines Act 1968 created an offence of strict liability particularly as other section in the Act expressly required *mens rea* to be proved. Thus, by omitting section 58 from those sections of the Act, Parliament intended that there should be no implication of a requirement of *mens rea* in section 58 (2) (a). The outcome was that a pharmacist who supplied prescription of only drugs, as a result of being given a false prescription, was

---

[2] Michael Jefferson ,*Criminal Law*, 9th edn (England :Pearson Education Ltd, 2009) 134

[3] (1982) 73 Cr. App. R. 367

[4] (1986) 2 All ER 635

guilty of the offence albeit, he was not at fault. Section 58(2)(a) provides thus:

> (a) no person shall sell by retail, or supply in circumstances corresponding to sale, a medicinal product of a description, or falling within a class, specified in an order under this section, except in accordance with a prescription given by an appropriate practitioner.

Similarly, in *Kirkland* v. *Robinson,*[5] the appellant was convicted of possessing live wild birds contrary to section 1(2)(a) of the wildlife and Countryside Act 1981 on the basis that as section 1(1) includes the word "intentionally", but section 1 (2) does not, parliament must have intended it to be an offence of strict liability. Therefore, the court held that his claim that he did not know that the bird in his possession was wild did not provide him with a defence.

Strict liability is not of recent judicial creation. Its roots were firmly established in the nineteenth century and in series of cases from 1846 onwards judges showed little reluctance towards the creation of strict liability offences. In the case of *Cundy* v. *Le Cocq,*[6] a publican sold alcohol to a drunken person, an action which contravened section 13 of the Licensing Act 1872. He claimed that he had no knowledge that the customer was drunk. The Divisional Court upheld his conviction and declared section 13 to be one of strict liability. Stephen J. was of the view that the words of the section amounted to an absolute prohibition and that however genuine the publican's mistake regarding his customer's state of intoxication, this would not provide him with a defence. In *Callow* v. *Tillstone,*[7] a negligent

---

[5] (1987) Crim. LR 463
[6] (1884) 13 QBD 207
[7] (1900) 83 LT 411

examination of a carcass by a veterinary surgeon had resulted in a butcher selling meat which was unfit for human consumption. He, of course, had relied upon the veterinary surgeon's certificate that the meat was good and would have no reason to assume that he was breaking the law. The butcher was convicted on the basis that the offence was one of strict liability. He had, in fact, sold meat which was not fit for human consumption. To compound his misery, the veterinary surgeon, who was charged with aiding and abetting the offence, had his conviction quashed on the basis that aiding and abetting required knowledge of the facts and an intention to encourage. Although he had been negligent in his examination of the animal, it could not be proved that he knew the meat was no good for human consumption.

It will be apparent that it is not just minor regulatory crimes to which strict liability will apply. Although it has been consistently stressed by the judiciary that the more serious the crime the less likely the presumption in favour of *mens rea* will be displaced, this presumption was recognised in the nineteenth century and specially alluded to in *Sherras* v. *De Rutzen*[8] by Wright J. The following words have been quoted and accepted as correct by the higher courts on numerous occasions. For example, see *Lim Chin Aik* v. *R*[9] and *Sweet* v. *Parsely* (*supra*) that:

> there is a presumption that *mens rea* is an essential ingredient in every offence; but that presumption is liable to be displaced either by the words of the statute creating the offence or by the subject matter with which it deals and both must be considered.

Where there is an obvious danger to the community as a result of engaging in a particular activity, the courts are more

[8] (1895) 1 QB 918
[9] (1963) AC 160

likely to deny that the presumption in favour of *mens rea* should apply. In *R* v. *Howels,*[10] the appellant had in his possession a firearm which he believed to be an antique, and he therefore concluded that he did not require a firearm certificate for the gun. In fact, the gun was a modern reproduction and did require a certificate. He was found guilty of contravening section 1 (1) of the Firearms Act of 1968 which makes it an offence for a person to have in his possession, or to purchase or acquire a firearm without holding a firearm certificate in force at that time. Howells argued that section 1 should not be construed so as to make it a strict liability offence and that an honest and mistaken belief should be recognised as a defence.

The Court of Appeal had no doubts that the section should be construed strictly for the following reasons:

(a) the wording of the section would appear to indicate such a conclusion;

(b) the danger to the community from those possessing unlicensed firearms is so great as to warrant an absolute prohibition against their possession without proper authority;

(c) to allow a defence based upon an honest and reasonable belief that the firearm was antique and therefore did not need a certificate would defeat the clear intention of the Act. In *R.* v. *Blake,*[11] the defendant was found guilty of an offence under section 1 (1) of the Wireless Telegraphy Act 1949 of using any apparatus for wireless telegraphy without licence. Investigation offices were concerned that pirates' broadcasts were frequently interfering with emergency service radio communications. They raided the premises of Raga FM and discovered DJ Casanova playing music. The Court of Appeal concluded that the fact that offenders were potentially subject to imprisonment must indicate

[10] (1977) 2 All ER 417

[11] (1977) 1 All E.R 963

that parliament viewed such broadcasts to be a matter of serious social concern which it wished to prevent in the interests of public safety. They concluded therefore that the offence was one of strict liability.

STRICT LIABILITY OFFENCES IN NIGERIA

As stated earlier, offences are classified as strict liability offences where the prosecution need not prove the *mens rea* of the offence in order to secure a conviction. Again, an offence may be classified as a strict liability offence where, on *prima facie* evaluation, the accused person is irresistibly linked to the commission of an alleged crime. It appears that the Nigerian position is not fundamentally different from the law stated above.

Offences in Nigeria are statutorily based. Therefore, there can be no liability for an alleged offence not created by any statute or existing law in Nigeria. Consequently section 36(12) of the 1999 Constitution (as amended) provides that:

> subject as otherwise provided by this constitution a person shall not be convicted of a criminal offence unless that offence is defined and the penalty therefore is prescribed in a written law, a written law refers to an Act of the National Assembly or law of a state, any subsidiary legislation or instrument under the provisions of a law.

Similarly, the provisions of section 4 of the Criminal Code and sections 2 and 3 of the Penal Code are to the same effect that a person cannot be tried or punished in Nigeria except the offence under which the person is been tried is statutorily provided for. Meanwhile, these statutory provisions have been given judicial approval in the case of *Aoko* v. *Fagbemi.*[12] In that case, the accused person was charged and convicted for coming adultery. On appeal, his conviction was quashed on the

[12] (1961) 1 All NLR 400

ground that the offence of adultery was unknown to the provisions of the Criminal Code under which the accused was purportedly being tried.

It may be difficult to predict whether a court would decide that the offence is strict or not. Yet, persons are convicted and imprisoned for these offences. The criminal law is only a way of controlling harmful activities.[13]

THE BASIS FOR STRICT LIABILITY OFFENCES

The difficulty of proving the guilty mind of an accused person may have provided the justification for strict liabilities offences. But this may not be so after all. As stated by Mike Molan,[14] there are several other reasons while the courts should recognise strict liability offences. Accordingly, Mike Molan concludes:

(a) that it helps to prevent prohibited acts because it keeps people on their toes and in this way ensures higher standards than would otherwise prevail;

(b) that without it many of those charged with such offences would plead not guilty and the prosecuting authorities have neither time or the personnel to litigate each case through the courts in the face of a large number of such pleas. This would lead to additional costs to the state and increased delays in the criminal justice system;

(c) those responsible for enforcement usually exercise their discretion and rarely prosecute in the complete absence of fault; and

(d) the existence of specific statutory defences in some cases helps to alleviate possible injustice.

Consequently, certain activities must be prohibited in the interest of public welfare. Activities likely to harm the society

[13] Lacey, B. *et al.*, *Reconstructing Criminal Law* 3rd edn, Lexis Nexis (2003) 50

[14] Mike Molan *et al.*, *Modern Criminal Law*, 5th ed (London, Cavendish Publishing Ltd, 2003)

must not be allowed. This may have informed Lord Parker position in the case of *Yeandel* v. *Fisher*[15] where he said:

> Drugs are a great danger today and legislation has been tightening up, the control of drugs. The courts are looking for socially dangerous activities when they implement the doctrine of strictly liability.

In a similar vein, the court in *Searle* v. *Randolph*[16] found the accused guilty of possessing cannabis when he knew that he had a cigarette end, but not that it contained cannabis.[17] Again, guilty people will not escape through lack of evidence.

However, there are strong arguments against strictly liability offences. It is the contention that unless a contrary intention appears, a person does not commit a code offence unless he acts intentionally, knowingly or recklessly in respect of each of its elements other than fault elements.[18] In the Privy Council case of *Gammon (Hong Kong) Ltd* v. *Attorney-General for Hong Kong,*[19] Lord Scarman provides what is considered as valuable approach to the application of strict liability when he stated:

i. there is a presumption of law that *mens rea* is required before a person can be guilty of a criminal offence;
ii. the presumption is particularly strong where the offence is truly criminal in character;
iii. the presumption applies to statutory offences, and can be displaced only if this is clearly or by necessary implication the effect of the statute;
iv. the only situation in which the presumption can be displaced is where the statute is concerned with an issue of social concern, public safety in such an issue;

---

15 (1966) 1 QB 440
16 (1972) Crim. LR 779
17 Leonard Leigh, *Strict and Vicarious Liability* (London, Sweet and Maxwell, 1982)
18 See section 24(1) of the 1985 version of the English Draft Criminal Code, Law Commission Report No. 143
19 (1985) A.C.1

v. even where the statute is concerned with such an issue, the presumption of *mens rea* stands unless it can be shown that the creation of strict liability will bc effective to promote the objects of the statute by encouraging greater vigilance to prevent the commission of prohibited act.[20]

The decision and reasoning in *B (A minor)* v. *DPP,* is perhaps rather surprising for its rejection of strict liability and welcome for its approach to the issue of mistake in criminal law. However, it is doubtful whether it will have any major impact on the general approach to the imposition of strict liability.

CONCLUSION

In this chapter, we examined strict liability offences. It was posited that strict liability offences require no *mens rea* as an essential element for a conviction. The basis for such offences was also examined. However, we acknowledged the arguments against the application of the strict liability rule. *Mens rea* therefore need not exist in every crime in relation to each element of the *actus reus*. Such, indeed, is the definition of strict liability.[21] It is our opinion that the application of strict liability in certain offences is not a violation of any enactment and as such, where a *prima facie* case is made against an accused person, the proof of the requisite *actus reus*, without more should suffice for a conviction.

---

[20] See the decisive comments in *B (A minor)* v. *DPP* (2000) 1 All ER 833 on the issue of strict liability offence.

[21] Michael Jefferson, *supra*, note 2 at 160

Chapter 4

CORPORATE CRIMINAL LIABILITY

INTRODUCTION

The concept of corporate criminal liability is a creation of the criminal law and is meant to regulate corporations whose corporate activities are capable of having harmful effect on the generality of the society. However, it was earlier doubted whether a corporation, not being a natural person, could form the *mens rea* required by the criminal law for it to be liable to punishment. This has now been laid to rest in the case of *Salomon* v. *Salomon*,[1] where it was held that, although a corporation has no human existence, it is a separate legal person. It is only those who are employed by the corporation that can be held liable for any criminal conduct of the corporation.

To put simply, a corporation is a registered company with perpetual succession and full legal rights to sue and be sued. So, in law, a company is a legal person.

Corporate liability is important because many defective products produced by companies are in the market and cause injury to persons. Also, pollution of the environment is caused by companies and accidents at workplace occupied by companies cause injury to employees.[2] Those who manage the affairs of the company are regarded as embodying the company itself.[3] The result is that a corporation may face

---

[1] (1897) AC 22

[2] Michael Jefferson, Criminal *Law* (England, Pearson Education Ltd, 2009) 218

[3] Legislating the Criminal Code: Involuntary Manslaughter Law.com. 237, 1996

criminal liability for virtually any offence as the *mens rea* of those embodying the company will be determined by reference to the state of mind of such individuals.

In *Deutsche Genossenschafts Bank* v. *Burnhopet*[4] Lord Steyn held that a company can be indicted for an offence of which *mens rea* is an ingredient. Indeed, a company can be guilty of theft of property. If that is so, there can be no reason in principle why a company cannot be guilty of burglary. After all, the essence of burglary is simple theft while trespassing on the property of another. Thus, if the chairman of a company dishonestly instructs an innocent employee to enter a warehouse and remove a bag containing valuables, the company may be guilty of burglary.

More importantly, it should be stressed that a corporation may be held liable in several ways. First a statute may impose liability on a company just as on anyone. If a statute imposes a duty on companies to ensure the health and safety of employees and sub-contractors and a breach of this duty occurs, the company will be criminally liable. This was the decision of the court in the case of *Gateway Food Markets Ltd* v. *DPP*,[5] where a company was held liable when it failed to ensure the safety of a lift and an employee was killed. A statute may impose liability, either expressly or by necessary implication.

Similarly, a corporation, as the owners of a vehicle, may be guilty of the various offences committed by the driver of the vehicle.[6]

Again, a company can be liable for crimes of *mens rea.* In *Mousell Bros* v. *LNWR*,[7] a company was found guilty of fraudulently evading freight charges. A company will be liable

---

[4] (1995) 4 All ER 717
[5] (1997) 2 Cr App R 4, CA
[6] See section 31 of English Transport Act, 1982
[7] (1917) 2 KB 836

for tax evasion, not fencing machinery as required by law, not holding a car licence, selling contaminated food, and so on.[8]

Under the doctrine of identification, which is also known as the *alter ego* doctrine, the liability of the company is personal and not vicarious. It is deemed to have committed the offence by itself. The doctrine makes a company liable for *mens rea* offences. The knowledge of the person to whom full delegation is made is treated as being the knowledge of the company under this doctrine. A company is liable even when a natural person would not be liable.

In *Tesco Supermarkets Ltd* v. *Nattrass,*[9] Lord Reid succinctly puts the doctrine of corporate criminal liability in this perspective:

> A living person has a mind which can have knowledge or intention or be negligent and has hands to carry out his intention. A corporation has none of these: it must act through living persons. Then the person who acts is not speaking or acting for the company. He is acting as the company...He is not acting as a servant, representative, agent or delegate...If (his mind) is a guilty mind, that guilty is the guilt of the company.

A company, being a legal institution, cannot operate without human intervention. It cannot take action or have a state of mind. This principle, known as the *alter ego* doctrine, was also given a judicial flavour in the case of *DPP* v. *Kent & Sussex Contractors Ltd,*[10] where Macnaghten J. stated thus:

> if a responsible agent of the company puts forward on its behalf a document which he knows to be false and by which he intends to deceive... his intention and belief must be imputed to the company.

---

[8] See *Chuter* v. *Freeth & Pocock Ltd* (1911) 2 KB 832

[9] (1972) AC 153

[10] (1944) KB 146

A company, in many ways, may be likened to a human body. It has a brain and a nerve-centre which controls what it does. It also has hands which hold the tools and act in accordance with directions from the centre. Some of the people in the company are mere servants and agents who are nothing more than hands to do the work and cannot be said to represent the mind or will. Others are directors and managers who represent the directing mind and will of the company, and control what it does. The state of mind of these managers is the state mind of the company and is treated by the law as such.[11]

However, it may not be absolutely clear who the controlling officers of a company are, particularly if the company is large. Lord Reid in the *Tesco* case thought that a company could be criminally liable for the acts of its board of directors, the managing director and other superior officers who carry out the functions of the company.[12] Lord Reid postulated that the test of identification applied where there was a substantial delegation of the functions of management. Only a few people such as the managing director and the members of the board are in such positions. The majority looked for those who represent the directing mind and will of the company and control what it does. The phrase, "directing mind and will", which is often used nowadays, comes from a civil case.[13]

In *Meridian Global Funds Asia Ltd* v. *Securities Commission*,[14] Lord Hoffmann, advised that whether a company was liable for a statutory offence depended on the terms of the enactment, its content and its policy. The issue was whether a company was liable for the acts of its senior investment managers done without its knowledge. The judicial committee decided that it was, after investigating the policy of the statute, which was to

---

[11] See, Denning LJ, in *HL Bolton Engineering Co. Ltd v. TJ Graham & Sons Ltd* (1957) 1 QB 159

[12] Mike Molan, *et al.*, *Modern Criminal Law*, 5th edn (London, Cavendish publishing Ltd, 2003) 126

[13] *Lennards Carrying Co. Ltd* v. *Asiatk Petroleum Co Ltd* (1915) AC 705

[14] (1995) 2 AC 500

compel disclosure of the identity of persons who had acquired substantial security. In a company, those persons were those who had the company's authority to acquire the security. Therefore, the company was liable. Similarly, in *Worthy* v. *Gordon Plant (Services) Ltd,*[15] the *actus reus* and *mens rea* of a traffic manager were imputed to the company and in the Nigerian case of *R* v. *Anglo-Nigerian Tin Mines Ltd,*[16] it was held that a firm could be prosecuted for certain offences under the old Minerals Ordinance. In *R.* v. *I.C.R. Haulage,*[17] the suggestion was made that a corporation should be liable for an offence involving violence committed by one of its servants and, in *Moore* v. *Bresler,*[18] a company was convicted in respect of the fraudulent act of its agent, even though he intended to defraud the company. According to Okonkwo and Naish,[19] there is no special legal reason why in principle a corporation should not be convicted under the Criminal Code. Practically every offence in the Code begins with the words "any person who" and the meaning of person as defined in section 3 of the old Interpretation Act, includes "any company or association or body of persons corporate or unincorporated."

The argument that *mens rea* cannot be attributed to a corporation was specifically rejected in *A.G. Eastern Region* v. *Amalgamated Press.*[20] In that case, a corporation was charged under section 14(1) of the Eastern Region Newspaper Law, 1955 which provides that any person who publishes or reproduces, or circulates in newspaper any statement, rumour or report, knowing or having reason to believe that such statement, rumour or report is false, shall be guilty of an offence. Ainle C.J held, *inter alia,*

---

[15] (1995) 2 AC 500
[16] (1989) RTR 7 (DC)
[17] (1944) KB 551
[18] (1944) 2 All ER 515
[19] *Criminal Law in Nigeria*, 2 edn (Ibadan, Spectrum Books ltd, 1980)126
[20] (1956-57) IERLR 12

> I make no doubt that a corporation can have knowledge of the falsity or otherwise of that which is published in a newspaper, and a corporation, through its agents, is clearly capable of publishing newspapers.

LIMITATION OF THE APPLICATION OF THE DOCTRINE OF CORPORATE CRIMINAL LIABILITY

It should be stated that the doctrine of corporate criminal liability does not apply to all offences to which there is a criminal sanction. A corporation, not being a natural person,[21] cannot be convicted for offences requiring death sentence or a term of imprisonment. But where a corporation cannot be found guilty of an offence because no sanction is applicable, other defendants may be guilty in the normal way.

Again, it appears that a company cannot also be tried for a crime of personal violence. In *Northern Strip Mining Construction Co. Ltd.,*[22] a company was tried for manslaughter, but the issue of the propriety of the indictment was not discussed and the firm was acquitted.

Furthermore, the offence of perjury cannot be committed by a company. The argument is that only a person who has been lawfully sworn can be guilty of perjury, and a company cannot lawfully be sworn. A company cannot equally be charged for the offences of rape, incest, bigamy, rogue and vagabond. These offences are regarded as personal crimes, to which only individual human beings could be said to have committed. A company cannot have an unlawful carnal knowledge of any person, and as such cannot be charged and convicted or rape. However, it has been posited that a company can be held liable for these offences. Some writers[23] gave the illustration thus: if Z, the Managing Director of X company Ltd, a film company,

---

[21] A corporation is a creation of law. The law regards it as an artificial legal personality. Therefore, a thin line must been drawn between an artificial legal person and a natural being.

[22] Unreported, 1965

[23] Reed, A and Fitz Patrick, B. , *Criminal Law*, 3rd edn (London: Thomson, Sweet and Maxwell, 2006) 168

supervises the filming of intercourse between M, an 18-year-old male, with N. a 15-year-old girl, there is no reason why Z and hence the film company should not be convicted as secondary parties to the unlawful sexual intercourse. For most crimes such as theft and burglary, there is no problem in finding the company liable. In *Deutsche Genossenschafts Bank* v. *Burnhope* (*supra*) Lord Steyn opined that if the chairman of a company dishonestly instructs an innocent employee to enter (a) warehouse and remove a bag containing valuables the company may be guilty of burglary.

CONCLUSION

The "corporate criminal liability" *per se* is not a novelty. There are many regulatory offences that can be committed by companies. It should be noted that the concept of corporate criminal responsibility is premised on the notion that failure to impose criminal sanction against a corporation constitutes an immunization of the offender who is the actual beneficiary of the illegal activity. It equally amounts to aiding and abetting evasion of criminal culpability.

Finally, it is now firmly established that corporation could be held criminally liable for the infraction of regulatory laws and for committing a criminal offence. However, there are still challenges in attributing culpability to corporation for some offences like murder, rape, etc. It must, however, be stressed that the consequences of corporate activities are the bases for corporate criminal liability.

Chapter 5

VICARIOUS LIABILITY

INTRODUCTION

By vicarious liability, we mean the imposition of liability on one person for the actionable conduct of another, based solely on a relationship between the two persons.[1] This could include indirect or imputed legal responsibility for the acts of another.[2] However, there has been some arguments as to the nature of the doctrine of vicarious criminal liability, as well as the reason for it. The orthodox view assumes that the master is vicariously liable for the servant only when the servant himself would be liable. The first question is to see whether or not the servant was liable. The second question is to determine whether the employer must be liable for the servant liability.[3]

However, the term "vicarious liability" appears to be more applicable in civil cases, especially matters bordering on tortuous acts of servants, where the employer may be vicariously held liable. Accordingly, the desirability of the concept in criminal law has also been questioned.[4] This is so because in criminal law, liability is usually personal and, one person cannot be held criminally liable for the actionable conduct of another.

---

[1] *Blacks Law Dictionary* 9th edition

[2] Atsegbua, L. and Aigbokhaevbo, V., *Law of Torts in Nigeria*, 2nd edn (Benin City, New Era Publication 2005)

[3] See *Young v. Edward Box & Co* (1951) 1 T.L.R. 789 at 1 793 per Denning L.J.

[4] Michael Jefferson , *Criminal Law*: 9th edn (England, Pearson Education Ltd, (2009) 210

In tort, employers are usually liable for the tort of their employees committed in the course of their employment. In criminal law liability is exceptional because as a general rule liability and therefore the stigma of being convicted of an offence is personal to the accused. The exceptions are aimed at obliging the accused to exercise control over other, but it may be unfair to penalize someone for what another has done and the accused may not be deterred in the future.

It should be noted that at Common Law, two main offences could give rise to vicarious liability. In *Stephen's* case,[5] it was stated that since the aim of the prosecution was not to punish the accused but to prevent the continuation of the nuisance. The accused was guilty when his servants had dumped rubbish into a river and thereby obstructed navigation. The court argued that the proceedings were in substance civil in character. It was as if the civil law doctrine of vicarious liability applied. It is assumed that if the proceedings are in truth criminal, the doctrine may not apply. It is difficult to distinguish criminal and civil objectives. Certainly, *Stephen's* case is not applicable to statutory nuisances, where the accused is guilty only when the words of the statute so demand.

The other common law crime importing vicarious liability is criminal libel. In *R* v. *Holbroook,*[6] it was held that the accused person is guilty for authorising another to publisĥ the defamatory material.

Again, a statute could equally make one party vicariously liable for the acts or omissions of another. Furthermore, the principal is liable for the physical acts of his agent, but not for his mental element. In the *Duke of Leinster,*[7] an undisclosed bankrupt was convicted under Section 155 of the Bankruptcy Act of 1914 for obtaining credit of more than £10 without

[5] (1866) LR 1 QB 702
[6] (1978) 4 QBD 42
[7] (1924) 1 KB 311

disclosing his financial situation. He was found guilty even though he had told his agent not to obtain such credit. As earlier noted, the employer is liable for breach of a duty which statute has placed on him. Without this doctrine, defendants could escape criminal liability by delegating their duties and the criminal law would be rendered unenforceable. In *Allen* v. *Whitehead,*[8] the accused employed a manager to run a café in London. He instructed him not to allow prostitutes to gather on the premises, and visited the café once or twice daily. On eight consecutive days, prostitutes stayed there from 8p.m to 4.a.m. He was held guilty of knowingly permitting prostitutes to remain in a place of refreshment, contrary to section 44 of the Metropolitan Police Act 1839. He was guilty even though his manager had flouted his instructions, even though he had put up notices telling prostitutes not to sit in the café and even though he did not know that prostitutes had gathered together. Lord Hewart CJ, said that if the accused was not guilty, this statute would be rendered nugatory. If there is a delegation, the accused is guilty whether he is in the next room or in the next country, the accused is liable vicariously even for the acts of employees low in the hierarchy and even though he is well away from the premises. The doctrine ensures that natural and juristic person do not escape liability when they have delegated a duty to low-level workers, but it should be noted that the doctrine applies even though the accused has taken great care in selecting his employees.

While affirming the doctrine of vicarious liability, Viscount Reading CJ in *Mousell Bros. Ltd* v. *London and North Western Rly Co,*[9] stated thus:

> it may be the intention of the legislature, in order to guard against the happening of the forbidden thing to impose a

[8] (1930) 1 KB 211
[9] (1917) 2 KB 836

> liability upon a principal even though he does not know of and is not party to, the forbidden act done by his servant. Many statutes are passed with this object.

Meanwhile, judicial interpretation will be the determiner or of whether a statute is deemed to impose vicarious liability as it is with strict liability offences. The offences in question are likely to be regulatory in nature as, for example, those imposing duties on licensee. It would be unreasonable to expect the licensee of a public house to carry out all the duties assigned to him under the terms of his licence. In practice, he will delegate the majority of functions to his employees but this would not absolve him of responsibility should there be a breach of the law. The delegation principle therefore imputes the *mens rea* of the employee upon whom the responsibility for complying with the duty has been delegated, to the employer making him liable for the breach of the duty. In simple terms, the delegator will, through his employee, have brought about the *actus reus* with the requisite *mens rea.* This will only apply where the offence is one which requires *mens rea.* If it is an absolute liability offence then *mens rea* will be irrelevant and the delegation principle will be redundant. If it is a strict liability offence where *mens rea* to one or more aspects of the offence need be established, then provided the employee possesses the necessary guilty mind, liability will rest with the delegator. In *Somerset* v. *Hart,*[10] Lord Coleridge CJ, said that a man may put another in his position so as to represent him for the purpose of knowledge.

However, it has been posited that to convict a person who has no *mens rea* of an offence requiring knowledge is unfair and if Parliament wishes to impose liability, it ought to draft legislation making it clear how this is to be achieved without recourse to what is the essence a legal fiction. This view is

---

[10] (1884) 12 QBD 360

supported by the Law Commission in its Draft Criminal Code thus:

> ...the delegation principle was regarded as anomalous by members of the House of Lords in *Vane* v. *Yiannopoullos* and our working party proposed its abolition. Parliament will have to provide clearly for the attribution to one person of the fault of another if it wishes to occur.[11]

Employers would not be using a vehicle when the accused was on folic of his own, such as when he is driving his family to the seaside on a summer Sunday. It should be noted that this extensive construction principle has been said not to apply to licensing offences[12]

It has been surmised thus:

> It seems that under the extensive construction principle only the act of the employee, etc., and not his *mens rea*, can be imputed to the employer, etc. the result is that the principle is limited to offences of strict liability. Where...a strict liability offences requires *mens rea* as to (some) elements, the employer must have *mens rea* as to those elements before (the) can be vicariously liable.[13]

In *Vane* v. *Yiannopoullos,*[14] the accused, a restaurateur, held a licence under which he could serve alcohol only to persons taking meals. He ordered his staff to stick to the terms of the licence. One waitress did not follow his instructions. By a three-to-two majority and with little enthusiasm for the doctrine, the House of Lords held that there was only a partial delegation, which was not sufficient for conviction. The accused was not on the floor where the alcohol was served, but was on the premises. And, in *Ogbuagu* v. *The Police,*[15] a newspaper

[11] The English Law Commission, 177 1989
[12] See *Mckenna* v. *Harding* (1905) 69 JP 265
[13] Card Cross and Jones, *Criminal Law*, 17th edn (OUP, 2006) 854
[14] (1965) Ac 486
[15] (1953) 20 NLR 139

proprietor, before leaving his premises, instructed the man he left in charge not to publish the paper while he was away. The man, in disobedience to the instruction, published a seditious article. In a charge, the proprietor was held not liable. The court further held that, in publishing the paper the servant was not acting as agent of the proprietor, therefore it cannot be said that the proprietor was publishing anything *per alium*.

It appears that an attempt to commit a crime would not attract vicarious liability. In *Gardner* v. *Ackroyd,*[16] it was held that there can be no vicarious liability for attempting an offence even when that crime is one which imposes vicarious liability, when completed. In addition, it was held in *Ferguson* v. *Weaving,*[17] that the doctrine did not apply to aiding and abetting an offence, even though that offence imposed vicarious liability on the principal offender. To be guilty as a secondary offender, the accused must know the essential facts constituting the offence, even a crime of strict liability.

CONCLUSION

The liability of a principal for the actionable conduct of his servant has long been established.[18] It is agreed that the justification for this doctrine is social policy. Lord Reid has said that the effect was to oblige employers to choose employers who take care. However, employers are liable whether or not they took care in the selection of employees. Where the delegation has been total, defendants are guilty even if they have instructed their agents to comply with the law.

---

[16] (1952) 2 QB 743

[17] (1951) 1 KB 814

[18] Generally, however, the employer of an independent contractor is not liable for the acts committed by the contractor or his employees in the course of the job for which he is engaged. The law considers that's since the employer cannot control the way in which the contractor does the work, it is the contractor alone who is in position to guard against any risk incidental to the work and who must therefore alone answerable for any damage caused to third parties as a result of his failure to take due precaution.

The proponents of this doctrine have also posited that the employers may have financially benefited from their servants' wrongdoing and as such they are the proper persons to be held vicariously liable.

Lord Evershed, has in *Vane* v. *Yannopoullos, supra* observed:

> where the scope and purpose of the relevant Act is the maintenance of proper and accepted standards of public order in licensed premises or other comparable establishments, there arises under the legislation what Channell, J in *Ernary* v. *Nolloth* (1903) 2 KB 264 called a 'quasi- criminal offence' which renders the licensee or proprietor criminally liable for the acts of his servants, though there may be no *mens rea* on his part. On the other hand, where the relevant legislation imports the word "knowingly...the result will be different --- in the proof of actual knowledge, nevertheless, the licensee or proprietor may be held liable if he is shown effectively to have delegated his proprietory or management functions.

Further justifying the application of the doctrine of vicarious liability, Edwards, J. stated that so long as the criminal law is used as a means to securing the legislative standard of correct trading, business and social welfare behaviour, it is legitimate to have recourse to the principle of vicarious liability.[19]

On the other side of the divide, it is posited that as a fundamental principle of criminal law, criminal responsibility should be personal. Why should a blameless person be punished for something another has done? Devlin, J. put it succinctly in ***Reynolds*** v. ***G.H. Austin & Sons Ltd***[20] when he said:

> if a man is punished because of an act done by another, whom he cannot reasonably be expected to influence or control, the law is engaged not in punishing thoughtless or inefficiency thereby promoting the welfare of the community, but in pouncing upon the most convenient victims.

---

[19] Edwards J., *Mens Rea in Statutory Offences* (Macmillan, 1955 243

[20] (1951) 2 KB 135

Chapter 6

THE OFFENCE OF SEDITION

INTRODUCTION

Every citizen of a country has a right to freedom of information and opinion. This freedom extends to the right of expression. Therefore, an individual can hold any opinion within the permissible limit of the law. The permissible limit to which an expression may be held was aptly demonstrated by Ademola C.J. in the case of *DPP* v. *Obi*[1] when he said:

> ...A person has a right to discuss any grievance or criticize, canvass and censure the acts of Government and their public policy. He may even do this with a view to effecting a change in the party in power or to call attention to the weakness of a Government, so long as he keeps within limit of fair criticism. It is clearly legitimate and constitutional by means of fair argument to criticize the Government of the day. What is not permitted is to criticise the Government in a malignant manner as described above, for such attacks, by their nature tend to affect the public peace.

The 1999 Constitution creates and guarantees the right to freedom of information, expression and the press.[2] Section 39 of the 1999 Constitution provides:

> 39(1) Every person shall be entitled to the freedom of expression, including freedom to hold opinion and

[1] (1961) 1 All N.L.R. 186

[2] Recently the National Assembly enacted the Freedom of Information Act., 2011. This Act seeks to provide protection and guaranteed assess to information. However, such information does not include the disclosure of sensitive security information

to receive and impact ideas and information without interference.

(2) Without prejudice to the generality of subsection (1) of this section every person shall be entitled to own, established and operate any medium for the dissemination of information, ideas and opinions.

The Constitution however provided a proviso thus:

If no person other than the Government of the Federation or of a State or any other person or body authorized by the president on the fulfilment of conditions laid down by an Act of the National Assembly shall own, establish or operate a television or wireless broadcasting station for any purpose whatsoever.

(3) Nothing in this section shall invalidate any law that is reasonably justifiable in a democratic society:

a. for the purpose of preventing the disclosure of information received in confidence, maintaining the authority and independence of courts or regulating telephony, wireless broadcasting, television or the exhibition of cinematography firms; or

b. imposing restrictions upon persons holding office under the Government of the Federation or of a State, members of the Armed Forces of the Federation or members of the Nigeria Police Force or other Government security services or agencies established by law.

However, it has been argued that the purpose of this section is to protect all persons, including the media, to write and to print as they will and, together, news for such publication without interference.[3] The section does not, however, authorised the publication of false and unverified information.

SEDITION

The offence of sedition is contained in both the Criminal Code and the Penal Code. Section 51 of the Criminal Code provides:

1. Any person who:
   (a) does or attempts to do, or makes any preparation to do, or conspires with any person to do, any act with a seditious intention;
   (b) utters any seditious words;
   (c) prints, publishes, sells, offers for sale, distributes or reproduces any seditious publication
   (d) imports any seditious publication, unless he has no reason to believe that it is seditious; for a first offence to imprisonment for two years or to a fine of two hundred naira or to both such imprisonment and fine and for a subsequent offence to imprisonment for three years and any seditious publication shall be forfeited to the state.

(2) Any person who without lawful exercise has in his possession any seditious publication is guilty of an offence and shall be liable on conviction for a first offence to imprisonment for one year or to a fine of one hundred naira or to both such imprisonment and for a subsequent offence to imprisonment for two years and such publication shall be forfeited to the state.

The offence of seditious has both the mental and the physical element of a crime. The mental element which is the *mens rea* must combined with the physical element the *actus reus*, for the offence of seditious to be complete or said to have been committed. For example, it must be established that

[3] Akpotaire V., *Criminal Law in Nigeria*, (Benin City, Sylva Publication Ltd 1999) 42

there is a seditious intention to publish the offending publication and the actual publication. Once these two elements are present, the offence of sedition could be said to have been committed.

THE MENTAL ELEMENTS OF SEDITION

Under Section 50(2) A "Seditious intention": is an intention:

(a) To bring into hatred or contempt or excite disaffection against the person of the President or of the Governor of a state or the Government of the Federation, or
(b) To excite the citizens or other inhabitants of Nigeria to attempt to procure the alteration, otherwise than by lawful means, of any other matter in Nigeria as by law established, or
(c) To raise discontent or disaffection amongst the citizens or other inhabitants of Nigeria, or
(d) To promote feelings of ill will and hostility between different classes of the population of Nigeria.

But an act, speech or publication is not seditious by reason only that it intends:

(i) to show that the President or the Governor of a state has been misled or mistaken in any measure in the Federation or a State as the case may be or,
(ii) to point out errors or defects in the Government or Constitution of Nigeria, or any State thereof, as by law established or in legislation or in the administration of justice with a view to

the remedying of such errors or defects; or

(iii) to persuade the citizens or other inhabitants of Nigeria to attempt to procure by lawful means the alteration of any matter in Nigeria as by law established, or

(iv) to point out, with a view to their removal, any matters which are producing or have a tendency to produce feelings of ill-will and enmity between different classes of the population of Nigeria.

(2) In determining whether the intention with which any act was done, any words were spoken, or any document was published was not seditious, every person shall be deemed to intend the consequences which would naturally follow from his conduct at the time and under the circumstances in which he so conducted himself.

Meanwhile, in a democratic society with a multiparty system of government, usually, the opposition party often offer criticisms against the government of the day by trying to point out their errors and weaknesses. These, the Criminal Code says are not seditious. But such criticism may be designed to ridicule the ruling government and its party. Could this not amount to sedition? The case of *Inspector General of Police* v. *Anagbogu,*[4] appears to be a pointer in this direction, when it was observed thus:

> He who writes an article with a seditious aim as defined in (a) to (d) cannot by including in the article criticism which is legitimate under (i) to (iv) be excused from a charge of writing a seditious article...often enough a seditious article does

---

[4] (1954) 21 NLR 26 at 27

> contain parts which are not seditious. These parts do not excuse the article from being seditious.

According to Okonkwo and Naish,[5] provided that the seditious intention is clear, a publication does not cease to be seditious merely because it does not tend to incite people to violence. This position was given a judicial approval in the case of *R* v. *Johnson Wallace*[6] when it was stated that:

> Violence may well be no doubt often is the result of wild and ill-considered words, but the code does not require proof from words themselves of any intention to produce such a result.

There can be no doubt that the absence of need to prove an intention to excite violence is a great impediment to freedom of speech.

In another development, it has also been opined that seditious intention could be inferred from the nature and manner in which an article was published. In *Nwobiala* v. *The Inspector General of Police,*[7] the appellant sent telegram to the premier of the then Eastern Region, who was also the National President of the party in power in the Region accusing leaders of his party of acts which brought discredit on the Government and calling on him to restrain them. His appeal against conviction was allowed on the ground that there was no seditious intention either in the words of the telegram or in the method of publication. But in *Ogidi* v. *COP,*[8] where the appellant sent a telegram to the Minister of Justice and a copy of which was also sent to the print and electronic media, wherein he accused the customary courts of a division of being the creatures of a political party, and of discriminating against

---

[5] *Criminal Law in Nigeria* , 2nd edn (Ibadan, Spectrum Books Ltd, 1980) 342

[6] (1939) 5 WACA, 56 at 61

[7] (1960)5 FSC, 243. A contrary decision was reached in the case of *R* v. *African Press* (1951) W.N.L.R. 1

[8] (1960) F.S.C. 251

the opponents and that citizens were not safe with the courts. It was held that the publication was strongly calculated to bring to hatred and contempt the administration of justice and that the intention behind the publication, which was communicated to the world at large, was certainly seditious.

It has also been held that seditious intention may be inferred from the circumstances surrounding the publication, the class of persons to whom it is addressed and the prevailing situation in the country.[9] Provided that seditious intention is established, there is no need to show that the publication intends to incite people to violence. This is perhaps the most significant difference between sedition under the Nigerian codes and the English Law.[10] Under the English Law, failure to establish intention to incite people to violence is fatal to the case of the prosecution. In *R.* v. *Burns,*[11] it was stated as follows:

> ...The privilege of pointing out errors and defects must often be illusory if the intention to excite violence need not be proved, since the dispassionate pointing out of errors may well excite hatred and contempt against those responsible for them. And the more grievous the errors or defect, the more likely it is that hatred and contempt will be excited.

Similarly, in *R.* v. *Aldred,*[12] Coleridge J. has this to say:

> In arriving at a decision of this test, you are entitled to look at all the circumstances surrounding the publication with the view of seeing whether the language used is calculated to produce the results imputed: that is to say, you are entitled to look at the audience address, because language which would be innocuous, practically speaking, if used to an assembly of professors or divines, might produce a different result if used before an excited audience of young and uneducated men. You

---

[9] *R* v. *Agwuna* (1949) 12 WACA, 456

[10] *R* v. *Johnson Wallace, supra*, at n.6

[11] (1886) 2 T.I.R., 510

[12] (1909) 22 Cox 1

> are entitled also to take into account the state of public feeling. Of course, there are times when a spark will explode a powder magazine, the effect of language may be very different at one time from what it would be at another.

In particular, section 50(3) provides that in determining whether the intention with which any act was done, any words were spoken or any document was published, was or was not seditious, every person shall be deemed to intend the consequences which would naturally follow from his conduct at the time and under the circumstances in which he so conducted himself.

Okonkwo and Naish[13] argued that on a strict interpretation of this provision, it would seem to follow that if a person utters seditious words, but has no seditious intention, he would be convicted because his intention must be inferred from the words. Consequently, a person may be guilty of sedition even though he honestly did not intend to commit that offence. It is suggested that the provision must be interpreted to include an element of foresight. The accused must foresee that his words are calculated to have a seditious effect. If a member of a political party is addressing a rally and he is requested by the organisers to read out a letter which unknown to him is seditious, and he reads out nearly all of it before he realises that it is seditious and stops, it would be harsh to convict him of sedition. Clearly, he has uttered seditious words, but he did not intend to do any of the things set out in section 50(2).

The Federal Supreme Court has held in *Director of Public Prosecution* v. *Obi supra* that the purpose of section 50(3) is to enable the prosecution to rely upon the words or publication itself, to prove intent, without having to call extrinsic evidence. The subsection, the court held, cannot be interpreted so as to

---

[13] Supra, note 5 at 344

deprive a person of his right to show that his only intention is one of those set out in the second paragraph of section 50(2).

THE PHYSICAL ELEMENT OF SEDITION

By physical element of sedition, we mean the *actus reus.* That is the actual act that was seditious. The conduct of the accused person, which may constitute the *actus reus* of sedition, are actually printing, publishing, offering for sale, distributing, reproducing or importing of the seditious publication. Under the Penal Code, the actual publication of the seditious material is *sine qua non* to the commission of the offence. It is, however, doubted whether it is the same position under the Criminal Code. Under the Criminal Code, there are indications that the offence may be committed without the publication of the seditious material.

It has been noted that a person who makes preparation to print a seditious document with the intention of distributing the same to the public with a view to exciting the populace may be guilty under Section 57(1) of the Criminal Code. Yet there is no publication.[14]

In another vein, the offence of possession of seditious materials without lawful excuse under section 51(2) of the Criminal Code clearly does not require any communication to any person of the materials.

Meanwhile, the consent of the Attorney General (Federal or State as the case may be) is necessary for a prosecution for sedition, which must be commenced within six months after the commission of the offence.[15] And no person shall be convicted of uttering seditious words on the uncorroborated testimony of one witness.[16]

---

[14] Akpotaire ,*supra,* note 3

[15] Section 52(1) and (2) The signature by the A-G personally of an information is sufficient compliance with this provision and it is not necessary for a document consenting to the institution of the prosecution to be filled in addition.

[16] See the provision of section 52(3) of the Criminal Code

Conclusively, it is settled that sedition is a crime against the state. It is therefore suggested that an act which is done maliciously in order to bring the government of the day to ridicule and disrepute should be treated as sedition. This is because such conducts are capable of painting the whole nation in a bad light to the rest of the world.

Chapter 7

INCHOATE OFFENCES

INTRODUCTION

An offence attempted is commonly classified as an inchoate offence. According to Clarkson and Keating,[1] an inchoate offence is committed when the defendant takes certain steps towards the commission of a crime. With attempt, the defendant must have tried to commit the offence and got relatively close to achieving his objective. It is argued in this chapter that when an offence is attempted, there is a harm against to the victim. At least, there is a threat to life and security. It is, therefore, opined that, an attempted crime should attract the same punishment as that completed because an accused person who attempts to commit a criminal offence has the *mens rea* to bring about the commission of the actual crime.

The chapter will equally examine the liability for criminal conspiracy to bring about the commission of a crime. It will be contended that a common agreement between two or more persons to do an unlawful act or to do a lawful act by unlawful means must attract the maximum criminal sanction as may be prescribed by law.

WHAT IS ATTEMPT?

It is interesting to note that both the Criminal Code and the Penal Code provide a clear definition for attempt. It has been argued that between the conception and the completed crime,

---

[1] *Criminal Law, Text and Materials*, 3rd ed (London, Sweet & Maxwell, 1998) p. 442

there exist a terrain in which there is the preparation to commit or an attempt to commit the offence.

Section 4 of the Criminal Code[2] provides that:

> when a person intending to commit an offence, begins to put his intention into execution by means adopted to its fulfilment and manifests his intention to such an extent as to commit the offence, he is said to attempt to commit the offence.

On its part, section 95 of the Penal Code[3] provides among others that whoever attempts to commit an offence punishable with a term of imprisonment or with a fine shall be so punished with such a fine or both. In effect, the Penal Code punishes an attempt to commit a crime.

In England, there are many other offences that might qualify as inchoate offences in the sense that they penalise conduct that might be preparatory to the commission of other offences, for example possession of firearms.[4] In English Law, attempt is a crime in itself, as it is indictable as such without reference to any further offence.

However, only about 20 per cent of attempts are ever reported to the police and therefore the proportion coming through the courts is much smaller. It is speculated that about half of the attempts failed because the level of security, and that the proportion of attempts has increased in recent years.[5]

To constitute an offence in the Nigerian context, the act of the accused person must be immediately connected with the commission of the particular offence and must be something more than mere preparation for the commission of the offence.[6]

---

[2] Cap C 34 Laws of the Federation of Nigeria 2004

[3] Cap P 3 Laws of the Federation of Nigeria 2004

[4] Sections 16-22, The English Firearms Act 1968

[5] Molan M., *et al*, *Modern Criminal Law*, 5th ed, (London, Cavendish Publishing Ltd) (2003) 159

[6] *Jegede* v. *The State* (2001) 14 NWLR (pt 733) 264 SC

THE LAW ON ATTEMPTS

It is now a settled law that, where a crime is attempted, there is a harm and a threat to life and security. In our society, we all have rights to bodily and proprietary security. An attempt to commit a crime represents a danger to these rights. Our right to security may have been infringed upon. This infringement of our rights constitutes in itself a harm that the criminal law seeks to punish. Gross expresses the view when he said:

> Where there is only attempt, liability, the conduct itself may usefully be regarded as a second order harm, in itself. It is the sort of conduct that normally presents a threat of harm, and that by itself, is a violation of an interest that concerns the law. The interest is of in security from harm and merely presenting a threat of harm violates that security interest.[7]

The laws in England and Nigeria both made provisions for the offence of attempt. Section 1(4) of the English Criminal Attempts Act 1981 provides that, there can only be criminal liability for attempts to commit "any offence which if it were completed would be triable...as indictable offence." It is observed that criminal liability for attempts to commit summary offences was excluded because there is "no social need to extend the punishment of attempt outside the class of serious crimes."[8]

As earlier noted, the Nigerian Criminal Code and the Penal Code both provide for the offence of attempt, which is also punishable either with a term of imprisonment, fine or both.

Section 508 of the Criminal Code provides that any person who attempts to commit a felony or misdemeanour is guilty of

---

[7] *Theory of Criminal Justice* (1979) p. 125

[8] In the *Attorney General's Reference* (No. 3 of 1994) 2 All ER 21, Schiemann J expressed the rationale underpinning the law on attempt when he said: "one way of analysing the situation is to say that a defendant, in order to be guilty of attempt, must be in one of the states of mind required for the commission of the full offence and did his best as far as he could, to supply what was missing from the completion of the offence. It is the policy of the law that such people should be punished notwithstanding that in fact the intention of such a defendant have not been fulfilled.

an offence which unless otherwise stated is a misdemeanour. Furthermore, section 509 the Criminal Code punishes an attempt to commit a felony of any kind.

Section 229 of the Penal Code applies to offences punishable with a term of imprisonment. With attempts, criminal liability can be imposed in the absence of any direct harm. Thus, when dealing with serious offences we are arguably justified in dispensing with the requirement of harm.

Meanwhile, Glazebrook has suggested that we do not need a general law of attempt. According to him, each substantive offence could be defined, or redefined, so as to include attempts to commit that offence.

It should be stressed that under section 4(1) of the Criminal Attempts Act 1981, a person guilty of attempting to commit an offence shall (a) if the offence attempted is murder or any other offence the sentence for which is fixed by law, be liable on conviction on indictment to imprisonment for life.

More so, under the California Penal Code, section 664(3) provides that if the offence so attempted is punishable by a fine, the offender convicted of such attempt is punishable by a fine not exceeding one-half the largest fine which may be so imposed upon a conviction of the offence so attempted.

It is suggested that an attempted crime should attract the same punishment as that completed in that a defendant who attempt to commit murder has the intention to kill.

THE *MENS REA* OF ATTEMPT

By virtue of section 4 of the Criminal Code, the required *mens rea* for attempts is the direct intention to commit the offence to which an accused person is alleged to have attempted.[9]

---

[9] In *R* v. *Mohan* (1975) 2 All ER 193, the Court of Appeal concluded that attempt was a crime of specific intent and defined that it means a ..... decision to bring about, in so far as it lies within the accused's power, the commission of the offence which it is alleged the accused attempted to commit, no matter whether the accuse deserved the consequences of his act or not.

Similarly, section 1(1) of the Criminal Attempts Act 1981, provides to the effect that, the defendant must act with the intent to commit an offence.

The effect of these provisions is that the prosecution must prove that the accused person has the intention to commit the offence which is alleged against him. It is not enough that the accused attempted the alleged offence, but that he has the intention to bring about the act alleged and had taken further steps towards achieving his objectives. In the Nigerian case of *Bassey Akpan Iden* v. *The State,*[10] the appellant was convicted on the charge of attempted murder. He appealed, contending that the trial court did not make any specific findings on whether or not the appellant had the intention to kill. While, dismissing the appeal and upholding the decision of the lower court, the Court of Appeal held that the *mens rea* in a charge of attempted murder is the intention to kill.

In *R.* v. *Mohan,*[11] James, L.J. has this to say:

> In our judgment, it is well established law that intent (*mens rea*) is an essential ingredient of the offence of attempt...An attempt to commit a crime is itself an offence. Often it is a grave offence...It is as morally culpable as the completed offence which is attempted but not in fact committed...

Similarly, in *R* v. *Whybrow,*[12] the defendant constructed a device and administered an electric shock to his wife while she was bathing. The Court of Appeal held that while an intention to kill or to cause grievous bodily harm would suffice for the completed crime of murder, for attempted murder an intention to kill was necessary. This is because for attempted murder, the intent becomes the principal ingredient of the crime.

---

[10] (1994) 8 NWLR (pt 365) P 719, CA

[11] (1976) Q.B. Pg 1

[12] (1951) 35 CR APP R, 141

In *Nwankwo* v. *Federal Republic of Nigeria,*[13] it was held that an attempt to commit a crime is an act done with the intent to commit that crime which forms part of a series of acts, which would constitute its actual commission if it were not interrupted.[14]

In another English case of *R* v. *Khan,*[15] the appellant attempted to have sexual intercourse with a non-consenting girl, but failed. The Court of Appeal, Russell L.J. held, *inter alia*:

> In our judgment...The words with intent to commit an offence, to be found in section 1 of the 1981 Act mean, when applied to rape, with intent to have sexual intercourse with a woman in circumstances where she does not consent and the defendant knows or could not care less about her absence of consent...He commits the offence because of the circumstances in which he manifests that intent.

Therefore, we are of the opinion that the mere intent to commit an offence suffices for the crime alleged. It is immaterial whether the accused succeeded in committing the actual offence or not.

THE *ACTUS REUS* OF ATTEMPT

The acts of the accused person that constitutes the *actus reus* of attempt must be acts directly and immediately connected to the offence attempted. By the provisions of section 4 of the Criminal Code, the following elements can be said to constitute the *actus reus* of attempt. These are:

---

[13] (2003) 4 NWLR (pt 809) Pg. 1 CA

[14] It is incumbent upon those analysing this area of the law to be aware that whatever the *mens rea* for the completed offence, only intention will suffice for a charged of attempt as evidenced in *R* v. *O' Toole* (1987) Crim LR 759 where reference in the indictment to recklessness on a charge of attempted criminal damage meant that the conviction had to be quashed. The accused must be doing everything in his power to bring about the completed offence and this is inconsistent with the concept of recklessness

[15] (1990) 2 All ER 783

(a) to begin to put the intention into execution by means adapted to its fulfilment;
(b) to manifest the intention by some overt acts, even though the actual offence is yet to be committed;
(c) that the accused has the intention to bring about the commission of the actual crime.

Section 1(1) of the Criminal Attempts Act, provides that "if with intent to commit an offence to which the section applies, a person does an act which is more than merely preparatory to the commission of the offence, he is guilty of attempting to commit the offence."[16]

Therefore, if attempt must be held as threats to people's lives and security, the accused person must be closely connected to the completion of the alleged crime. Until that is established, it cannot be said that there is a threat to the security of lives and property. In *R* v. *Gullefer,*[17] the appellant during a race at a greyhound-racing stadium climbed onto the track in front of the dogs and attempted to distract them by waving his arms. He told the police that he had attempted to stop the race because the dog on which he had staked £18 was losing. He was convicted of attempted theft. He appealed to the Court of Appeal contending that his act was not sufficiently proximate to the completed offence of theft to be capable of comprising an attempt to commit theft. While allowing the appeal, Lord Lane, CJ has this to say:

> ...might it be properly be said that when he jumped onto the track, he was trying to steal £18 from the bookmaker? Our view is that it could not properly be said that at that stage he was in the process of committing theft...In our view there was

---

[16] The law on attempts is to be found in the Criminal Attempt Act 1981, having until then been ruled by the common law. The law on attempts primarily addresses the issue of failure, that is, the inability to make a success of the proposed criminal enterprise. It acknowledges that the accused failed to bring about the *actus reus* of the particular crime he or she has in mind.

[17] (1990) 91 Cr App R 356

> insufficient evidence for it to be said that he had, when he jumped onto the track gone beyond mere preparation...

Similarly, in *R.* v. *Eagleton*,[18] Per Parke B, observed as follows:

> Some act is required and we do not think that all acts towards committing a misdemeanour are indictable. Acts remotely leading towards the commission of the offence are not to be considered as attempts to commit it, but acts immediately connected with it are.

In the recent case of *Aminu* v. *The State*[19] the Court of Appeal held that the act that amounts to an attempt is one that must be immediately connected with the possible commission of the substantive offence. The court further held that the appeal must be dismissed on the ground that the prosecution has not been able to prove that there was a clear and unequivocal nexus between the overt act of attempt and the substantive offence of murder.

Furthermore, in *R.* v. *Robinson*,[20] the Court of Appeal held that what the appellant did was a preparation for the commission of a crime and that there was no further step to the commission of the offence. The court observed:

> If he had made a claim of the money from the underwriters, or had communicated to them the facts of the pretended burglary upon which a claim was to be subsequently based, he clearly could have been convicted.

It is, however, conceded that the overt act of the accused person must be contemporaneous with the actual crime alleged for the offence of attempt to be established and sustained.

---

[18] (1885) 6 Cox C.C. 559
[19] (2005) 2 NWLR (PT 908) 180, CA
[20] (1915) 2 KB 342

IMPOSSIBILITY

One may be faced with the question whether or not a defendant should be held criminally liable for attempting the impossible.

The impossibility may be legal, physical or otherwise. Section 1 (2) of the Criminal Attempts Act 1981, provides to the effect that "a person may be guilty of attempting to commit an offence to which this section applies even though the facts are such that the commission of the offence is impossible."

The legal implication of this provision is that there can be criminal liability for attempting the impossible, irrespective of the category of impossibility.

However, where the law creates an impossibility for the commission of in an offence, there could be no criminal liability. In *Haughton* v. *Smith,*[21] the defendant was charged with attempting to handle stolen goods contrary to section 22 of the Theft Act 1968. The defendant had actually handled the goods but, unknown to him, they were not stolen goods. The House of Lords held that there could be no liability for attempt in such circumstances. Lord Reid was apt in saying:

> The crime is impossible in the circumstances, so no acts could be proximate to it...He took no step towards the commission of a crime because there was no crime to commit.

Again, where it is physically impossible for the accused person to commit the alleged offence, there can be no attempt. In *Partington* v. *Williams,*[22] it was held that there could be no liability where in the circumstances of the case, the substantive offence is impossible of being committed.

Furthermore, apart from the impossibility rule, it is now provided in section 4 of the Criminal Code that it is irrelevant to

---

[21] (1975) A.C. 476

[22] (1975) 62 CR. APP R. 220

liability that the fulfilment of the offender's intention was prevented by circumstances independent of his will.

There could be no attempt if the alleged offence is impossible to be committed due to the defendant's ineptitude, inefficiency or his adoption of insufficient means to bring about the commission of the actual offence.

But in *R.* v. *White*,[23] the defendant tried to kill his mother with poison but used an insufficient quantity of poison for that purpose. He was convicted of attempted murder. Lord Reid observation is apt when he said:

> A man may set out to commit a crime with inadequate tools. He finds that he cannot break in because the door is too strong for him or he uses poison, which is not strong enough. He is certainly guilty of attempt; with better equipment or greater skill, he could have committed the full crime.[24]

It is now agreed that there should be liability in certain obvious cases of attempts to bring about the commission of the actual crime. Accordingly, attempting is not just an event of inner experience; it is an effort in the real world to accomplish one's objective. Therefore, when the act is aptly related to that of the actor's objective, the courts should perceive a manifest attempt to commit an offence.

PUNISHMENT OF ATTEMPTS

In Nigeria, as well as in England and the United States of America, attempt to commit a crime is punishable.

In the United States of America, the California Penal Code provides that every person who attempts to commit any crime, but fails, or is prevented or intercepted in the preparation thereof is punishable.

Section 664(2) of the California Penal Code provides thus:

---

[23] (1910) 2 KB 124

[24] *Haughton* v. *Smith*, *supra*, note 21

> If the offence so attempted is punishable by imprisonment in a county jail, the person guilty of such attempts is punishable by imprisonment in a county jail for a term not exceeding one-half the term of imprisonment prescribed upon a conviction of the offence so attempted.

The basis for imposing punishment on attempted crimes is to serve as deterrence to those who may contemplate the commission of a crime of any sort, who if not prevented would take further steps towards achieving their objective of committing the actual crime.

In England, the completed crime of theft carries a maximum of seven years imprisonment[25] and attempted theft can similarly be punished up to this maximum of seven years. But in California, if theft is committed, it carries a presumptive penalty of seven years imprisonment in the state prison, while attempted theft would carry a presumptive penalty of three and a half years imprisonment.

In Nigeria, both the Criminal Code and the Penal Code provide punishment for attempts. In certain offences, the punishment for attempt is specified. It should be pointed out that the punishment for attempt varies according to whether the offence attempted was a felony punishable with death or 14 years imprisonment or any other kind of felony, a misdemeanour or a simple offence.

Section 508 of the Criminal Code makes every attempt not otherwise specifically provided for, a misdemeanour. Meanwhile section 512 of the Criminal Code reduces by half the punishment of attempt where it is shown that the accused voluntarily desisted from the completed crime. The Criminal

[25] See section of Theft Act of 1968

Code, under section 221 punishes both attempt and the crime of defilement equally with 2 years' imprisonment.

Under the Penal Code, section 229 punishes an attempted culpable homicide punishable with death with life imprisonment or any less term or with fine or both. By the provisions of sections 298-299 of the Penal Code, the completed offence of robbery attracts up to fourteen years imprisonment while the attempt is punishable with up to seven years imprisonment.

Finally, it is no longer a gainsaying than that the law punishes attempt to commit an offence. This is reflected both in the English Criminal Attempt Act, the California Penal Code and the Nigeria Criminal and Penal Codes respectively.

CONSPIRACY

Conspiracy has been defined[26] to mean a secret plan by a group of people to do something harmful or illegal. For there to be conspiracy, there must be an agreement between two or more persons to prosecute an unlawful purpose through unlawful means.[27]

In England, the development of conspiracy from a narrow, circumscribed crime of agreeing falsely to accuse another, to one where agreeing to do any unlawful act fell with its ambit, and its use in particular against the early trade union movement is well documented.[28] Conviction for conspiracy usually depends on interferences from overt acts said by the

---

[26] The *Oxford Advanced Learner's Dictionary* 6th edn.

[27] In *Sule v. State* (2009) 17 NWLR (pt 1169) 33 SC, Ogbuagu JSC held, an offence of conspiracy can be committed where persons have acted either by an agreement or in concert. A bare agreement to commit an offence is sufficient. The actual commission of the offence is not necessary. Thus, conspiracy to commit an offence is a separate and distinct offence and it is independent of the actual commission of the offence to which the conspiracy is related.

[28] Per Lord Diplock in *D.P.P* v. *Bhagwan* (1972) AC 60 at 79, where he observed; The development of conspiracy from a narrowly circumscribed crime of agreeing falsely to accuse another to one where agreeing to do any unlawful act feel within its ambit, and its use in particular against the early trade union movement has been well documented.

prosecution to have been performed in pursuance of the agreement. In practical terms, liability arises by virtue of overt acts done in pursuance of the agreement.

In the United States of America, the Model Penal Code of the American Law Institute provides that no person may be convicted of conspiracy to commit a crime, other than a felony of the first or second degree, unless an overt act in pursuance of such conspiracy is alleged and proved to have been done by him or by a person with whom he conspired.

According to *Phillip Johnson,*[29] conspiracy is also an inchoate or preparatory crime, permitting the punishment of persons who agree to commit a crime even if they never carry out their scheme or are apprehended before their objective.

At Common Law, conspiracy was an agreement between two or more persons to do an unlawful act or to do a lawful act by unlawful means. Thus, it was not necessary to prove that there was an agreement to commit a crime. Agreement to commit other unlawful acts, such as fraud, some torts or corruption of public morals clearly sufficed.[30]

Section 1 of the Criminal Attempts Act of 1981, provides that if a person agrees with any other person or persons that a course of conduct shall be pursued which if the agreement is carried out in accordance with their intentions either:

(a) will necessarily amount to or involve the commission of any offence or offences by one or more of the parties to the agreement; or

(b) would do so but for the existence of facts which render the commission of the offence or any of the offence impossible, he is guilty of conspiracy to commit the offence or offences in question.

---

[29] "The Unnecessary Crime of Conspiracy" (1973) 61 Col. L. Rev. 1137 at 1157 - 1158

[30] In *Kamara* v. *D.P.P.* (1974) AC 104, an agreement to commit the tort of trespass to land, if accompanied by an intention to inflict more than merely nominal damage was held to be a criminal conspiracy

In *R.* v. *Reed,*[31] it was held that if A and B agree to rob a bank, if when they arrive at the bank, it seems safe to do so, their agreement will necessarily involve the commission of the offence of robbery, if it is carried out in accordance with their intentions, accordingly they are guilty of the statutory offence of conspiracy.

Similarly, in *R.* v. *Anderson,*[32] the defendant agreed for a fee to supply diamond wire to cut through bar in order to enable another to escape from prison. He claimed that he only intended to supply the wire and then go abroad. He believed that the plan could never succeed. The appellant' s conviction for conspiring with others to effect the release of one of them from prison, claiming that as he did not intend or expect the plan to be carried out, he lacked the *mens rea* for the offence of conspiracy. The appeal was dismissed.

And in Nigeria, the offence of conspiracy is a creation of both the Criminal and Penal Codes. Although the Codes avoid the temptation of defining the term conspiracy, they however render liable to punishment anyone who conspires with another to effect an unlawful purpose by unlawful means.[33]

In *Majekodunmi* v. *R.,*[34] the West African Court of Appeal adopted the definition of Willes J. in *Mulcahy* v. *R.*[35] when it held, *inter alia,*

> conspiracy consists not merely in the intention of two or more persons, but the agreement of two or more to do an unlawful act or do a lawful act by unlawful means.

Under the Criminal Code, conspiracy to commit treason is provided for by virtue of section 37(2), while section 126(1) deals

---

[31] (1982) Crim L.R. 819

[32] (1986) AC 27

[33] See generally the provisions of sections 516 to 518 Criminal Code

[34] (1952) 14 WACA, 64

[35] (1868) L.R. 3 H.L. 306 at 317

with conspiracy to pervert the cause of justice. Conspiracy to defile a woman is provided under section 227 of the Criminal Code. The Criminal Code punishes conspiracies to commit felonies with a maximum of seven years imprisonment, and the punishment for the certain other conspiracies is two years imprisonment. Sections 7 and 8 of the Criminal Code deals with cases of common intention to commit an offence. Conspiracy can be inferred from certain criminal acts of the parties concerned, if done in pursuant of an apparent criminal purpose in common between the parties. For proof of conspiracy, the acts or omissions of any of the conspirators in furtherance of the common design, may be and very often are given in evidence against any of the conspirators. In essence, conspiracy is invariably an offence that is inferentially deduced from the acts of the parties thereto which are focused towards the realisation of their common or mutual criminal purpose.

In *Oduneye* v. *The State*,[36] the appellant was charged with conspiracy to murder the deceased. On appeal, the Supreme Court held, dismissing the appeal, Per Ejiwunmi JSC has this to say:

> In the instance case, the necessary inference that must be drawn upon the facts disclosed in the record is that the deceased, was lured to the proposed site of the fishpond by the appellant and confederate, Faseyitan to be killed. I will further add that in arriving at this conclusions, it must be borne in mind that apart from PW1 and PW2 the only persons who knew about the arrangement to visit the site on that day with the deceased was the appellant and Faseyitan his confederate. There is nothing to suggest that PW1 and PW2 informed any other person about the visit. The only two people who could tell anyone else of the visit remained the appellant and Faseyitan. It is therefore to be inferred that having regard to what happened leading to the murder of the deceased, that it was either or both of them that prepared the ground for the people who turned up at the site, and who apparently killed

[36] (2001) 2 NWLR (pt 697) 311

> the deceased. It is also important to note that the appellant and his confederate having lured the deceased to the site did nothing to save the deceased from those who attacked him. It is in my view clear that the action and or inaction of the appellant as shown above established beyond reasonable doubt that the appellant conspired with others to effect the murder of the deceased.[37]

In *Ebenezer Aje* v. *The State,*[38] the Court of Appeal held that when two or more persons form a common intention to prosecute an unlawful purpose in conjunction with one another and in the prosecution of such purpose an offence is committed of such a nature that its commission is a probable consequence of the prosecution of such purpose, each of them is deemed to have committed the offence.

For the offence of conspiracy to commit an offence, it must be shown that what was agreed to be done constitutes a crime in law. In *Otegheri* v. *I.G.P.,*[39] it was held that there was no conspiracy because what the accused agreed to do did not disclose any offence.

In *Usufu* v. *The State,*[40] the appellant and two others were charged with conspiracy to commit robbery and armed robbery. At the end of the trial, they were found guilty. Dissatisfied with the judgment, they appealed to the Court of Appeal. Allowing the appeal, the court held that, where the prosecution relies on the commission of the substantive offence by an accused person and others to infer conspiracy, and the accused person is convicted, the conviction for the

---

[37] But in *Ogugu* v. *State* (1990) 2 NWLR (pt. 134) 539, it was held that it takes two to conspire. A person cannot be convicted of conspiracy if the others alleged to have conspired with him are acquitted and discharged. To convict only one person for conspiracy suggest that the others were equally guilty of conspiracy, though acquitted and discharged. See also the case of *Suleiman* v. *State* (2009) 15 NWLR (pt 1161) 263 where it was held that a single person can not be charged for conspiracy of an unknown alleged act without the persons he was alleged to have conspired with.

[38] (2006) 8 NWLR (pt 982) 345

[39] (1957) W.R.N.L.R., 8

[40] (2007) 3 NWLR (pt 1020) 94

conspiracy will fail if the conviction for the substantive offence is set aside on appeal.

But in *Omotola* v. *The State,*[41] the Supreme Court held that it is not the requirement of the law that a person charged with the offence of conspiracy to murder and murder must first be found guilty of the conspiracy before he can be found guilty of the offence of murder.[42]

CONCLUSION

Finally, it can be concluded that, *prima facie*, an agreement by two or more persons to execute an unlawful purpose is an offence. We, are, therefore of the firm opinion that once there is a *consensus ad idem* between two or more persons to execute an unlawful purpose, the offence of conspiracy is established.

---

[41] (2009) 7 NWLR (pt 139) 148

[42] In *Yakubu* v. *FRN* (2009) 14 NWLR (pt 1160) 154, Augie, JCA held that conspiracy as an offence is the agreement by two or more persons to do or cause to be done an illegal act or a legal act by illegal means. In the instant case, the roles of the appellants in the alleged transaction are connected and intertwined. The trial court was therefore right when it held that the persons who recommended, approved the recommendation and effected the transfers are responsible for the transfers.

Chapter 8

PARTICIPATION IN CRIME

INTRODUCTION

Where two or more persons formed a common intention to commit a criminal offence, they are said to be parties to the commission of the crime. However, the degree of their participation in the commission of the crime may differ. But the law holds all or each party to the crime criminally liable in the same manner if the result of their action was criminal. The law regards all the participants as partners in the commission of the crime. This is expressed in the Latin maxim, *particeps criminis*. All the law requires of the prosecution is to prove and establish the common intention of all the participants in the commission of the crime.

Section 8 of the Criminal Code[1] provides that, when two or more persons form a common intention to prosecute an unlawful purpose in conjunction with one another, and in the prosecution of such purpose an offence is committed of such a nature that its commission is a probable consequence of the prosecution of such purpose, each of them is deemed to have committed the offence. It is immaterial whether the offence actually committed is the same as that counselled or a different one.[2] Those who aid, counsel and those who carry out the actual crime are jointly and severally liable.

---

[1] Cap C 28 Laws of the Federation of Nigeria, 2004

[2] See Section 9 of the Criminal Code

PRINCIPAL OFFENDERS

The principal offender is the person who actually commits the offence or causes it to be committed.

According to Mc Alhoe and Huxley-Binns, the principal is the person who stabs the victim in a wounding offence, penetrates the non-consenting victim in rape, damages another's property in a criminal damage or causes the death of the victim in homicide.[3] However, there may be more than one principal to an offence. That is, two or more defendants may fatally stab a victim.

Furthermore, the principal offender is usually described as the one whose acts is the most immediate cause of the physical injury suffered by the victim. The principal offender is the person who shoots and kills the deceased in a crime of murder.

Meanwhile, under section 8 of the Accessories and Abettors Act 1861, all the parties to a crime may be tried, indicted and punished in the same way.[4] Again, section 7 of the Criminal Code leaves us not in doubt when it provides:

> When an offence is committed, each of the following persons is deemed to have taken part in committing the offence and to be guilty of the offence and may be charged with actually committing it-
>
> (a) Every person who actually does the act or makes the omission which constitutes the offence;
>
> (b) Every person who does or omits to do any act for the purpose of enabling or aiding another person to commit the offence;

---

[3] See *Criminal Law, The Fundamentals*, 2nd edn (London, Thomson Sweet and Maxwell, London, 2010) at 340

[4] It should be noted that until 1967, principals were known as principals in the first degree and secondary parties as principals in the second degree if they were present at the crime and accessories if they were not. The Criminal Act 1967 effectively abolished the distinction.

(c) Every person who aids another person in committing the offence;
(d) Any person who counsels or procures any other persons to commit the offence.

It should be stressed that a conviction for counselling or procuring the commission of an offence entails the same consequences in all respects as a conviction of committing the offence. The law is therefore settled that all the participants in a criminal offence will be held liable jointly and severally for their common intention to bring about the commission of the alleged offence. Their degree of participation in the commission of the criminal offence may be immaterial.

In *Oyakhire* v. *The State,*[5] the Supreme Court held that once it is firmly established that two or more persons formed the necessary common intention to prosecute an unlawful purpose and in the prosecution of such purpose an offence of such nature, that its commission was probable consequence of the prosecution of such purpose is committed, each of them is deemed to have committed the offence. The Supreme Court stated further that in such circumstances, once the execution of the common intention or design is established, the court would be right in asserting that it did not matter on such facts which of the accused persons did what. This is for the simple reason that under such circumstances a fatal blow, though given by one of the accused persons involved, is deemed in the eye of the law to have been given by the rest of his co-accused persons. The person actually delivering the blow is regarded to be no more than the hand by which the others all strike.

Similarly, in *Bashaya* v. *The State,*[6] the Supreme Court held that, by virtue of section 79 of the Penal Code, when a criminal act is done by several persons in furtherance of a common

[5] (2006) 15 NWLR (pt 1001) pg 161
[6] (1998) 5 NWLR (pt 550) 353

intention of all, each of such persons is liable for that act in the same manner as if it were done by him alone. In such a situation, it would not matter who did what if the result of the action of those who acted was criminal.[7]

It was also held in *Okonkwo* v. *The State*[8] that where there was a common intention to prosecute an unlawful purpose in conjunction with one and another, each of those who joined in the prosecution of the unlawful purpose is deemed to have committed the offence committed in the prosecution of the unlawful purpose.

It should be acknowledged that a person may not actually commit an offence himself, but may still cause it to be committed. And, therefore, is still principal where he acts through what is known as "innocent agent". In such circumstances, the perpetrator is the innocent agent and the principal is the person who causes the innocent agent to commit the crime. An innocent agent is someone who is innocent of the crime. A person may be an innocent agent in one way or the other. In the first instance, he may lack the *mens rea* for the crime. In *R.* v. *Stringer*,[9] the principal was an employer who dictated a fraudulent letter to his secretary to type and post. The secretary was held to be the innocent agent as she did not know that the letter was to enable a fraudulent transfer. Again, the perpetrator of an offence will be an innocent agent where he lacks the required capacity to commit the offence itself because he is a minor under ten years of age or is insane. In *R* v. *Michael*,[10] the principal was a mother who wished to kill her baby. She gave her nurse a bottle of poison, telling her that it was medicine and asking her to administer it to the baby. The nurse did not do so and left the poison on a

---

[7] See also the case of *Nwali* v. *The State* (1971) 1 NMLR 78
[8] (1998) 4 NWLR (Pt 544) 149
[9] (1991) Crim L.R. 639
[10] (1840) 9 Car & P.

shelf. A child later removed the poison and gave it to the baby killing him. The child was held to be an innocent agent. However, the position would not have been different if it was the nurse who administered the said poison to the child (the dead child).

In a more recent case of *R.* v. *Yemoh,*[11] the defendants were members of a gang involved in the stabbing of the deceased. The principal offender was never identified, and they were all convicted on the basis of their participation in a joint enterprise. On appeal, the defendants argued that although some of them had known that a member of their group had been in possessed of a Stanley knife, they had not known that any other sort of knife might be used. Their appeal to the Court of Appeal was rejected. While rejecting the appeal, Lord Justice Hooper has this to say:

> ...it cannot be said as a matter of law that the knife used to kill in this is more lethal than a Stanley knife, to adopt the words of Lord Hutton in Powell and English, we therefore reject this submission also.

Furthermore, in the Nigerian case of *Atiku* v. *The State,*[12] the Court of Appeal held that when two or more persons actively participated in the commission of a crime, in the execution of a common intention, each of them would be liable for the offence and it does not matter who did what in the commission of the offence. In the instance case, the 2nd and 3rd appellants were shown by the unassailable evidence to have actively and fully participated in the beating of the deceased during which the 1st appellant delivered the fatal blow. Consequently, each and every one of them was responsible for the acts which eventually resulted or led to the death of the deceased.

---

[11] (2009) E WCA Crim 930

[12] (2010) 9 NWLR pt 119 241 at 248

Therefore, it is our opinion that all the participants in a criminal offence are as liable as the principal offender. Their degree of involvement in the commission of the crime is immaterial.

SECONDARY OFFENDERS

Different persons may be involved in the commission of a criminal offence. There are those who aid, counsel, procure and those who commit the actual offence, all of whom are *particeps criminis*. The law treats those who aid, abet, counsel or procure the commission of an indictable offence as secondary offenders.

Under section 8 of the English Accessories and Abettors Act 1961, whosoever shall aid, abet, counsel or procure the commission of an indictable offence is liable to be tried, indicted and punished as a principal offender.

In *R* v. *Bryce,*[13] the Court of Appeal held that, in charging secondary parties, "it is frequently advisable to use the 'catch-all' phrase 'aid, abet, counsel or procure', because the shades of difference between them, are far from clear."

However, it is pertinent to note that the mere presence of an accused person at the scene of a crime without more may not necessarily qualify as having aided or encouraged the commission of the crime. It must be proved that he intended to give encouragement or indeed encouraged the commission of the crime. This was the view of Megan L.J. in the case of *R.* v. *Clarkson,*[14] when he observed as follows:

> ...In my opinion, to constitute an aider and abettor some active steps must be taken by word, or action, with the intent to instigate the principal, or principals. Encouragement does not of necessity amount to aiding and abetting...It is no criminal

[13] (2004) 2 Cr App R 35 at 39
[14] (1971) 55 Cr. App.R. 445

offence to stand by, a mere passive spectator of a crime, even of a minder...

By the provisions of Section 10 of the Criminal Code, a person who receives or assists another who is, to his knowledge, guilty of an offence in order to enable him to escape punishment is said to become an accessory after to the offence. While under section 7(b) of the same Code, liability only exist where the defendant acts with the intention of enabling and aiding the commission of the criminal offence. Section 83 of the Penal Code defines an abettor as a person who intentionally aids or facilitates the commission of a criminal offence.

However, in *Alor* v. *The State*[15] the Supreme Court held that, it is immaterial whether the offender is found guilty as a principal offender or as a participant or as an aider or abetter or a person who has counselled or procured the commission of the offence or a conspirator who has committed the offence.[16]

Elsewhere, it has been argued that for a secondary offender to be held liable for the commission of a criminal offence, there must be a proof of his intention to bring about the *actus reus* of the alleged crime. His mere presence at the scene of the crime is not enough. This reasoning must have informed the decision of the court in the case of *Milar* v. *The State,*[17] where it was held that it is unsafe and improper to convict an accused person merely because he was present when an alleged offence of crime was committed without more. A similar decision was reached in the case of *Akanni* v. *R.*[18] In that case, members of a crowd stood by and watched a burning house with an old

[15] (1997) 49 LRCN, pg 944

[16] See also *Okosun & Ors* v. *Attorney General, Bendel State* (1985) 11 SC, pg 194 and *Iyaro* v. *The State* (1988) NWLR (pt) 691 p. 256 where it was stated that if the accused was among the robbery gang that committed the offence, it does not matter that he himself was not armed.

[17] (2005) 8 NWLR (Pt 927) pg 236

[18] (1959) WRNLR, pg 103

woman trapped inside. The Supreme Court of Nigeria stated thus:

> they behaved disgracefully, but that does not bring them within the provisions of section 7 (Criminal Code) as to be regarded as participants in murder.

It appears that under the provisions of section 7(b)(c) and (d) of the Criminal Code, where a principal offender cannot be convicted for the commission of a criminal offence, either on a procedural ground or on the ground of incapacity, a secondary offender may, however, be convicted once it is established that a crime was in fact committed. The decision in *Obosi* v. *The State*[19] must have found justification and judicial approval for the above assertion. In that case, the principal offenders in a case of murder were discharged for want of evidence, but a self-confessed co-conspirator present during the killing was convicted of murder.

In the final analysis, we are of the view that once a common intention is established against the participants in a criminal act, they should be held liable jointly and severally.

MODE OF PARTICIPATION

From the provisions of section 7(c) and (d) of the Criminal Code,[20] it can rightly be said that there are three major ways through which an accused can be said to have participated in the commission of a criminal offence. These are:

1. aiding and abetting;
2. counselling; and
3. procuring.

---

[19] (1965) NMLR 119

[20] Every person who aids, counsels or procures any other person to commit a criminal offence is deemed to have taken part in committing the offence and may be charged with actually committing it.

Aiding and Abetting

To aid and abet, according to the *Black's Law Dictionary*,[21] means to assist or facilitate the commission of a crime or to promote its accomplishment. It may also involve acts of encouragement, instigating or inciting the commission of an offence.

It should be noted that the terms 'aid' and 'abet' are frequently used interchangeably, although they are not synonymous. To aid is to assist or help another. On the other hand, to abet means literally excite to bait or execute. Meanwhile, in its legal sense, it means to encourage, advise, or to instigate the commission of a crime.[22]

In *Enweonye* v. *R.*,[23] the West African Court of Appeal held, *inter alia*,

> We are of the opinion that to bring a person within this section (section 7(c) "there must be clear evidence that...the appellant did something to facilitate the commission of the offence.

Also, in *Upahar* v. *State*,[24] the court held that by virtue of section 85 of the Penal Code, whoever abets any offence shall, if the act abetted is committed in consequence of the abetment and no express provision is made by the Penal Code or any other law for the time being in force for the punishment for such abetment, be punished with the punishment provided for the offence.

In England, the position is not anything different. In *R.* v. *Coney*,[25] it was held that non-accidental presence at the scene of the crime is not conclusive of aiding and abetting. According to Hawkins J., what must be proved to establish that a person

---

[21] 9th edition, 2009

[22] See Charless E. Torcia, Wharton's *Criminal Law* (15th ed. 1993) pg 181

[23] (1955) 15 WACA at page 1

[24] (2003) 6 NWLR pt 1000 pg 230 at 239

[25] (1882) 8 Q.B. D 534

aided or abetted the commission of a crime, is obvious in his judgment, in Coney's case when he said:

> ...in my opinion, to constitute an aider and abettor, some active steps must be taken by word, or action with the intent to instigate the principal, or principals. Encouragement does not of necessity amount to aiding and abetting.

To be culpable, it must be proved that the accused person has the intention to aid, or actually aided or encouraged the commission of the criminal offence. This was the position of the Court of Appeal in *R.* v. *Tait*[26] where it was held that both an intention to encourage and the encouragement in fact must be established.

Conclusively, it is our observation that the present law's insistence upon actual encouragement tends to support instead a causal theory of complicity. Elsewhere, where a gang of boys went and engaged in a fist fight, it was held that if one of them produced a gun and shot another, the remaining boys would not be liable as the action of shooting was beyond the scope of the joint unlawful enterprise.[27]

Counselling

In criminal law, to counsel means to advise or assist in the commission of a criminal act. But according to Clarkson and Keating, counselling refers to the help given before the commission of a crime and may take the form of advice, information, encouragement or the supply of equipment. They further argued that the form of help given is not crucial and may, in fact, be fairly minimal.

In the Nigerian case of *Amoo* v. *R*,[28] where a political group thought that their leader has been killed and set out armed with

---

[26] (1993) Crim. L.R. 538

[27] See the case of *Davies* v. *D.P.P.* (1954) AC at page 378

[28] (1959) 4 F.S.C.

dangerous weapons to avenge his death, it was held that anyone who joined knowing its purpose is criminally responsible.

In *R.* v. *Calhaem,*[29] Parker L.J. had this to say:

> We must therefore approach the question raised on the basis that we should give the word counsel its ordinary meaning, which is as the judge said 'advise', 'solicit', or something of that sort. There is no implication in the word itself that there should be any causal connection between the counselling and the offence. It is true that, unlike the offence of incitement at common law, the actual offence must have been committed and by the person counselled. To this extent there must clearly be first contact between the parties, and secondly a connection between the counselling and the murder...

Delvin J. concludes in *N.C.B.* v. *Gambe*[30] that:

> an indifference to the result of crime does not of itself negative abetting. If one deliberately sells to another a gun to be used for murdering a third man, he may be indifferent whether the third man lives or dies and interested only in the cash profit to be made out of the sale, but he can still be an aider and abettor. To hold otherwise would be to negative the rule that *mens rea* is a matter of intent only and does not depend on desire or motive.

Interestingly, it is now a settled law that those who counsel the commission of an offence are similar to those who do an act for the purpose of enabling or aiding the commission of the actual crime. And by virtue of the provisions of section 7 of the Criminal Code, all participants in the commission of a criminal offence are *particeps criminis.*

---

[29] (1985) 1 Q.B. 808

[30] (1959) 1 Q.B. 11 at 23

Procuring

Procuring in this context is used in its restricted legal sense, to mean the act of persuading or inviting another for the purpose of committing an offence. The law is that, anyone who attempts to procure the commission of an offence is guilty of the offence and may be punished accordingly.

Again, to procure means to produce by endeavour. You procure a thing by setting out to see that it happens and taking the appropriate steps to produce that happening. There are instances in which a person may be said to procure the commission of a crime by another even though there is no sort of conspiracy between the two, even though there is no attempt at agreement or discussion as to the form which the offence should take. In the *Attorney General's Reference,*[31] the defendant was charged with aiding, abetting, counselling and procuring the offence of driving with an excess quantity of alcohol in the blood under section 6(1) of the Road Traffic Act, 1972. The reference concerned the question of whether there had to be a shared intention between the parties or encouragement of the offence. The Court of Appeal held that, giving the words their ordinary meaning in English and asking oneself whether in those circumstances the offence has been procured, we are in no doubt that the answer is that it has. It has been procured because, unknown to the driver and without his collaboration, he has been put in a position in which in fact he has committed an offence which he never would have committed otherwise.

It is submitted that if one accepts that to procure is to produce by endeavour, then it is impossible to avoid the conclusion that intention is required and that there is some merit in continuing to regard procuring in this way. It is, however, stressed that the word 'procuring' must involve some

---

[31] (1975) Q.B. 773

positive act of encouragement to those who commit the offence. In *Idika* v. *R.*[32] it was held, that if members of a society meet and being faced with orders to kill a particular man, they decide unanimously to obey these orders, each man present at the meeting encourages his fellow to kill the victim.

It is, however, not enough to prove that a man knew that some crime was intended. Again, it is also not altogether easy to lay down a precise form of words which will cover every case that can be contemplated. But, the view has been held that it must be proved that there was knowledge of the type of crime intended and committed. It is irrelevant, however, that an accused did not know that a particular offence on a particular date and at a particular premises was intended.

Meanwhile under section 82 of the Penal Code, where several persons are engaged in the commission of a criminal act, each one may be guilty of a different offence or offences by that act. But section 7(d) of the Criminal Code says that, anyone who procures another to commit a crime is a principal offender.

It is, however, clear that a person does not assist in the commission of an offence merely because he fails to prevent the commission of the offence. A person may still be guilty even though he does not know the time and place of the commission of the offence, provided he knows or believes that an offence is to be committed. An accused will also be guilty if he knows or believes that the principal intends to commit one of a number of offences and does any act that he knows or believes will assist the principal in committing whichever of those offences the principal in fact intends.

Meanwhile, it is now established that a defendant need not know the identity of the principal, nor have any particular principal or group of principals in mind, provided that he

[32] (1959) 4 FSC, 106

intends his communication to be acted on by any person to whose attention it becomes. A defendant can be convicted of the new offence if they encouraged an offence without intending that it should be committed at a specific time or place.

It is thus our opinion that a person could be said to have committed the offence of encouraging the commission of a crime, if he solicits, commands or encourages another to do or causes to be done an act or acts which if done will involve the commission of an offence by the principal.

THE LIMITS OF LIABILITY FOR JOINT PARTICIPATION IN A CRIMINAL OFFENCE

Criminal liability can only arise where it has in fact been established that a criminal offence has been committed. It is only those who actively participated in the commission of such offence that will be liable. Innocent persons merely present at the scene of a crime would not be victims of criminal liability. But, a cursory look at the provisions of section 2 of the Penal Code, an abettor is criminally liable whether or not the offence abetted was in fact committed.

According to Turner J, the principal may be acquitted through lack of evidence or because of some procedural defect that applied to him, secondary parties may nevertheless be convicted if the evidence shows clearly that there was a crime. The principal may be acquitted and the court applies the doctrine of innocent agency to justify the conviction of the secondary party. In such a case, the secondary party is in fact deemed to be the principal offender. Again, the principal may be acquitted because he has a defence, or because either the *mens rea* or the *actus reus* of his crime has been negatived. In certain circumstances, the secondary party may nevertheless be convicted.

Meanwhile, an examination of section 10 of the Criminal Code leaves us with some limits to which criminal liability can be extended. Section 10 of the Criminal Code provides to the effect that a wife is not an accessory if she assists her husband to escape punishment, and that a husband is not also liable for assisting his wife. But according to Okonkwo and Naish,[33] this rule is clearly based on a consideration of the various emotions which might arise between husband and wife on such occasions, such as love, compassion or fear.

However, in *R.* v. *Bourne*[34] where the defendant terrorised his wife into committing burglary with a dog, he was convicted of aiding and abetting his wife to commit burglary with a dog. His appeal to the Court of Criminal Appeal was dismissed. While dismissing the appeal, Lord Goddard C.J. said:

> ...the evidence was that he caused his wife to have connection with a dog, and he is guilty, whether you call him an aider and abettor or an accessory, as a principal in the second degree.

Similarly, in *R.* v. *Cogan and Leak,*[35] Leak compelled his wife to have sexual intercourse with Cogan, who believed that she consented. As Cogan's conviction was quashed on the strength of his belief, it became necessary to decide whether Leak's conviction as aider and abettor could stand. Leak's appeal against conviction was based on the proposition that he could not be found guilty of aiding and abetting Cogan to rape his wife, if Cogan was acquitted of that offence, as he was deemed in law to have been, his conviction was quashed. His appeal against conviction was dismissed. Dismissing the appeal, Lawton L.J. observed:

---

[33] *Criminal Law in Nigeria* (Ibadan, Spectrum Books Ltd, 1980)

[34] (1952) 36 Cr App. R 1251

[35] (1976) QB 217

> ...In the language of the law, the act of sexual intercourse without the wife's consent was the *actus reus*; it had been procured by Leak who had the appropriate *mens rea*, namely his intention that Cogan should have sexual intercourse with her without her consent. In our judgment, it is irrelevant that the man whom Leak had procured to do the physical act himself did not intend to have sexual intercourse with the wife without her consent. Leak was using him as a means to procure a criminal purpose...in the circumstances of this case, it would be an affront to justice and to the common sense of ordinary folk. It was for these reasons that we dismissed the appeal against conviction.

Again, Chapman J., concludes in *R.* v. *Humphrey*,[36] that it would be anomalous if a person who admitted to a substantial part in the perpetration of a misdemeanour as aider and abettor could not be convicted on his own admission merely because the person alleged to have been aided and abetted was not or could not be convicted.

According to Smith and Hogan, once the *actus reus* of an offence is established, the criminal responsibility of each secondary offender must depend on their respective *mens rea.* In *R.* v. *Howe,*[37] on the issue whether a secondary party can be convicted of murder despite the conviction of the principal for manslaughter, Lord Mackay said:

> ...I consider that the reasoning of Lord Lane C.J. is entirely correct and I would affirm his view that where a person has been killed and that result is intended by another participant, the mere fact that the actual killer may be convicted only of the reduced charge of manslaughter for some reason special to himself does not, in my opinion, in any way result in a compulsory reduction for the other participants.

---

[36] (1963) 3 All ER, 689 at 692

[37] (1987) 1 AC 477

In conclusion, it is necessary to question the assumption that accessories are as blameworthy as principal offenders and deserve comparable punishment. At a superficial level, of course, the rationale for this is obvious; the accessory's role may have greatly facilitated the commission of the crime. They may sometimes be guiltier than the perpetrator.

Chapter 9

HOMICIDE

INTRODUCTION

Homicide is the killing of one person by another. The legal term for killing a person, whether lawfully or unlawfully, is homicide. Unlawful homicide at Common Law comprises the two crimes of murder and manslaughter.[1] What makes homicide unique is causing the death of another. While all personal injuries and destruction of property are irreversible harms, causing death is a harm of a different order. Killing another human being is not only a worldly deprivation, in the Western conception of homicide, killing is an assault on the sacred natural order. In the biblical view, the person who slays another was thought to acquire control over the blood, the life force of the victim.[2]

In the law of homicide, the focal point is neither the act nor the intent, but the fact of death. This overpowering fact is the point at which the law begins to draw the radius of liability.

According to Seidman in his book, *Source Book of Criminal Law in Africa,* in considering the law of homicide,

> the value protected is obvious, human life, but the law does not punish every killing. The problem is to determine which killings are criminal and which are not, and in every case to discover the rule or principle that determines which side of the line a particular killing will fall. The question a student should therefore always ask is this killing criminal or not. What is the reason given by the court for making the killing of another

[2] George P. Fletcher, *Rethinking Criminal Law* (1978)

unlawful? How does that reason justify the underlying objectives of criminal punishment?

In this chapter, we examine the liability for homicide. We will also consider the two major classifications of homicide, i.e., murder and manslaughter and the legal basis for such classification will also be examined.

MURDER

Murder is the killing of a human being with malice aforethought. But according to Coke, murder is when a man of sound memory and of the age of discretion unlawfully kills within any country of the realm any reasonable creature is *rerem natura* under the King's breach, with malice aforethought, either expressed by the party or implied by law, so as the party wounded, or hurt, etc., dies of the wound or hurt, etc., within a year and a day after the same.

Section 308 of the Criminal Code provides that any person who causes the death of another, directly or indirectly, by any means whatever is deemed to have killed that other person. Also, section 220 of the Penal Code provides that whoever causes death:

(a) by doing an act with the intention of causing death or such bodily injury as is likely to cause death; or
(b) by doing an act with the knowledge that he is likely to cause death; or
(c) by doing a rash or negligent act commits the offence of culpable homicide.

Also, if a person who is charged with the duties to provide necessaries of life fails to do that to any person under him or her by virtue of age, sickness, unsoundness of mind, detention or any other cause and as a result of that omission a consequence affects the life or health of that person, he or she will be held guilty. Again, section 302 of the Criminal Code imposes a heavy duty on masters or mistresses who have contracted to provide necessary food, clothing or lodging for any servant or apprentice under the age of 16 years. Hence, if death occurs as a result of this omission, such a master or mistress will be guilty of homicide.

More importantly, section 316 of the Criminal Code provides for the circumstances under which a person could be said to have killed another person, and therefore guilty of the offence of murder. Section 316 provides:

> a person who unlawfully kills another under any of the following circumstances, that is to say–
>
> 1. if the offender intends - to cause the death of the person killed, or that of some other person;
> 2. if the offender intends to do to the person killed or to some other person some grievous harm;
> 3. if death is caused by means of an act done in the prosecution of an unlawful purpose, which act is of such a nature as to be likely to endanger human life;
> 4. if the offender intends to do grievous harm to some person for the purpose of facilitating the commission of an offence which is such that the offender may be arrested without warrant, or for the purpose of facilitating the commission of an offence which is such that the offender may be arrested without warrant, or for the purpose of facilitating the flight of an offender who has committed or attempted to commit any such offence;
> 5. if death is caused by administering any stupefying or overpowering things for either or the purposes last aforesaid;

6. if death is caused by wilfully stopping the breath of any person for either of such purpose is guilty of murder.

Furthermore, any person who by threats or intimidation or by deceit, causes another person to do an act or make an omission which results in the death of that person is deemed to have killed him or her.[3]

Flowing from the analysis, it can be said that death can result from the malicious intent to kill, to cause grievous bodily harm, or through the negligence and reckless conduct of the accused person. Death can also result from acts of omission.

Intent to Kill or Cause Grievous Bodily Harm

For the prosecution to succeed in a case of murder, it must be established that the accused person presumed or premeditated the killing of the deceased. The intention to kill or cause grievous bodily harm to the person of another is the *mens rea* of murder. Thus, it must be established that:

1. the accused intends to cause death;
2. intends to cause grievous bodily harm.

However, the onus is on the prosecution to prove intent. It may rely on the presumption that a man intends the natural consequences of the act,[4] but is open to the accused to show that death occurred in purely accidental circumstances and that he had no intent to kill or cause grievous bodily harm to any person.[5] In *Hyman* v. *D.P.P.*,[6] it was held that foresight of death or grievous bodily harm as a highly probable consequence of one's action was sufficient to constitute the mental element for murder. In that case, the accused was discarded by her lover

---

[3] See section 10 of the Criminal Code Cap C 38 Laws of the Federation of Nigeria, 2004.

[4] *R* v. *Ningu* (1953) 14 WACA

[5] See Okonkwo and Naish, Criminal *Law in Nigeria*, 2nd edn (Ibadan, Spectrum Book Ltd 1980) 232

[6] (1974) 2 All ER, 41. This case and others were discussed extensively in Chapter 2.

who began to pay his respect to another woman. At about 2 am one morning, the accused was driven by jealousy to set fire to the house in which the other woman lived with her three children. Two of the children were burnt to death. The accused pleaded that her only intention was to frighten the other woman into leaving the neighbourhood and that she had no intention to cause death or grievous bodily harm.

While rejecting the plea, Lord Hailsham observed:

> ...If a man, in full knowledge of the danger involved and without lawful excuse, deliberately does that which exposes a victim to the risk of the probable grievous bodily harm...or death and the victim dies, the perpetrator of the crime is guilty of murder and not manslaughter to the same extent as if he had actually intended the consequences to follow, and irrespective of whether he wishes it.

Meanwhile, a survey of the laws on murder, both under the English Common Law and some other codified systems that derived therefrom, the following are the requirements to establish the mental element for murder:

a. an intention to cause death;
b. intention to inflict grievous bodily harm;
c. recklessness as to the causing of death;
d. recklessness as to infliction of grievous bodily harm; and
e. state of mind which does not contemplate the causing of death or the infliction of grievous bodily harm, but which may suffice to constitute murder under certain technical rules.

The argument whether an intent to inflict grievous bodily harm should serve as an alternative to intent to kill in murder causes has generated heated debate with diverse opinions. The proponents of the debate that intent to inflict grievous bodily harm as an alternative to intent to kill, reasoned as follows:

(a) it is in accord with the general sense of justice that a man who causes death by the intentional infliction of grievous bodily harm, although not actually intending to kill, should not only be punished as severely as a murderer but should be treated in law as a murderer;
(b) grievous harm is a relatively simple concept which can be readily explained. Any attempt to define 'grievous bodily harm' as, for example, harm likely to endanger life, or further to require that the accused should know that the harm inflicted is likely to endanger life, would make the judge's function more difficult;
(c) to eliminate the intent to inflict grievous bodily harm from the intent to kill in murder would encourage the ruthless criminal who kills in furtherance of some purpose other than killing and, it may be said, does not intend to kill but only to inflict such grievous bodily harm as will enable him to carry out that purpose.[7]

On the other hand, the antagonists of the proposition that intent to inflict grievous bodily harm as an alternative to the intent to kill in murder cases reasoned thus:

(a) murder is commonly understood to mean the intentionally killing of another human being and unless there are strong reasons which justify a contrary course, it is generally desirable that legal terms should correspond with the popular meaning;
(b) if the intent to inflict grievous bodily harm is to be retained in the law of murder at all, harm referred to is harm likely to kill. In this respect, it should be noted that Viscount Kilmuiri, L.C.M. in *D.P.P.* v. *Smith,* specifically declined to make a distinction between grievous bodily harm in its relation to intent in murder and in connection with the statutory

[7] See Owoade M.A., *Law of Homicide in Nigeria* (OAU Press Ltd (1990), 41

offence of inflicting grievous bodily harm under section 18 of the Offences Against the Person Act 1861 (in which latter context, it is clear that it is not limited to bodily harm likely to kill);

(c) furthermore, a man should not be regarded as a murderer if he does not know that the bodily harm which he intends to inflict is likely to kill;

(d) if there are practical difficulties in determining what harm is likely to endanger life and in ascertaining the accused's knowledge of such likelihood, it does not follow that the present law must therefore remain unchanged. It may precisely for this reason be desirable to eliminate altogether the intent to inflict grievous bodily harm as an alternative to the intent to kill;

(e) the view that the intent to inflict grievous bodily harm as an alternative to intent to kill in murder, covers the cause of the ruthless criminal who does not stop at killing in furtherance of some other purpose is too indiscriminate in its approach. A distinction must be made between the man who is not wiling to kill, even if he intends to inflict grievous bodily harm which in fact results in death, and the man who is willing to kill, even if he hopes to avoid, or is indifferent whether he causes death.

In reviewing the foregoing arguments, the Law Commission in England, conceded that the present law relating to the intent to inflict grievous bodily harm in murder is unsatisfactory, but concluded that any change in the law should await a general review of the unsatisfactory state of the law of manslaughter.

Unlike the Criminal Code, section 22 1(a) of the Penal Code provides that homicide punishable with death includes homicide committed with the intention of causing death. And section 221(b) states that homicide punishable with death if the doer of the act causing the death knew or had reason to know that death would be the probable and not only likely consequence of his act or of any bodily injury which the act was intended to cause in this connection, it will be necessary to stress the distinction between 'probable' and 'likely'. An act is said to be likely to have a certain consequence or to cause a certain effect if the occurrence of that consequence or effect would cause no surprise to a reasonable man, while an event is said to be a probable consequence of an act if the occurrence of that consequence would be considered by a reasonable man to be the natural and normal effect of that act.[8]

Under section 308 of the Criminal Code, killing may be direct or indirect by any means whatsoever, therefore is not a precondition for killing. In a charge of murder, what is important under the Nigerian Criminal Law is that the act of the accused person resulting in the death of the deceased must be unlawful. In *Idiok* v. *State, supra* the court held that for the prosecution to succeed in a murder charge under section 319(1) of the Criminal Code, it must be proved beyond reasonable doubt that:

(a) there was a killing;
(b) the killing was unlawful as prohibited by section 316 of the Criminal Code;
(c) it was the act or omission of the accused person that caused the death of the deceased;
(d) the accused intended to cause the death of the deceased.

To establish that the accused killed the deceased, the prosecution must adduce cogent evidence linking the accused with the death of the deceased showing either a positive act or negative omission of the accused causing injury to the deceased, which in turn resulted directly in the death of the deceased.[9]

---

[8] Section 19 Penal Code. See also the case of *Maijamaa* v. *State* (1964) 1 All NLR, 21

[9] See *Akinfe* v. *State* (1988) 3 NWLR (pt 85) 729, *Okoro* v. *State* (1988) 5 NWLR (pt 94) 255, *Nnunukwe* v. *State* (2003) 14 NWLR (Pt 840) 219, Onah v. State (1985) 3 WLR (pt 12) 236.

Similarly, in *Mbang* v. *State*,[10] the appellant and his co-accused were alleged to have killed one Mary Obongha at Ekori. Consequently, they were charged for the murder of the deceased contrary to section 319 (1) of the Criminal Code Law of River State. At the end of the trial, the appellant was found guilty as charged and sentenced to death by hanging. Dissatisfied with the judgment, the appellant appealed to the Court of Appeal which held that the offence of murder is one of the heinous and abominable crimes of our land, that when committed and the culprit is charged, tried and found guilty upon all the available evidence presented before the court including his defence thereto, it attracts nothing but a death sentence to the accused. It is in consequence of this that the law itself deeply entrenched the criteria the prosecution must meet before a conviction for murder can be secured. By virtue of section 312 of the Criminal Code the person who caused bodily injury to another person, caused the death of the person injured. It is immaterial that, that might have been avoided by proper precaution on the part of the person injured or that death from that injury might have been prevented by proper care or treatment. Section 313 of the Criminal Code is to the effect that when the injured person has resources to surgical or medical treatment and death results either from the injury or medical treatment, the person who does the grievous bodily harm to the deceased is deemed to have killed that other person, although the immediate cause of death was the surgical or medical treatment, provided that the treatment was reasonably proper under the circumstances and was in good faith.

For an accused person to be sentenced for culpable homicide punishable with death under the Penal Code, the persecution must prove:

---

[10] (2010) 7 NWLR (pt 1194) 431

(a) the death of the deceased;
(b) that death resulted from the act of the accused person;
(c) that the accused knew that his act will result in death or did not care whether the death of the deceased will result from his act.[11]

Similarly, under section 20(a) of the Penal Code the offence of culpable homicide punishable with death is committed by a person who causes death by doing an act with intention of causing death or such bodily injury as is likely to cause death. In *State* v. *Babawuro Usman,*[12] the Court of Appeal held that to secure conviction in a charge of murder or culpable homicide, the prosecution must prove beyond reasonable doubt that:
(a) the deceased had died;
(b) his death was caused by the accused; and
(c) the act of the accused which caused death was intentional, having the knowledge that death or grievous bodily harm was the probable consequence of the act.

The court further held that where death is caused instantaneously by a blow on the neck with a formidable weapon cutting through the windpipe, intention to cause death would be said to have been proved. In the instance case, the deceased died instantaneously from the injury caused her by the respondent. The accused was hereby found guilty of the offence of culpable homicide punishable with death under section 221(a) of the Penal Code as charged.

In law, a man intends the consequences of his voluntary act when he desires it to happen, whether or not he foresees that it probably will happen. Whether he desires it or not,[13] knowledge on foresight or compels a jury to draw the necessary inference as to intention.[14]

---

[11] *Akpan* v. *State* (2008) 14 NWLR (pt 1106) 72
[12] (2005) 1 NWLR (pt 906) 80
[13] *R* v. *Moloney* (1985) AC 905
[14] Lord Hailsham of St. Marylebone L.C. in *Reg* v. *Hyman* (1975) AC 55.

The *Actus Reus* of Murder

As with all crimes, the *actus reus* is the external element of the crime – the objective requirement necessary to constitute the offence. Thus, the *actus reus* of the offence of causing death by dangerous driving is causing the death of another person by driving a mechanically propelled vehicle on a road or other public place. Here, it is necessary to establish that the same dangerous driving caused the forbidden consequence specified in the *actus reus*, namely, the death of another person.

Therefore, the *actus reus* of murder is causing the death of a human being in circumstances which are not authorised, justified or excused by law.[15] The victim of murder must be a human being. Hence, Coke defines murder as the killing of a person in *rerum natura*. This definition eliminates all human-like structures that cannot be classified as natural human beings. A person or child becomes a human being in law when it has completely proceeded in a living state from the body of its mother, whether it has breathed or not, and whether it has an independent circulation or not, it is not in fact necessary for the navel string to have severed.[16] In *R.* v. *West*,[17] it was held that if a person intending to procure abortion does an act which causes a child to be born such earlier than the natural time that it is born in a state much less capable of living and afterwards dies as a consequence of its exposure to the external world, the person who by her misconduct so brings a child into the world and puts it merely into a situation in which it cannot live is guilty of murder.

Where, however, there is no proof that a child was born alive, a conviction for its murder cannot be secured. In *State* v. *Linus Akpan*,[18] the accused persons who were members of a

---

[15] See section 306 of the Criminal Code

[16] See *R* v. *Castles* (1969) QWN 36. See also section 307 of the Criminal Code. See Williams, *The Sanctity of Life and the Criminal Law* (London: Faber & Faber, 1958), pg.1

[17] See Malle, J in *R* v. *West* (1848) 2 C & K, 748, 175 E R 329

[18] (1972) 2 U.I.L.R. 457

religious sect were charged with killing a child in consequence of an act omitted to be done during child birth contrary to section 247 of the Criminal Code.[61] Counsel to the accused person made a no-case submission to give the woman a medical attention and that it was an essential ingredient of the offence to prove that the child was born alive but that this had not been proved. The court held that since there was no proof that the child was born alive, the essential ingredient of the offence had not been proved and consequently the accused persons were discharged and acquitted.

Meanwhile, taking a cue from the English law, poisoning, striking, starving, and drowning are part of the innumerable ways of killing a human being. The cause of death can be proved by direct or circumstantial evidence. It can also be inferred where the person injured or attacked died immediately. Suspicion, however strong, cannot take the place of legal proof as it does not amount to proof. Once there is any doubt, the slightest doubt in the mind of the trial court that some person other than the accused committed the offence, the court must as a matter of the Nigerian criminal justice system and the law, resolve the doubt in favour of the accused person. So, when the prosecution fails to prove beyond reasonable doubt that the act of the accused caused the death of the deceased, a verdict of discharge and acquittal must be entered. In *Teggivonor* v. *State,*[20] it was held that in a charge of murder, if the cause of death has not been proved, it is futile and illogical to proceed to consider whether it was the accused who caused the death of the victim attacked. The primary inquiry into the cause of death of a person is an inquiry into the biological cause of death. The pertinent question at this stage of inquiry is *what* caused the death and not *who* caused the death. When *what* caused the death has been ascertained, the

[61] Cap C 38, Laws of the Federation of Nigeria, 2004
[20] (2008) 1 NWLR (Pt 1069) 630

issue of *who* caused the death becomes relevant or one of causal connection between the act of the accused person and the biological cause of the death.

The law presumes that the person last seen with a deceased bears the full responsibility for his death. Thus, where the accused person was the last person to be seen in the company of the deceased and circumstantial evidence is overwhelming and leads to no other conclusion, it leaves no room for acquittal.[21] In *Idiok* v. *State*, it was held that when a person is charge with the murder of another person and there being no direct evidence of the killing of the deceased, recourse may be had to circumstantial evidence, and this includes any evidence which tends to connect that person with the probable cause of death. In the instant case, the evidence of PW4 was that she saw the appellant tying the deceased up with climbing ropes. PW3 also saw the deceased tied up and attempted to free the deceased before he was challenged. PW1's manner showed that the deceased met a violent death. The evidence of PW4 was cogent, unequivocal, positive and conclusive. The conclusion was that the evidence of PW4 led to the guilt of the appellant.[22]

However, by virtue of section 314 of the Criminal Code a person is not deemed to have killed another if the death of that other person does not take place within a year and a day of the cause of death. Such period is reckoned inclusive of the day on which the last unlawful act contributing to the cause of death is done. That is, a person cannot be convicted of murder where the death of the deceased does not occur within a year and a day of the infliction of the injury. In *R.* v. *Dyson*,[23] the accused, on 13th November, 1906 beats his three-month-old child into unconsciousness and fractured its skull. On 29th December,

---

[21] *Mbang* v. *State supra*
[22] *Igho* v. *State* (1978) 3 SC, 87
[23] (1908) 24 K.B. 454

1907, he beat the child again, bruising it severely about the head and face. On 17th February, 1908 at which time the bruises inflicted in 1907 had disappeared, the child was admitted to the hospital, suffering from traumatic meningitis. It died on March, 1908, the accused was found guilty of manslaughter. The appeal against conviction to the Court of Criminal Appeal was quashed.

Causation

It is trite law that there must be a causal connection between the cause of death and the act or omission of the accused person which caused the death of the deceased. The causal link between the act of the accused person and the resultant consequence must remained unbroken. As earlier noted, a person cannot be held liable for murder if there is no direct link between the act of the accused person and the actual cause of death. That is, there must not be a break in the chain of causation. It means therefore that, *actus novus intervenien* should also not be inferred from the circumstances of the case. According to the provisions of section 314 of the Criminal Code, for an accused to be held liable to have caused the death of the deceased, the prosecution must prove and establish that death occurred within a year and a day. If death is caused by an omission, the period includes the day on which the omission ceases, which event is the later. However, it has been argued that section 315 of the Criminal Code which provides for the twelve months rule in the determination of the criminal responsibility anticipates a situation where the accused is guilty of the offence of murder or manslaughter.

It is equally the argument of others that in the determination of the cause of death, the duration between the suspected act of death, that is the *actus reus*, and the death is not important. They further argued that an accused could be guilty of the offence of murder or manslaughter even if the duration is long.

In so far as the court comes to the conclusion correctly that the act of the accused caused the death of the deceased, a conviction and sentence will be proper in law. Conversely, even if the period between the act and the death of the deceased are proximate, a court can still not find the accused guilty if there are more than one possible causes of death. What is essential is that there must be evidence that the act of the accused resulted in the death of the deceased.

The situation appears to be different in the United States of American. In *Commonwealth* v. *Ladd*,[24] the Supreme Court of Pennsylvania held that the year and a day was no more than a rule of evidence or procedure only and might therefore be displaced by adequate proof causation, although another American court[25] has reached a similar result through statutory interpretation. On the whole, while the application of the rule appears certain in the traditional crimes of murder and manslaughter, it is not clear whether the rule applies to modern statutory offences of homicide, such as causing death by driving or is limited to the Common Law felonies of murder and manslaughter. It seems, however,[26] that the Criminal Code provisions will be inapplicable where a person is, for example, charged with the offence of causing death by dangerous driving under the Federal Highways Decree of 1971.

Section 308 of the Criminal Code embodies the broader problems of causation by providing that death may be caused directly or indirectly. The problems of causation are not limited to homicide nor to criminal law generally. In fact, it first reared its troublesome head in the area of the tort.[27] In recent times, however, it has featured prominently in crime especially in the homicide cases. In an insurance case of *Becker Arey and Co.* v.

---

[24] (1960) 116 A 2d, 501

[25] *People* v. *Brengard* (1934) 265 NY, 100

[26] See Owoade, M.A. ,*Law of Homicide in Nigeria* (OAU) Press Ltd 1990) pg 22

London Assurance Co.,[28] where the issue of proximate cause of an accident of a ship arose, the court remarked, *inter alia*, that:

> causation is as old as Aristotle, its doctrines are applicable in both civil and criminal law and it is no more than a commonsensical approach to the issue of cause and effect in any particular issue.

In *R.* v. *Blaue,*[29] the appellant stabbed the deceased to death. The deceased was taking to the hospital where she was told that she needs blood transfusion to save her life. This she refused on the ground that as a Jehovah's Witness, she could not take blood transfusion. She subsequently died the next day as a result of over bleeding. The appellant was convicted of manslaughter and appealed arguing that the deceased's refusal to have blood transfusion was unreasonable and had broken the chain of causation The Court of Appeal upheld the conviction on the ground that the stab wound was an operative cause of death. Lawton L.J. has this to say:

> It has long been the policy of the law that those who use violence on other people must take their victims as they find them. This in our judgment means the whole man, not just the physical man. It does not lie in the mouth of the assailant to say that his victim's religious beliefs which inhibited him from accepting certain kinds of treatment were unreasonable. The question for decision is what caused her death. The answer is the stab wound. The fact that the victim refused to stop this end coming about did not break the causal connection between the act and death.

It should, however, be noted that a person who inflicts a grievous wound on another person is not liable for subsequent death of that other person where such death results neither

---

[28] (1918) AC 101
[29] (1975) 3 All ER 446

from the wound nor from medical treatment but the cause of death is only accidentally or remotely connected with the wound. But a person whose conduct accelerates the death of another person who, at the time of such conduct, is labouring under some disorder or disease arising from another cause, is deemed to have killed that other person. In every case where it is alleged that death has resulted from the act of a person, a causal link between the death and the act must be established and proved in a criminal proceeding beyond reasonable doubt. The first and logical step in the process of such proof is to prove the cause of death. Where there is no certainty as to the cause of death, the enquiry should proceed no further. Where the cause of death is ascertained, the next step in the enquiry is to link that cause of death with the act or omission of the person alleged to have caused it. These are factual questions to be answered by a consideration of the evidence. In *Oforlete* v. *The State,*[30] the appellant was involved in a fight with the deceased. The appellant hit the deceased on the head with a kitchen stool. The head of the deceased was swollen three months later. The deceased was taken to the hospital where he spent about two weeks. He was subsequently referred to a psychiatric hospital where he died. What was gathered from the contradictory evidence of the two medical doctors was that there existed the possibility of an intervening factor which might have made the condition of the deceased worse, thereby leading to his death. The trial court held that it was the act of the appellant that caused the death of the deceased. The Court of Appeal upheld this finding. Dissatisfied, the appellant appealed to the Supreme Court. While allowing the appeal, the Supreme Court held that in establishing a causal link between the act of an accused person and the relevant consequence, as a factual question, no aspect of the enquiry should be left to

[30] (2000) 12 NWLR (pt 681) 415

assumption, speculation or conjecture. Where a long period has transpired between the act and the consequence alleged, much stronger evidence is required to show an unbroken link between act and consequence than when the act and consequence are contemporaneous or proximate in matter of time.

Per Ayoola, JSC observed as follows:

> the truth of matter is that the whole case was poorly investigated, and poorly prosecuted. Proper investigations should have revealed some degree of continuity between the blow to the deceased's head resulting in a swelling on the head and the eventual resort to medical treatment three months later – proper. Prosecution should have ensured that adequate evidence of causal link of the cause of death and the appellant's act was presented at the trial. The prosecutor should have ensured, but did not ensure that medical evidence was presented in an intelligible form leaving nothing to speculation and conjecture. The gap between the incident and the first contact of the deceased, three months later, with the first medical witness (PW2) should have put the investigator and the prosecutor on inquiry whether the swelling occasioned by the blow inflicted on the deceased by the appellant persisted and was troublesome to him until medical help was sought.

In many practical situations, the net effect of the 'proximate cause rule' might not be different with the 'but for' rule of causation. That was for example, adopted by the Model Penal Code[31] draft Hart and Honoree expressed preference for the 'Common-sense' approach, which has marked past American and British judiciously experience in the field of causation, though they do obviously insist on reconciliation of inconsistencies which after all need not exist. As far as homicide cases are concerned, causation could arise in terms of for

[31] American Law Institute, Model Penal Code tentative draft No, 41,203.

suitability of consequence, or in the determination of whether the action of the accused is a substantial or contributory cause of the death of the deceased. In all the situations, the issue is essentially on whether or not for the conduct of the accused, the death of the deceased would not have occurred. This was cloaked with greater theoretical formulation by Wingersky,[32] whose treatise can be summed up in the three basic propositions:

i. the ultimate harm suffered is linked by caused relation, to the perpetrating act;
ii. the resultant harm is imputed to an accused if it is the proximate consequence of his act remission;
iii. a sense actor is presumed to intend the natural, probable and reasonable consequence of his own deliberate, voluntary acts.

Section 310 of the Criminal Code provides that a person is deemed to have killed another if, by threats or intimidation by deceit, he causes that other person to do an act or make an omission which results in his death. In *R.* v. *Nwoaka,*[33] the trial judge applied section 310 of the Criminal Code and held the accused guilty of manslaughter. In that case, the accused person pointed a *juju,* called *Onye Uku,* at the deceased who owed him money and uttering words to that effect that since you refuse to pay me my money this juju will kill you, or since you refuse to pay me, you shall no more eat or drink. He left the *juju* at the deceased's house and although there was no evidence that she stopped eating or drinking, the deceased became very depressed and six days later she went out and hanged herself on a high tree. On appeal, the West African Court of Appeal held, quashing the conviction, that there was no evidence that the particular *juju* used had ever resulted in a person killing herself and no evidence that the accused knew

---

[32] Wingersky, Clark and Marshall, *Law of Crimes* ,6th Ed.1958
[33] (1939) 5 WACA, 120

that his conduct was reasonably or likely to have led the deceased to commit suicide.

In *Emmanuel Ben v. the State,*[34] the appellant was charged with the murder of the deceased. The appellant struck the deceased on the head with a big stick. The deceased fell down unconscious and never regained consciousness until he died a few hours later before he could be treated at the hospital. It was held that where in fact the death of the deceased occurred from the act of the appellant within the period of one year and a day, it was the presumption that the act of the appellant was the cause of death except it could be shown that the deceased died from a cause other than the act of the appellant. That the consequence is not different even if he did not intend to kill the deceased. In the instant case, the death of the deceased was caused by the injuries he sustained through the act of the appellant and not whether from the medical point of view, death was caused by such injuries.

However, it must be acknowledged that causation problems may be more difficult in cases where the accused person having inflicted a wound on the deceased, some external factors for which the accused is not responsible supervene or occur to cause death.[35] If X inflicts a grievous wound on Y and subsequently other causes occur which aggravate the wound and cause Y's death, X will be liable for causing Y's death provided the wound inflicted by X is a contributing cause of death.

In *R.* v. *Smith,*[36] Lord Parker, C.J, has this to say:

> it seems to the court that if at the time of death, the original wound is still an operating cause and a substantial cause, then the death can properly be said to be the result of the wound, albeit that some other cause of death is also operating only if it

---

[34] (2006) 16 NWLR (Pt 1006) 582

[35] See Owoade, M.A,. *supra*, note 26 at page 26

[36] (1959) 2 All E.R.193

> can be said that the original wound is merely the setting in which another cause operates can it be said that the death does result from the wound.

By the virtue of the provisions of section 312 of the Criminal Code, once the victim's death is traceable to the injury inflicted by the accused, it will avail him nothing to show that the deceased's death might have been prevented by proper care or treatment. But, Owoade, however, argued that this may be relevant considerations in civil but not in criminal proceedings.

A prosecutor who must succeed in a charge of murder against an accused, must prove and establish that it was the act or omission of the accused person that caused the death of the deceased. That is, there must be a nexus between the act of the accused person and the eventual cause of death. The chain of causation must remain and unbroken. Meanwhile, if there exist other intervening factors that are the immediate cause of death, a conviction for murder may be quashed on appeal.

Punishment for Murder

It is a common saying that he who kills by sword, must himself be killed by sword. In effect, it may be translated in this context to mean that he who unlawfully kills another must himself be killed. Thus, the punishment for murder should be a death sentence. But whether this position is what is obtainable in all jurisdictions, only a further analysis would reveal.

In England, the Murder (Abolition of the Death Penalty) Act 1965, abolished capital punishment for murder and substituted it with a mandatory life sentence for those convicted for murder. This, in essence, abolished the death penalty as punishment for murder. Therefore, the mandatory life imprisonment is the punishment for murder in England, although there are still arguments whether all kinds of murder should attract the same length of imprisonment. However, in *R.*

v. *Lichinak,*[37] the House of Lords held that the indeterminate life sentence was not contrary to Article 3 (Inhuman or Degrading Treatment) or Article 5 (Right to Liberty) of the European Convention on Human Rights.

It should be stressed that the Murder (Abolition of the Death Penalty) Act, 1965 was supported by the Government at that time for two basic reasons. First that murder was a unique offence and should be marked by a unique penalty. Secondly, that to permit determinate sentencing for the offence could be risky, since there might be cases in which the Home Secretary would have to release a prisoner who has served a determinate sentence, less remission, even though he might feel that it was unsafe to do so.

One of the arguments of those who believe that murder merits a unique penalty is that the mandatory life sentence reflects the retributive view that anyone who murders another must place his life at the disposal of the State to the extent that both his release and his liberty to remain at large will always be subject to executive decision. This view is usually associated with the argument that to sentence murderers in the same way as other offenders would be to devalue murder as an offence and to reduce the deterrent effect of the existing penalty.[38] Meanwhile, a trial judge has no discretion to vary the sentence of life imprisonment. However, the Home Secretary may release such a person on licence at any time during the term, but the trial judge has the power to make a recommendation that such a step should not be taken for a certain number of years. Thus, the court may, in sentencing the convicted murderer to life imprisonment, recommend that he should serve at least 20 years before being released. This type of recommendation will be made when the judge feels that he is

---

[37] (2003) 1 AC, 903

[38] See the Report of the Advisory Council on the Penal System Sentences of Imprisonment (A Review of Maximum Penalties) (1978) para 236-237

dealing with, for example, a particular brutal murder. The Home Secretary is clearly not bound to follow such a recommendation, although failure to do so would most certainly increase the presumption for a return of the death penalty.[39] This procedure has, in effect, been replaced by a process under which the trial judge who has imposed a mandatory life sentence writes, via the Lord Chief Justice, to the Home Secretary informing him of what he considers would be an appropriate period to meet the requirements of retribution and deterrence.

In Nigeria, the punishment for murder is the death sentence. This is provided for under section 319 of the Criminal Code. Section 319 (1) of the Criminal Code provides that any person who commits the offence of murder shall be sentenced to death. In this respect, the trial judge has no discretion to do otherwise. Once an accused person has been found guilty of the offence of murder, the court shall pronounce a death sentence. These provisions of the law are mandatory. A person convicted of murder must be sentenced to death appears not applicable to all categories of persons. Young persons and pregnant women may not be punished with the death sentence if at the point of conviction the child has not attained the age of seventeen years or the women are said to be pregnant.

Section 319(2) of the Criminal Code provides that when an offender who, in the opinion of the court, had not attained the age of seventeen years at the time the offence was committed and has be found guilty of murder, such offender shall not be sentenced to death but shall be ordered to be detained during the pleasure of the President and upon such an order being made, the provisions of part 44 of the Criminal Procedure Act shall apply.

---

[39] See Sweet and Maxwell, *Criminal Law Textbooks Series* (London 1990) at page 308

Part 44 of the Criminal Procedure Act provides for the detention during the pleasure of the President. The Criminal Procedure Act in section 401(1) provides that when any person is ordered to be detained during the pleasure of the President, he shall notwithstanding anything in this Act or in any other written law contained be liable to be detained in such place and under such conditions as the President may direct and whilst so detained shall be deemed to be in legal custody. However, under section 401(2) of the Criminal Procedure Act (CPA), a person detained during the pleasure of the President may at any time be discharged by the President on licence. A licence may be in such form and contains such conditions as the President may direct.[40] Also, a licence may at any time be revoked or varied by the President and where a licence has been revoked, the person of the President may direct and if he fails to do so, may be arrested without warrant and taken to such place.[41]

Section 319(3) of the Criminal Code provides that where a woman who has been convicted of murder alleges she is pregnant or where the judge before whom she is convicted considers it advisable to have inquiries made as to whether or not she be pregnant, the procedure laid down in Section 376 of the Criminal Procedure Act shall first be complied with section. 376 of the CPA provides:

> 376(1) Where a woman convicted of an offence punishable with death alleges that she is pregnant, or where the court before or by which a woman is so convicted thinks fit so to do, the court shall, before sentence is passed on her, determine the question whether or not she is pregnant;

---

[40] See section 401(3) Criminal Procedure Act Cap C41 Laws of the Federation of Nigeria 2004

[41] Section 401 (4) of the Criminal Procedure Act (CPA).

> (2) The question whether the woman is pregnant or not shall be determined by the court on such evidence as may be laid before it on the part of the woman or on the part of the prosecution and the court shall find that the woman is not pregnant unless it is proved affirmatively to the satisfaction of the court that she is pregnant;
>
> (3) Where on proceedings under this section the court finds the woman in question is not pregnant, the court shall pronounce sentence of death upon her;
>
> (4) An appeal shall lie to the Supreme Court against such finding and that court, if satisfied that the finding should be set aside, shall quash the sentence passed on her and in lieu thereof pass on her a sentence of imprisonment for life;
>
> (5) The rights conferred by this section on a woman convicted of an offence punishable with death shall be in substitution for the right of such a woman to allege in stay of execution that she is quick with the child the last mentioned right having ceased exist;
>
> (6) The court shall report to the appropriate authority any case in which the court passes a sentence of imprisonment for life under this section.

In conclusion, although life imprisonment, as punishment for murder in England, is still being debated as to whether or not all categories of murder should carry the same length of punishment, it is, however, settled under the Nigerian Criminal Law that whosoever commits the offence of murder shall be sentenced to death, except where the convict is a child under the age of seventeen years or of woman who is said to be pregnant at time of conviction.

MANSLAUGHTER

Manslaughter is the twin brother of murder. Hence, section 317 of the Criminal Code provides that any unlawful killing which does not amount to murder is manslaughter. But, according to Clarkson and Keating, the crime of manslaughter is committed when a defendant (the accused person) commits the *actus reus* of homicide but the killing is not sufficiently blameworthy to warrant liability for murder.

Under the Penal Code, homicide offences are classified as culpable homicide punishable with death and culpable homicide not punishable with death. Although the later does not necessarily means manslaughter. But it could be seen that culpable homicide not punishable with death is a lesser offence as manslaughter under the Criminal Code. The offence of manslaughter is usually classified as voluntary and involuntary.

Voluntary Manslaughter

The offence of manslaughter is said to be voluntary when an accused person intentionally kills another under provocation. Therefore, the defence of provocation when successfully pleaded by an accused person may reduce a charge of murder to manslaughter. Thus, it is not uncommon for an accused person to raise the defence of provocation in a murder charge. And, it has inevitably become a common plea in the criminal courts especially in murder trial.[42] The major reason for having the defence of provocation in murder cases is that a murder charge attracts a fixed sentence, that is capital punishment.

Section 318 of the Criminal Code provides that if a person kills another in the heat of passion caused by sudden

[42] See the Home Office Research Statistics on Murder H.M.S.O. (1961)

provocation, and before there is time for his passion to cool, he is guilty not of murder but of manslaughter. On the other hand, section 222(1) of the Penal Code provides that culpable homicide is not punishable with death if the offender whilst deprived of the power of self-control by grave and sudden provocation, cause or causes the death of any other person by mistake or accident.

Section 283 of the Criminal Code defines provocation as follows:

> the term provocation used with reference to offence of which an assault is an element, includes, except as hereinafter stated, any wrongful act or insult of such a nature as to be likely, when done to an ordinary person, or in the presence of an ordinary person to another person who is under his immediate care, or to whom he stands on a conjugal, parental, filial, or fraternal relation, or in relation of master and servant, to deprive him of the power of self-control and to induce him to assault the person by whom the act or insult is done or offered.

Meanwhile, the law has traditionally accepted the claims of provocation as affecting criminal liability. Provocation may reduce murder to manslaughter, because it is felt unjust to subject the defendant to the full rigour of a conviction for murder. A conviction for manslaughter gives the courts the necessary flexibility to impose whatever sentence is deemed appropriate.

According to Conklin[43] victim precipitation of a crime means that the person who suffers the eventual harm from a crime

---

[43] Conklin J.E., *Criminology* (1981) at pp. 302 -304

may play a direct role in causing the crime to be perpetrated. For example, the homicide victim may be the first to use force. About one in four is victim precipitated, although one study found that 38 per cent of a sample of murders were caused in part by the victim. There is a continuum from deliberate provocation by the victim, to some involvement by the victim, to little or no victim contribution.

Conklin's claims appear to provide justification for the defence of provocation in murder cases. He argued that the victim may be the one who provoked the assault on him that led to his eventual death. As such, a charge of murder should be reduced to manslaughter. Section 3 of the English Homicide Act of 1957 provides that where on a charge of murder, there is evidence on which the jury can find that the person charged was provoked (whether by things done or by things said or by both together) to lose his self-control, the question whether the provocation was enough to make a reasonable man do as he did shall be left to be determined by the jury, and in determining that question the jury shall take into account everything both done and said according to the effect which, in their opinion, it would have on a reasonable man.

In *R.* v. *Doughty*,[44] the defendant was convicted of the murder of his 17-day old son. He had to look after both his wife (who had a caesarean operation), and the baby since their return from the hospital. The baby was extremely restless and cried persistently. The defendant agreed to have been a conscientious father who had done his best, finally tried to stop the crying by placing a cushion over the baby's head and then kneeling on it. The trial judge refused to allow the baby's crying immediately prior to the killing to go the jury as evidence of provocation. The defendant's appeal against the conviction was allowed. He was, however, convicted of manslaughter. And in *R.*

---

[44] (1986) 83 Cr. App. R. 319

v. *Senior,*[45] a midwife who was ignorant of the art he professed and unable to deliver the woman with safety to herself and the child, as might have been done by a person of ordinary skill, broke and compressed the skull of the infant and thereby occasioned its death immediately, after it was born. A conviction for manslaughter was upheld. Similarly, in *Duffy v. R.*,[46] Devlin J has this to say:

> provocation is some act, or series of acts done by the dead man to the accused which would cause in any reasonable person and actually causes in the accused, a sudden and temporary loss of self-control, rendering the accused so subject to passion as to make him or her for the moment not master of his mind.

Commenting on the loss of self-control as a vital ingredient of the defence of provocation, Coker, J.S.C. in *Ewo Akang* v. *The State*[47] opined as follows:

> provocation which reduces what would otherwise amount to murder to manslaughter is a legal concept. It is of paramount importance in the consideration of this concept that the act held out as a natural and justifiable reaction of the provoked person be done not in self-revenge but in ventilation of a natural, sudden and contemporaneous feeling of anger caused by the circumstances of the occasions.

Meanwhile, the ingredients of the offence of manslaughter which must be proved were stated in the recent case of *Maren* v. *The State,*[48] where it was held that by virtue of section 317 of the Criminal Code,[49] a person who unlawfully kills another in

---

[45] (1832) 1 Mood CC 346

[46] (1949) 1 All NLR 932. See also *Ogbodu* v. *State* (1987) 2 NWLR, 20 *Stephen* v. *the State* (1986) 5 NWLR, 978

[47] (1971) 1 All NLR 46

[48] (2010) 3 NWLR (pt 1181) 259

[49] Cap C17 Laws of Lagos State 2003

such circumstances as not to constitute murder is guilty of manslaughter. The ingredients of manslaughter which must be proved were listed as:

(a) that the death of a human being actually took place;
(b) that such death was caused by the accused;
(c) that the accused intended by such act to cause death or that he intended by such act to cause such bodily injury as was likely to cause death or that he caused the death by a rash negligent act.

In *R.* v. *Bassey*,[50] the appellant was attacked by three persons of whom the deceased was one. The appellant inflicted four blows on the deceased and she died. The trial judge found that the sudden attack on the appellant would cause a reasonable person of the appellant's standing in life considerable anger and cause him to strike the deceased once but that it did not excuse his continuing to deal deathblows on the deceased then incapacitated, for the second, third and fourth times in quick succession. The Federal Supreme Court disagreeing and finding provocation proved, pointed out that the finding of the trial judge implied that there was time for the appellant's passion to cool between the infliction of the first and other injuries, was unable to agree. "All four blows were delivered within a matter of seconds of each other and if the first blow was, as the learned judge found, given in the heat of passion caused by sudden provocation we cannot see how the other blows can be treated differently."

However, it is submitted that the nature of the act resulting from the provocation is merely a piece of evidence relevant in deciding whether there is indeed a loss of self-control. It has, therefore, been held that the words "provoked" and "provocation" are to be given their plain, ordinary meaning, unaffected by any technical legacies from the pre-1957

[50] (1963) 1 All NLR 280

Common law as to what may or may not constitute provocation. Therefore, it appears a settled principle of law that where it is proved that the deceased provoked the assault on him which led to his death, a charge of murder may be reduced to manslaughter. Manslaughter is thus a lesser offence when compared with murder.

Involuntary Manslaughter

An involuntary act is an act done unintentionally and which is independent of the will of the accused person. In respect of manslaughter, it can be said to be a situation where death occurs under such circumstances not contemplated by the accused person as capable of causing the death of another. According to Smith and Hogan, involuntary manslaughter occurs where a person causes death under such circumstance that he did not intend to kill and did not foresee death as a probable consequence of his conduct but there is some blameworthiness, such as some negligence in his conduct. It may also occur where death is the result of an unlawful act which involves the risk of harm to another. It should be noted that there can be no conspiracy to commit the offence of manslaughter, neither could there be an attempt to commit the offence. This is so because the offence of manslaughter is an *unintentional* killing of another by the accused person. So, the accused person lacked the necessary *mens rea*. However, his culpability lies on the *actus reus,* which occurs independently of his will. Section 24 of the Criminal Code provides to the effect that a person shall not be criminally liable for acts or omissions which occurred independently of his will. However, culpability in manslaughter finds expression in the fact that the acts of the accused caused the eventual death of the deceased.

Reckless Manslaughter

Reckless manslaughter is a new offence of causing death by dangerous driving. The offence of causing death by dangerous driving is created and punished by section 4 of the Federal Highways Act No. 4 of 1971. Section 4 of the Act provides:

> Any person who causes the death of another person by the driving of motor vehicle on federal highway recklessly, or at a speed or in a manner which is dangerous to the public having regard to all the circumstances of the case, including the nature, condition and the use of the federal highway, and the amount of traffic which is actually at the time or which might reasonably be expected to be on the federal highway, shall be guilty of an offence and liable on conviction to imprisonment for a term of seven years.

However, the interpretation given to section 4 of the Federal Highway Act of 1971 by Ayorinde, J. in *State* v. *Isaiah Ajayi*[51] appears doubtful. In that case, the accused person was charged with the offence of causing death by dangerous driving and dangerous driving contrary to sections 4 and 5(1) respectively of the Act. The question in dispute was whether the accused caused the death by driving his vehicle in a manner which was dangerous having regard to all the circumstances of the case. The trial judge, convicted only on the first count but in reaching his conclusion he felt that section 4 of the Act created three offences. They are the offences of causing death by driving a motor vehicle on a federal highway (a) recklessly or (b) at a speed, or (c) in a manner that is dangerous to the public, having regard to all the circumstances. Furthermore, where the charge under section 4 of the Act is for causing death in a manner which is dangerous to the public having regard to all the circumstances of the case for the prosecution to succeed, he does not have to show that the accused drove recklessly. It is difficult to agree with the learned trial judge's proposition that section 4 created three distinct offences. It is submitted that the only one offence is created, but it could be committed in

---

[51] Suit No. HIL/JC/81 (Unreported, High Court of Oyo State) delivered on 2nd March, 1982

any of the three ways indicated within the body of the provision.

Meanwhile, in the relatively recent case of *Moses* v. *the State,*[52] the court stated that the proof required to establish a case under section 4 of the Federal Highway Act, 1971 is not as high as the one required to establish a case of manslaughter under the Criminal Code. The court further held that dangerous driving which resulted to manslaughter was an offence of absolute prohibition into which no *mens rea* was required, and it was no answer to say "I did not mean to drive dangerously."

The necessary ingredients, which the prosecution must prove to establish the offence of causing death by dangerous driving under the Act, were aptly laid down by Ayoola J. in the case of *State* v. *Felix Usifo*[53] as follows:

a. there must be a death;
b. the accused's action could have been the substantial cause of death;
c. the accused must have driven his vehicle dangerously.

In England, section 1 of the Road Traffic Act of 1988, as amended by the Road Traffic Act of 1991, provides that a person who causes the death of another person by driving a mechanically propelled vehicle dangerously on a road or other public place is guilty of an offence. It should be stressed that the offence is triable only on indictment and is punishable by a maximum penalty of 10 years imprisonment. Before 1977, the offence covered causing death by reckless or dangerous driving. In 1977, it was narrowed down to causing death by reckless driving.[54]

Recklessness, as with negligence, must exist in relation to some particular consequence. If a defendant, for example, tosses a book out of a window onto the pavement below, this

---

[52] (2006) 11 NWLR (pt 992) 446
[53] (1977) 1 NMLR 72
[54] See section 50(1) of the Criminal Law Act of 1977.

might be recklessness as to causing a minor injury. But, if a defendant throws a 11 pounds lump of concrete from a bridge onto a busy motorway, he could be held to be reckless as to causing death or really serious injury.[55] It is widely argued that for a crime as serious as manslaughter, there should be recklessness as to the death or, at the very least, grievous bodily harm.

In *R.* v. *Lawrence,*[56] the respondent was riding his motorcycle along an urban street in Lowestoft. The street was subject to a 30 mph speed limit and there was a good deal of other traffic using it at the time. The driver ran into and killed a pedestrian who was crossing the road to return from an off-licence shop to her car that was parked on the opposite side of the street. The driver was in due course tried on indictment for the offence of causing her death by driving a motor vehicle on a road, recklessly, contrary to section 1 of the Road Traffic Act 1972. The respondent's case was that the motorcycle was being driven at between 60 and 80 mph and probably much nearer to the latter. The case of the defence was that the speed of the motorcycle was no more than 30 or at most 40 mph and probably near the former. His Lordship cited sections 1 and 2 section 50(1) of the Criminal Law Act of 1977:

> 1. A person who causes the death of another person by driving a motor vehicle on a road recklessly shall be guilty of an offence;
> 2. A person who drives a motor vehicle on a road recklessly shall be guilty of an offence.

He then contrasted these with the lesser offence of section 3 of the Road Traffic Act 1972:

---

[55] *R* v. *Green* unreported No 4475/C2/79/Court of Appeal, Criminal Division) 1980

[56] (1982) AC 510

> If a person drives a motor vehicle on a road without due care and attention, or without reasonable consideration for other persons using the road, he shall be guilty of an offence.

Lord Diplock has this to say:

> ...my Lords, this House has very recently had occasion in *Reg* v. *Caldwell* to give close consideration to the concept of recklessness as constituting *mens rea* in criminal law. The conclusion reached by the majority was that the objective 'reckless' when used in a criminal statute, i.e., the Criminal Damage Act 1971, had not acquired a special meaning as a term of legal art, but bore its popular or dictionary meaning of careless, regardless, or heedless of the possible harmful consequences of one's acts. The same must be true of the adverbial derivative 'recklessly'.

While dismissing the appeal, the court then held that the defendant was, in fact, driving the vehicle in such a manner as to create an obvious and serious risk of causing physical injury to some other person who might happen to be using the road or of doing substantial damage to property.

Similarly, in *R.* v. *Reid*,[57] the appellant was driving in the inside lane of a dual carriageway. He was trying to overtake another car on its nearside. Further down the road in the nearside lane there was an obstruction, a taxi-drivers' rest hut protruded some 6ft into the road. Lines were painted on the road to show that it was necessary to move towards the middle of the road to avoid the obstruction. The appellant's car struck the hut, killing his front seat passenger. He was convicted of causing death by reckless driving. His appeal against conviction was equally dismissed.

It should be noted, however, that recklessness includes cases where the defendant's perception is impaired by drink or by

---

[57] (1992) 95, Cr. App. R 393

blind rage or by some other excitement with the result that he fails to give any thought to the possibility of such risk. However, there may be other cases. For example, the defendant's state of mind may be such that he does not care whether any such risk exists or not, which has been described as an attitude of indifference or, of not caring less. In other cases, the defendant's state of mind may be one of wilful blindness where he simply closes his mind to the possibility of risk. In yet other cases, perhaps the most common, the defendant simply does not think about the matter at all, perhaps because he is acting impetuously on the spur of the moment without addressing his mind to the possibility of risk.

Gross Negligence Manslaughter

Negligence is described as the failure to exercise the standard of care that a reasonably prudent person would have exercised in a similar situation. It is also any conduct that falls below the legal standard established to protect others against unreasonable risk of harm, except for conduct that is intentionally wantonly, or wilfully disregardful of others' rights. The term denotes culpable carelessness. The term "gross negligence" refers to a lack of slight diligence or care. It is a conscious, voluntary act or omission in reckless disregard of a legal duty and of the consequences to another party who may typically recover exemplary damages. According to Hart, negligence is gross if the precautions to be taken against harm are very simple such as persons who are but poorly endowed physical and mental capacities can easily take.[58]

The decision in *R.* v. *Prentice & Ors*,[59] shows that there is clearly a crime of gross negligence manslaughter, quite separate from reckless manslaughter, in many respects though

---

[58] See Hart, H. A "Negligence *Mens Rea* and Criminal Responsibility," in *Punishment and Responsibility* (1968), 136 at 149

[59] (1994) 98 Cr App. R. 262

the test for the two offences is similar. The defendant must have been indifferent to, or have actually foreseen "an obvious risk of injury to heath" or have failed to advert to "a serious risk". It is, however, unclear whether the word "serious" here refers to a risk of serious injury or to a high risk of injury to health. However, a risk of injury to health is clearly broader than a risk of causing physical injury which is probably required for reckless manslaughter and, even more significantly, there is no lacuna in gross negligence manslaughter. A defendant who realises that there might be a risk but rules it out is not reckless, but can be grossly negligent.

The problem is thus one of determining when to employ gross negligence manslaughter as opposed to reckless manslaughter. Lord Taylor was careful to stress that the *Lawrence* recklessness test applies to motor manslaughter cases and that the gross negligence test applies in cases involving a breach of duty. In *Idris* v. *The State,*[60] the appellant was the driver of a trailer. On a certain date, at about 7pm, the appellant's vehicle broke down along the Abeokuta Shagamu Expressway. He left the vehicle on the middle of the road, cut some leaves and placed them a short distance away from the vehicle ostensibly as a sign of warning to other road users. He then left for Lagos to inform his employers about the development. He could not return the same day. The following morning when he returned to the scene, he discovered that a car had run into the rear of the vehicle and that the driver of the car was already dead. The appellant thereafter reported the incident to the police. He was subsequently arrested and charged to court on a two-count charge of negligence and manslaughter. It was held that for an act to constitute criminal negligence, the act must not be a simple lack of care or mere inadvertence but gross negligence. The higher degree of

[60] (2006) 2 FWLR (pt 311) 2360. See also *Adebunloye* v. *the State* (2002) 9 NWLR (pt. 773) 660

negligence, often described as gross, is required to convict for the offence of manslaughter in Nigeria. To constitute proof beyond reasonable doubt, negligence of the degree required to establish manslaughter must be revealed and proved.

To Okonkwo and Naish, the degree of negligence required to establish gross negligence manslaughter must be above the ordinary tortuous negligence. Accordingly, a simple lack of care or mere inadvertence such as would create civil liability is not sufficient. There must be gross negligence or recklessness. In *Uzoka* v. *State,*[62] it was held that under our law, it is an offence to do a lawful act in a negligent manner as to harm others. Thus, negligence negatives the defence of accident provided for under section 24 of the Criminal Code, and killing a person by negligent act would constitute manslaughter. Similarly, in *Akerele* v. *R.,*[63] the Judicial Committee of the Privy Council held that the standard of criminal negligence capable of a conviction for manslaughter must be gross and was not proved in this case. The accused was acquitted. In *R.* v. *Bateman,*[64] Lord Hewart C.J. stated as follows:

> in explaining to juries the test which they should apply to determine whether the negligence in the particular case amounted or did not amount to a crime, the judges have used many epithets, such as culpable criminal gross, wicked, clear, complete. But whatever epithet be used and whether an epithet be used or not, in order to establish criminal liability the facts must be such that in the opinion of the jury, the negligence of the accused went beyond a mere matter of compensation between subjects and showed such disregard to a crime against the state and conduct deserving punishment.

It should be stressed that a person who assumes a particular skill cannot avoid criminal responsibility if he turns out to be

---

[62] (1990) 6 NWLR (pt 158) 680

[63] (1942) 8 WACA, 5

[64] (1925) 19 Cr App. Rep 8 at 11

deficient in knowledge and competence. In *A.G Western Nigeria* v. *Oyelade,*[65] the accused native doctor had been invited to treat the deceased of his swollen scrotum. The accused began the treatment by pricking the swollen scrotum with a needle and squeezing out from the scrotum some liquid substance into a calabash. He later gave the deceased some medicine to drink. The deceased later died of the injuries to his test in the scrotum. The accused was charged with manslaughter and negligence contrary to sections 255 and 286(1)(e) respectively of the Criminal Code of Western Nigeria same as sections 317 and 343(1)(e) Criminal Code. He was convicted of manslaughter. Fakayode J. observed as follows:

> If a person takes upon himself the responsibility of attending to a patient when he is not qualified for the purpose and uses a dangerous drug, he is bound to bring skill to its use. If his education or employment makes the use of the dangerous drug amount to lack of skill and the patient dies, the person administering the drug is guilty of such criminal negligence as amounts to manslaughter.[66]

As shown above, it is admitted that the degree of negligence required establishing the offence of gross negligence manslaughter is higher than the ordinary tortuous negligence. The circumstances must be such that involve danger which put at risk the life of the victim.

The punishment for manslaughter

In England, prior to decision in *R.* v. *Boswett,*[67] the maximum penalty for manslaughter was five years imprisonment. In 1993, this was increased to ten years in response to a public outcry over deaths being caused by joyriders. In *Shepherd and Wernet*, it was held that the statement of principle and examples of

---

[65] (1966) WMLR 407
[66] (1946)12 WACA, 56
[67] (1984) 79 Cr. App. R. 277

aggravating and mitigating circumstances in *Boswell* still apply but the phrase "two years or more" should now read "upwards of five years" and in the very worst cases, if contested sentences, will be in the higher range of those now permitted by Parliament. However, an examination of the cases leaves one baffled as to when, if ever, a sentence of more than five years would be appropriate. For example, in *R.* v. *Tumer,*[68] the driver was described as an "absolute menace on the road" and sentenced to two years imprisonment in what was undoubtedly a very bad case. In the *Attorney General's reference* Nos. 17 and 18 of 1992, the Court of Appeal in a bad case of reckless driving involving a number of the aggravating factors enumerated in Boswell increased the sentence to three years imprisonment.

But in Nigeria, the punishment for manslaughter is life imprisonment. This is provided for by virtue of section 325 of the Criminal Code. The position of the law in Nigeria is that any person who commits the offence of manslaughter is liable to imprisonment for life. The Nigeria position, in regards to the punishment for manslaughter, appears more stringent. This is aimed at discouraging offenders from perpetuating crimes which are against the order of nature and human existence generally.

---

[68] (1988) 10 Cr App.R. 234

Chapter 10

PROPERTY OFFENCES

THE OFFENCES OF THEFT

Stealing

Prior to the enactment of the Theft Act in England, 1968, the offence of larceny existed. It shared similar characteristics with the offence of theft. However, the offence of larceny no longer exists in the English Law having been outlawed by the Theft Act of 1968.

In Nigeria, one may concede that the offence of theft in England bears similar features with the offence of stealing contained in section 390 of the Criminal Code. Section 1(1) of the English Theft Act of 1968 provides that a person is guilty of theft if he dishonestly appropriates property belonging to another with the intention of permanently depriving the other of it. Section 7 of the Theft Act, however, provides punishment for the offences of theft thus:

> A person guilt of theft shall on conviction on indictment be liable to imprisonment for a term not exceeding seven years.

Section 383 of the Criminal Code provides that a person who fraudulently takes anything capable of being stolen, or fraudulently coverts to his own use or to the use of any other person anything capable of being stolen, is said to steal that thing.

It should be noted that the *mens rea* of the offence of theft is dishonesty and intention permanently to deprive. The *actus reus* is appropriate property belonging to another.[1]

Appropriation

In England, under the old Law of Larceny, the thing had to be carried away. Accordingly, land could not be stolen. The new word was "appropriation", which it was hoped would be easily understood by the trials of fact. That hope has been dashed. Under the present law, an article can be stolen without being taken away. For example, if the accused puts his hand into the victim's pocket and grabs-hold of a watch, there is an appropriation because of the definition found in section 3(1) or the Theft Act 1968. Under section 3(1) of the Theft Act, any assumption by a person of the right of an owner amounts to an appropriation. Section 3(1) of the Theft Act provides that where a person comes by property, whether innocently or not, and later assumes the right of owner of that property, that subsequent assumption of the rights of the owner is an appropriation. While section 3(2) of the Theft Act provides that where a person assumes the right of the owner of goods because he has purchased them, for money or money's worth, in good faith, that assumption of rights is not to be regarded as an appropriation. In *R.* v. *Adams,*[2] the appellant was convicted for being in possession of stolen goods which he purchased. On appeal to the Criminal Court of Appeal his appeal was allowed. And, the court held that by virtue of section 3(2) of the Theft Act 1968 which provides that where a person has received property for value in good faith, no later assumption by him of right which he believed himself to be acquiring would by reason of a defect in title amount to theft. In *Corcoran* v. *Aderton,*[3] it

---

[1] Michael Jefferson, *Criminal Law* 7th edn (England: Pearson Education Ltd, (2006), P53
[2] (1993) Crim. LR 72 CA
[3] (1980) 71 Cr App R 104 (DC)

was held that grabbing a handbag is an appropriation, even though the accused dropped the bag immediately and did not get away with it.

Similarly, in *Lawrence* v. *MPC*,[4] the House of Lords held that the accused can steal even though the victim consents to the taking. One can assume the rights of the owner even though the owner permitted one to do so. The House of Lords' decision in *Lawrence* that there may be theft despite the owner's consent applied generally to all forms of consent. In *Lawrence,* the appropriation took place because an Italian student handed over extra money to a taxi driver who had deceived him as to a taxi fare, but *Lawrence* is not restricted to instances where the accused appropriated by deception. In *R.* v. *Rader,*[5] the Court of Appeal held that *Lawrence* applied even when the accused had taken the victim's money with his full consent. The victim gave him almost €10,000, on the latter's promise that he would return it on the due date with some sort of profit. The accused said that he was investing the money via an acquaintance in Miami, but that person had not repaid the money. His appeal was dismissed. The victim had consented to the taking but the facts constituted an appropriation.

Unlike taking, dealing with goods in a manner inconsistent with the right of the true owner amounts to a conversion, provided that it is also established that there is also an intention on the part of the defendant in so doing to deny the owner's right or to assert a right which is inconsistent with the owner's right.[6]

Accordingly, to destroy, alter, sell, pledge or use property belonging to another person is to convert it. But, in order that the conversion will amount to stealing, it must be done with

---

[4] (1972) AC 626

[5] (1992) Crim LR 663

[6] Atkin J. in *Lan Cashier & Yorkshire Railway Co.* v. *Machnicol* (1919) 88 L.J.K. B/. 601 at 605

one of the fraudulent intents specified in section 383.[7] If A merely uses B`s horse and redelivers it to him, this is conversion in tort but it is not stealing under the Code because it is not done fraudulently within the meaning of section 383(2). In *Oshinye* v. *COP,*[8] the accused obtained some goods from someone saying falsely that the owner had authorised him to take the goods. When he received them, he had no fraudulent intent but he later appropriated them to his own use. He was held guilty of stealing by conversion.

PROPERTY

Section 4(1) of the Theft Act, 1968 defines property to include money and all other property, real or personal, including things in action and other intangible property. Section 4(2) provides that a person cannot steal land, or thing forming part of land and severed from it by him or by his directions, except in the following cases, that is to say:

(a) when he is a trustee or personal representative or is authorised by power of attorney or as a liquidator or a company or otherwise, to sell or dispose of land belonging to another, and he appropriates the land or anything forming part of it, by dealing with it in breach of the confidence reposed in him; or

(b) when he is not in possession of the land appropriates anything forming part of the land by severing it or causing it to be severed, or after it has been severed; or

(c) when, being in possession of the land under tenancy, he appropriates the whole or part of any fixture or structure let to be used with the land.

For purposes of this subsection "land" does not include incorporeal hereditaments, "Tenancy"

---

[7] See Okonkwo & Naish, *Criminal Law in Nigeria*, 2nd ed. (Spectrum Books Ltd, Ibadan 1980) p. 289

[8] (1960) 5 F.S.C. 105

> means a tenancy for years or any less period and includes an agreement for such a tenancy, but a person who after the end of a tenancy remains in possession as statutory tenant or otherwise is to be treated as having possession under the tenancy, and let shall be construed accordingly.[9]
>
> (3) A person who picks mushroom growing wild on any land or, who picks flowers, fruits or foliage from a plant growing wild on any land does not (although not in possession of the land) steal what he picks, unless he does it for reward or for sale or other commercial purpose.
>
> (4) wild creatures, tamed or untamed, shall be regarded as property, but a person cannot steal a wild creature not tamed nor ordinarily kept in captivity or the carcass of any such creature, unless either it has been reduced into possession by or on behalf of another person and possession of it has not since been lost or abandoned, or another person is in course of reducing it into possession.

In *Oxford* v. *Moss,*[10] on 5th May, 1976, an information was preferred by the prosecutor against the defendant alleging that the defendant stole certain intangible property, namely confidential information being examination question for civil engineering examination to be held in the month of June 1976 at Liverpool University, the information being the property of the Senate of the university and the allegation being that the respondent intended permanently to deprive the said Senate of the said property. The question for the court's determination was whether confidential information can amount to property within the Theft Act, 1968. Smith J. held: "in my judgment, it is

---

[9] See Michael Molan, *Source Book on Criminal Law*, 2nd edn (Cavendish Publishing Ltd, London, 2001) pg 919

[10] (1978) 68 Cr App R 183 (DC)

clear that the answer to that question must be "No". Accordingly, I would dismiss the appeal."

Wien J. held that the right to confidential information is not intangible property within the meaning of Section 4(1) of the Theft Act, 1968. In *R.* v. *Hancock*,[11] the appellant was charged with theft from the Crown of 16 ancient coins found in an area which appeared to have been the site of a Romano-Celtic Temple. If the coins were a treasure trove, they belong to the Crown.

Auld, J held:

> it is not necessary for the offence of theft that the property alleged to have been stolen is in the possession, actual or constructive of the owner at the time when it is appropriated. Accordingly, we are of the view that it was for the jury in the trial of this matter to determine as part of their finding on the issue of guilt or innocence of the appellant whether the coins were in fact treasure trove and thus the property of the Crown. In their determination of that issue, they have to apply the ordinary criminal burden and standard of proof, namely they could only convict the appellant if they were sure that the coins in question were treasure trove, namely that they had been deposited by someone who had intended to retrieved them.

In *R.* v. *Kohn*,[12] the accused, an accountant, drew cheques on his employer's account. He was guilty of the theft. The causing of the bank account to be reduced was appropriation, and the account was property.

Generally, the power to prosecute for an offence is not determined by the ownership of the property allegedly stolen or misappropriated. The determining factors were recently adumbrated in the case of *Nyame* v. *Federal Republic of Nigeria*[13] as follows:

(a) who can exercise prosecutorial power of the offence;

---

[11] (1990) 2 WLR 640 CA

[12] (1979) 69 Cr App R 395

[13] (2010) 7 NWLR (pt 1193) p. 370

(b) the nature of the offence charged;
(c) where the offence was committed, that is the venue.

The court then held that it is not a defence known to law that an accused person cannot be prosecuted by the authority with prosecutorial powers on the ground that the prosecutor is not the owner of the stolen items. Criminal offence is an offence against the state. A state prosecutor need not have interest in the subject matter of the complaint before he can prosecute an accused person. Protecting the state and its citizens and every prosecutor or authority or agency vested with the power to prosecute should be encouraged to carry out their duties, provided the due process is maintained and followed.

It should, however, be stressed that, it is not everything that is capable of being stolen. Section 382 of the Criminal Code contains a list of things capable of being stolen. Every inanimate thing which belongs to some person and which is capable of being made movable is capable of being stolen as soon as it becomes movable, although it is made movable in order to steal it. The section contains provision about tame animals and animals wild by nature. As noted earlier, land cannot be stolen. In *Ojiko* v. *Inspector General of Police,*[14] A received money from B in order to buy land in A's name and then transfer it to B. A bought the land but refused to transfer it to B. it was held that A is not guilty of stealing the money because he had used it for the purpose for which it was intended. The court further held that A was also not guilty of stealing the purchased land because land property can also not be stolen, an ownerless property can also not be stolen. However, under section 3 of the Lagos Criminal Code, a thing in action is capable of being stolen.[15] Meanwhile, under section 5(4) of the English Theft Act of 1968, where A receives money

[14] (1956) 1 F.S.C., 62
[15] Criminal Justice (Misc. Provisions) Decree, No. 84 of 1966

from B as a result of a mistake on B's part and A is under a legal obligation to return some or all of that money to B, the money which should be returned to B is regarded as property belonging to B for the purchase of theft.

Taking with Dishonesty Property Belonging to Another
Section 2 of the Theft Act of 1968 provides:

> (1) A person's appropriation of property belonging to another is not to be regarded as dishonest;
> (a) if he appropriates the property in the belief that he has in law the right to deprive the other of it, on behalf of himself or of a third person, or,
> (b) if he appropriates the property in the belief that he would have the other's consent if the other knew of the appropriation and the circumstance of it, or,
> (c) (except where the property came to him as trustee or personal representative) if he appropriates the property in the belief that the person to whom the property belongs cannot be discovered by taking reasonable steps.
> (2) A person's appropriation of property belonging to another may be dishonest not withstanding that he is willing to pay for the property.

In *R.* v. *Holden,*[16] the appellant was charged with theft of scrap tyres from Kwik-fit, where he had worked. He claimed that other people had taken tyres with the permission of a superior. The depot manager gave evidence that taking tyres was a sackable offence. The jury had been directed that the test for dishonesty was whether the defendant had a reasonable belief that he had a right to take the tyres. It was held that reasonable belief was not the relevant test of dishonesty. A

[16] (1991) Crim LR 478 (CA)

person was not dishonest if he believed, reasonably or not, that he had a legal right to do what was alleged to constitute an appropriation of property.

In *Attorney General Reference*[17] (Nos. of 1982), the court was asked to determine whether a man in total control of a limited liability company is capable of stealing the property of the company, and whether two men in total control of a limited liability company are capable of jointly stealing the property of the company. It was submitted that since the defendants were the sole owners of the company and through their shareholding the sole owners of all its property, they could not in effect be charged with stealing from themselves. In particular, it was submitted that there was no issue to go to the jury on the ingredient of 'dishonesty'. The defendants were the sole will and directing mind of the company. The company was therefore bound to consent to all to which they themselves consented.

The court held, *inter alia*, Kerr, LJ:

> We entirely disagree with both these propositions...
> In our view there is no substance whatever in the submission that section 2(1) (b) would preclude a jury from concluding, as a matter of law, that the defendants had acted dishonestly in these cases. Nor can we accept for one moment that any jury would be bound to conclude, on the facts alleged, that dishonesty had not been established...it does not by any means follow that the members and directors of a company which is wholly owned by them cannot properly be charged with theft of the company's property...

At Common Law, it has been asked whether it can be a defence in law for a man charged with theft and proved to have taken money to say that when he took the money, he intended to repay it and had reasonable grounds for believing and did

[17] (1984) QB 624 (CA)

believe that he would be able do so. In *R.* v. *Freely*,[18] the appellant took £30 from his employer's safe. He did not put an IOU in the safe, nor make any record to show what he had done, nor tell his employer what he had done. Four days later, a shortfall of £40 was discovered. The appellant then gave an IOU for that amount. When interviewed by the police, the appellant said:

I. that he would have paid the money back; and
II. that his employer owed him about £70, more than enough to cover what was taken. Lawton, LJ held, *inter alia*, "...people who take money from tills and the like without permission are usually thieves; but if they do not admit that, they are pleading not guilty. It is for the jury, not the judge, to decide whether they have acted dishonestly."

It may, therefore, be asked whether is "dishonestly" in section 1 of the Theft Act 1968 intended to characterise a course of conduct. Or, is it intended to describe a state of mind? If the former, then we can well understand that it could be established independently of the knowledge or belief of the accused. But if, as we think, it is the latter, then the knowledge and belief of the accused are the root of the problem. In *R.* v. *Ghosh*,[19] Lord Lane C.J. said:

> ...if we are right that dishonesty is something in the mind of the accused... then if the mind of the accused is honest, it cannot be deemed dishonest merely because members of the jury would have regarded it as dishonest to embark on that course of conduct. So, we would reject the simple uncomplicated approach that the test is purely objective, however attractive from the practical point of view that solution may be...

Again, can it be said that an accused acted dishonestly for receiving stolen property if at the time of the reception is

[18] (1973) QB 530
[19] (1982) QB 1053

neither aware that such were stolen property? Section 427 of the Criminal Code[20] provides that any person who receives anything which has been obtained by means of any act constituting a felony or misdemeanour...and which is an offence under the laws in force in the place where it was done, knowing same to have been so obtained is guilty of a felony. The section stated further that if the offence by means of which the thing was obtained is a felony, the offender is liable to imprisonment for fourteen years, except in the case in which the thing so obtained was postal matter, or any chattel, money, or valuable security contained therein, in which case the offender is liable to imprisonment for life. In *Abacha* v. *Federal Republic of Nigeria,*[21] the court held that the ingredients to found a conviction for receiving stolen property of an offence punishable under section 317 of the Penal Code are as follows:

a. that the property in question is stolen property;
b. that the accused received or retained such property;
c. that he did so dishonestly;
d. that he knew or had reason to believe that the property is stolen property.

Similarly, section 319 of the Penal Code punishes the offence of concealing stolen property. In *Abacha* v. *FRN supra*, the court equally listed the ingredients of the offence of concealing stolen property punishable under section 319 of the Penal Code as follows:

(a) that the property in question is stolen property;
(b) that the accused assisted in concealing or disposing of or making away with the property;
(c) that he did so voluntarily;
(d) that he knew or had reason to believe that the property is stolen property.

[20] Cap C38 Laws of the Federation of Nigeria 2004
[21] (2006) 4 NWLR (pt 970) 260

In *Okoroji* v. *The State,*[22] the Court of Appeal held that receiving stolen property is manifested when:

(a) there is proof of stealing of the goods in question;

(b) there is proof that the person charged, dishonestly received the goods allegedly stolen which is manifested when he either physically received the goods or that they were in the possession of person over whom he had control and the person charged must have had the thing in his possession, whether alone or jointly with another or has actually aided in concealing or disposing of it when he knew that it was stolen;

(c) there is evidence of guilty knowledge which in effect means that at the time the person charged received or bought the goods, he knew them to be stolen.

The evidence required to establish guilty knowledge according to the court may be stated as follows: The evidence required to established guilty knowledge, according to the court may be stated as follows:

i. the manner of the receipt of the goods stolen;
ii. the time delivered;
iii. the actions upon delivery; and
iv. the price paid for the items.

In all cases, dishonesty must be proved. The fact of deception does not *per se* prove dishonesty. In *R.* v. *Potger,*[23] the accused falsely represented that he was a student who was taking part in a competition to sell the "Most magazines". He was not, in fact, a student. The court held that he was guilty despite the fact that the magazine was worth the purchase price.

Again, an accused person who obtains the property of another under a false pretence will equally be guilty of the offence of stealing.

---

[22] (2002) 5 NWLR (pt 759) 21

[23] (1970) 55 Cr. App R. 42

Fundamentally, the offence of obtaining by false pretence means knowingly obtaining another person's property by means of a misrepresentation of facts with intent to defraud. Section 419 of the Criminal Code provides for the offence of obtaining by false pretences that any person who by false pretence and with intend to defraud, obtains from any other person anything capable of being stolen or induces any other person to deliver to any person anything capable of being stolen is guilty of a felony, and is liable to imprisonment for three years. For the offence of obtaining by false pretences to be committed, the prosecution must prove that the accused had an intention to defraud and the thing is capable of being stolen. An inducement on the part of an accused to make his victim part with a thing capable of being stolen or to make his victim deliver a thing capable of being stolen will expose the accused to imprisonment of the offence.

In *Onwudiwe* v. *Federal Republic of Nigeria*[24] the Supreme Court of Nigeria held that in order to succeed in a charge of obtaining by false pretence, the prosecution must prove the following:

(a) that there is a pretence;
(b) that the pretence emanated from the accused person;
(c) that it was false;
(d) that the accused person knew of its falsity or did not believe in its truth;
(e) that there was an intention to defraud;
(f) that the thing is capable of being stolen;
(g) that the accused person induced the owner to transfer his whole interest in the property.

The offence could be committed by oral communication, or in writing, or even by conduct of the accused person. However, an honest belief in the truth of the statement on the part of the

---

[24] (2006) 10 NWLR (pt 988), p 394

accused which later turns out to be false cannot found a conviction on false pretence.[25]

Per Jobi, J.S.C.:

> The false pretence on the part of the appellant was very clear. At the time he was in the so-called business conversation with Mrs. Justina Nkechi Nwaogu, he knew that neither the Ivory Merchant Bank Limited nor himself had US$345,000 to exchange for ₦16.56million. And that made the pretence false. And because he had intention to defraud, the appellant kept away from P.W.1 and P.W. 2 the fact that he had no dollar value or content of the ₦16.56 million. By his action and conduct, appellant had an intentional perversion of truth for the purpose of inducing P.W. 1 and P.W.2 to part with ₦16.56 million without a dollar. By section 419, the ₦16.56 million is capable of being stolen and it was stolen by the appellant...In my view, the prosecution proved the offence of obtaining by false pretence against the appellant and I so hold.

The gist of the above argument is that any person who dishonestly or while acting under false pretences takes the property belonging to another person is guilty of the offence of stealing or theft.

Intention of Permanent Deprivation

Section 383(2)(a) & (b) of the Criminal Code provides for intention of permanent deprivation of property belonging to the person of another.

Section 383(2) provides that a person who takes or converts anything capable of being stolen, or is deemed to do so fraudulently if he does so with...

(a) an intent permanently to deprive the owner of the thing of it;

[25] See *Alake* v. *State* (1991) 7 NWLR (pt 205) p. 567, *Akosa* v. *COP* (1950) 13 WACA 43, *Oshin* v. *IGP* (1961) 1 SCNLR 49

(b) an intention to permanently deprive any person who has any special property interest in the thing of such property.

It should be noted that the term "special property" includes any charge or lien upon the thing in question and any right arising from or dependent upon holding possession of the thing in question, whether by the person entitled to such right or by some other person for his benefit.

Section 6 of the English Theft Act 1968, has similar provisions with section 383(2) of the Nigerian Criminal Code. Section 6(1) & (2) of the Theft Act 1968 provides as follows:

(1) A person appropriating property belonging to another without meaning the other permanently to lose the thing itself is nevertheless to be regarded as having the intention of permanently depriving the other of it if his intention is to treat the things as his own, to dispose of regardless of the other's rights, and a borrowing or lending is for a period and in circumstances making it equivalent to an outright taking or disposal.

(2) Without prejudice to the generality of subsection (1) above, where a person having possession or control (lawfully or not) of property belonging to another, parts with the property under a condition as to its return which he may not be able to perform, this (if done for purposes of his own and without the other's authority) amounts to treating the property as his own to dispose of regardless of the other's right to it. In *R.* v. *Warner*,[26] the defendant took some tools belonging to another. He said that he intended to return the tools to their owner, but had not decided when he was going to do so. The fundamental legal issue that was raised on appeal was whether the accused man had ever formed the intention to deprive

[26] (1970) 55 Cr App R 93 (CA)

the owner indefinitely of the use of his tools. It was held that there can be no theft without the intention of permanently depriving another of his property. Meanwhile, in *R.* v. *Velumy*,[27] the appellant who was an employee of a company took the sum of £1,050 from a safe at work without any authority and in breach of the company's rules of operation. At the end of the trial, he was convicted and appealed to the Court of Appeal. Dismissing the appeal the court held that there had been an appropriation by the appellant's assumption of the rights of the owner of the money because he had no intention to return the objects which he had taken. His intention had been to return objects of equivalent value, which intention was relevant to the question of dishonesty which was not in issue.

Similarly, *Ndukwe* v. *Legal Practitioners Disciplinary Committee*,[28] the Supreme Court held that from the provisions of section 383 of the Criminal Code, what is prescribed is the act of dealing with goods or property which lawfully come into the possession of a person in a manner inconsistent with the right of the true owner, provided that it is also established that there is an intention on the part of the defendant or accused in so doing, to deny the owner's right or assert a right which is inconsistent with that of the owner. However, in *Ukana* v. *COP*,[29] the appellant in this case was an employee under the Akoko-Edo Local Government Area of the then Bendel State (now Edo State). He obtained his employment with the council with a primary school leaving certificate. He was later dismissed for an alleged stealing of the primary school leaving certificate belonging to one Onimisi Adeche with which he obtained his employment with the council. The Court of Appeal held,

[27] (1989) CRIM LR 299 (CA)
[28] (2007) 4 FWLR (pt 393) 6440 SC
[29] (1995) 8 NWLR (pt 416) 705 CA

dismissing the appeal in part, that to sustain a charge of stealing against an accused, the prosecution must prove the following:

(a) that the thing stolen is capable of being stolen;
(b) that the accused has the intention of permanently depriving the owner of the thing stolen;
(c) that the accused was dishonest;
(d) that the accused has unlawfully appropriated the thing stolen to his own use.

It should be stressed, however, that if the intent is merely to deprive the owner temporarily of the use of it, it will not amount to stealing unless there is also any of the other interests set out in section 383(3) of the Criminal Code.

In *R.* v. *Easom,*[30] the accused took a handbag with the intention to steal money from it. The accused searched the bag but could not find money but cosmetics and other items. He returned the bag. His conviction for stealing the handbag and its contents was quashed because he did not intend to deprive her permanently of them. A similar decision was reached in *R.* v. *Holloway*[31] where a dresser of skins removed skins from his employer's warehouse to a different part of the premises in the pretence that he had not been paid for work done on them. It was held that the accused was not guilty of the offence charged as he merely intended to obtained payment for the work done.

Intent to Permanently Deprive Any Person Who Has Any Special Interest in Such Property

A person who has a special interest in a property may not be the owner of such property but the law protects the rights of such person. There are, however, some reasons why the law recognised his interest in the property. The person in possession of such a property may claim to have a lien or other rights as the law may permit. A person can also be said to have

[30] (1971) 2 All ER 945
[31] (1849) 2 C & K 949

a special interest on property if he intends or has the power to exercise physical control over them. This was the decision of the court in the case of *Hibbert* v. *Mckiernan.*[32] However, an intention to return sooner or later is not such an intent. To be precise, "intention" and "intent permanently to deprive" are not defined in the Act. Presumably, intention bears the same meaning as it does after *R.* v. *Woollin.*[33] It should be noted that section 6 of the English Theft Act merely gives three extensions to the concept of intent permanently to deprive; it, however, does not define it. Meanwhile, the word "permanently", prevents most unauthorised borrowings from being regarded as theft. Therefore, dishonest borrowings, even for a long time are not theft. Consequently, the moral considerations of dishonest borrowings are different from those of theft. Usually, a borrowing is not as serious as a permanent taking. Such borrowings were not very common. And as such, criminalising them would cover trivial matters, such as neighbours quarrelling over a lawnmower. There are, however, some contrary arguments. These arguments are:

(a) if the crux of theft is the dishonest appropriation of another's property, the intention permanently to seems otiose;
(b) the social importance of the accused's conduct does not depend on such an intention. After all, there are many trivial thefts;
(c) if the victim wants the thing during the time when the accused has dishonesty borrowed it, he cannot use it, whether or not the accused intends permanently to deprive. If a student wants his textbooks for an examination in January, it is not to the point that he will get them back in February;

---

[32] (1948) 2 KB, 142
[33] (1999) AC 82

(d) such an intent is not needed in most other theft acts offences such as obtaining a pecuniary advantage by deception (s. 16);

(e) as we have seen, an intention to repay or substitute may be dishonest because the defendant cannot replace the very thing taken, yet if he intends to return the property itself, he is not guilty of the theft because he does not have the intention permanently to deprive;

(f) some items such as puff bull skirts or gypsy tops are fashionable at one time but not trendy after appropriating a child's toy and handing it back after its popularity has plummeted exemplifies the situation;

(g) it is not thought that the courts would be overwhelmed with cases.

The main argument to the contrary is that in respect of many items, their value lie in the ability to use them at a particular time. Returning a lawnmower in February is no use when one wished to cut the grass over the previous summer.

It has been argued that where there is no intent permanently to deprive, a conspiracy charge may lie. There may be one situation where an intention temporarily to deprive is caught by section 6(1) of the Theft Act. This possibility occurs where the victim has only an interest limited in time in the item and the accused intends to borrow it longer than that person. For example, if the victim skips from its owner for a week and the accused takes it away for longer than a week intending to return it, he has intended to deprive the victim of his whole interest. Towards him, there is an intent permanently to deprive and there is theft from him.

It is, therefore, our view that there need not be actual permanent deprivation for an accused person to be found culpable of the offence of theft or stealing. The *mens rea* suffices. Therefore, the *actus reus* is not necessarily important.

Consequently, a person can be guilty of theft even though the owner gets the property back at some other time.

CONSPIRACY TO DEFRAUD

By conspiracy to defraud, we mean an agreement between two or more persons to do or cause to be done some illegal act, or some act which is illegal by illegal means. In *Abacha* v. *Federal Republic of Nigeria (supra),* the court held that it would be conspiracy to defraud under section 97 of the Penal Code, where the agreement is other than an agreement to commit an offence, that some act besides the agreement was done by one or more of the parties in furtherance of the agreement specifically, that each of the accused persons individually participated in the conspiracy.

However in *R.* v. *Ninedays,*[34] the accused and some others conspired to obtain payment for some bags of cocoa belonging to a marketing board by representing to it that the cocoa came from the United Africa Company. It was held that they could not be convicted of stealing those bags of cocoa since they did not intend to deprive the board of the property in the cocoa. But, according to Okonkwo and Naish, this decision cannot be supported because the owner of the cocoa was permanently deprived of property in it.

The motive of gain is not essential in deciding whether a permanent deprivation is fraudulent.[35] Therefore, it would be theft if two or more persons form a common intention to permanently deprive the owner of the use of his property. It is immaterial that the accused intended to return it. It would still be stealing, even if the accused person formed the intention to return it, but is yet to execute it. So, the offence of conspiracy

---

[34] (1959) 4 FSC 192

[35] See the decision in the case of *R.* v. *Cabbage* (1815) R & R 292. Perhaps, if A takes B's property and in return leaves him some more valuable property this may be stealing.

to defraud is premised on the *mens rea*, the *actus reus* is insignificant.

Chapter 11

OTHER PROPERTY OFFENCES

BURGLARY AND AGGRAVATED BURGLARY

Section 411 of the Criminal Code provides for the offence of house breaking, i.e., burglary. Section 411(1) of the Criminal Code provides thus. Any person who –

(1) breaks and enters the dwelling house of another with intent to commit a felony therein, or

(2) having entered the dwelling house of another with intent to commit a felony therein, or having committed a felony in the dwelling house of another, breaks out of the dwelling house, is guilty of a felony, and is liable to imprisonment for fourteen years. If the offence is committed in the night, the offender is liable to imprisonment for life.

Furthermore, section 412 of the Criminal Code provides to the effect that any person who enters or is in the dwelling house of another with intent to commit a felony is guilty of a felony, and is liable to imprisonment for seven years. If the offence is committed in the night, the offender is liable to imprisonment for fourteen years.

In England, the offence of burglary is seen as one which is directed against criminal trespass to home and other buildings such as factories and shops.[1] By section 9 of the English Theft Act, 1968, as amended, regarding the offence of burglary:

> 1.A person is guilty of burglary if:
> (a) he enters any building or part of a building as a trespasser and with intent to commit any such offence as is mentioned in sub-section (2) below, or
> (b) having entered any building or part of a building as a trespasser he steals or attempts to steal anything in the building or that part of it or inflicts or attempts to inflict on any person therein any grievous bodily harm;
> (2) the offences referred to in subsection (1) above are offences of stealing anything in the building or part of a building in question, of inflicting on any person therein any grievous bodily harm therein and of doing unlawful damage to the building or anything therein.

It should be stressed that in England, the maximum penalty is 14 years imprisonment in the case of burglary in a dwelling and 10 years elsewhere, such as a shop, after conviction on indictment. It is unclear whether the accused is guilty of the more serious offence only if he knows that what he entered was a dwelling. An interesting aspect of the sentence is that an accused is guilty under section 9 (1) (a) even though he has not yet even attempted to steal in a house and is liable to 14 years imprisonment. Yet if he does actually steal, the maximum sentence for theft is seven years. The difference between dwelling and other buildings was introduced in 1991. There has not been a problem so far in distinguishing the two. A flat is

---

[1] Michael Jefferson, *Criminal Law* ,7th Edn (England, Pearson Education Ltd 2006) 621

undoubtedly a dwelling, but what of a house in the process of construction? It is uncertain whether the accused is subject to the higher penalty only if he knew that what he entered was a dwelling, whether he knew it to be so or not. Since, if the accused trespasses in a building and intends to steal (but has not stolen) he is guilty of burglary a maximum sentence of 14 years looks excessive in relation to the harm.

In Nigeria, a distinction is drawn between the offences of *burglary* and *housebreaking*, although they both have the same ingredients except that one is committed in the daytime and the other is committed at night. Night means the period between 6.30pm and 6.30 am.[2] In case of breaking in order to enter both, the breaking and the entry must be done at night. If the breaking is in the day and entry is at night or vice versa, the offence is not burglary. But the breaking and entering need not necessarily occur on the same night as the English case of *R.* v. *Smith,*[3] illustrates. Here the breaking was on a Friday night and entering on a Saturday night. In cases of breaking in order to get out after entering with intent to commit a felony or after committing a felony in the dwelling house, both the breaking and the entering need not be at night. Entry may be in the daytime but the breaking must be at night.

Meanwhile, section 410 of the Nigeria Criminal Code provides that a person who breaks any part, whether external or internal of a building, or opens by unlocking, pulling, pushing, lifting, or any other means whatever, any door, windows, shutter, cellar flap, or other thing, intended to close or cover an opening in a building or an opening giving a passage from one part of a building to another, is said to break the building. Again, a person is to enter a building as soon as any part of his body or any part of any instrument used by him is within the building. Therefore, a person who obtains entrance into a building by

---

[2] See Okonkwo and Naish at page 305

[3] (1820) R & R 417

means of any threat or artifice used for that purpose or by collusion with any person in the building permanently left open for any necessary purpose, but not intended to be ordinarily used as a means of entrance, is deemed to have broken and entered the building.

In *Chukwueke & Anor* v. *The State*,[4] some unknown persons broke into the house of Pastor Timothy Uwaechi (PW1) at Ohaozara Faith Tabernacle Church in Nduma, Umuahia. PW 1 later escaped and brought some of his relations who arrived whilst the robbers were still ransacking PW 1's house. During the process of overpowering the robbers, one of the robbers fired at PW 2 (Josiah Onyenweaku) who in turn threw a knife at the robber who shot him. None of the robbers was caught at the scene of crime but shortly after the incident the first appellant was caught near the scene of crime with some of the goods belonging to Pastor Timothy Uwaechi (PW 1). The first appellant was then handed over to the police and he made a statement. The second appellant was implicated by that statement and he was subsequently arrested.

During the trial at the High Court, the investigating Police Officer, PW 4, testified that he arrested the second appellant with members of his gang although the 1st appellant who stated that it was the 2nd appellant who brought him to the scene of crime could not locate the house of the second appellant when the first appellant was first taken to the second appellant's village. PW4 did not know the second appellant before he arrested him. The Court of Appeal while convicting the first appellant of stealing and burglary, per Ogundare J.C.A. (as he then was) held, *inter alia,*

> As the entry into the house of PW1 was burglarious and having regards, I am of the view that he ought to have been convicted of burglary contrary to section 411 of the Criminal

---

[4] (1991) 7 NWLR (pt 205) 604

Code, cap 30 Laws of Eastern Nigeria, 1963 applicable in Imo State.

According to Okonkwo and Naish, breaking is an essential ingredient of both the offence of burglary and housebreaking. In *State* v. *Onwemunlo,*[5] it was held that if a man leaves the door of his dwelling house open and a thief enters through the same open door, the offence is neither burglary nor housebreaking because the element of "breaking" is lacking. Breaking may be actual or constructive. There is actual breaking when a person breaks any part, whether external or internal, of a building or opens by unlocking, pulling, pushing, lifting or any other means whatever, any door, window, shutter, cellar flap, or other thing intended to close or cover an opening in a building or an opening giving passage from one part of a building to another.

On the other hand, constructive breaking occurs when entrance into a dwelling house is obtained by means of any threat or artifice used for that purpose or by collusion with any person in the building or where entry is made through a chimney or other aperture of the building permanently left open for any necessary purpose, but not intended to be ordinarily used as a means of entrance.

In *R.* v. *Walkinton,*[6] the accused was guilty under section 9 (1)(a) when he went into a three-sided partition in the middle of a shop where the till was. The area inside the partition was part of a building. There need be no physical separation between one part of a building and another. A sign is sufficient.

There may be difficulties in determining whether the accused has entered a part of a building. If he enters a shop, hides in a corner, comes out, when the members of staff have gone home, and steals some items, is he a burglar? In the

[5] (1967)-68) M.S.N.L.R. 137

[6] (1979) 2 All ER 716 CA

evening when he comes out, is his previously lawful presence converted into a trespassory entrance? Is he guilty only when he crosses some national line?

It should be noted that in section 9(1)(a) the statute speaks of "offence" of grievous bodily harm. It has been said in section 9(1)(b), which does not mention the term 'offence', grievous bodily harm does not necessarily mean the offences found in sections 20 and 23 of the Offence Against the Person Act 1861.[7] It would certainly be strange if the accused could be guilty of this form of burglary if he accidentally or, indeed, lawfully inflicted the harm, for all other ulterior offences in burglary require intent. It was sufficient in *Jenkins* that the victim was so shocked by the accused's presence that the victim suffered a stroke. There was no need for an assault. The accused need not know that the victim was present.

An alternative reading of *Jenkins* is to say that section 9 (1) (b) does require an offence involving the infliction of grievous bodily harm but the prosecution need not specify the offence. The House of Lords reversed the decision but not on this point.[8] It is suggested that *Jenkins* should not be followed. If the accused inflicts grievously bodily harm on the victim, without intending to do so and without being subjectively reckless, he is not guilty of non-fatal offence. It would equally be strange if he were guilty of burglary on those facts.

Finally, burglary is a serious offence, but the ruling in *Jenkins* inappropriately makes it a strict one in respect of grievous bodily harm.

AGGRAVATED BURGLARY

According to Jefferson,[9] the offence of aggravated burglary occurs when the accused has with him a firearm, imitation

---

[7] *R* v. *Jenkins* (1983) 1 All ER, 993. It should be stressed that section 18 requires the causing of grievous bodily harm

[8] *MPC* v. *Wilson* (1984) AC 242

[9] Michael Jefferson *supra*, note 1

firearm, weapon of offence or explosive. The time at which he must have it with him is the time when he stole, etc. If the burglary is the section 9 (1) (b) type, as in *R.* v. *O'Leary*[10] which was applied in *R.* v. *Kelly,*[11] where the accused had a screwdriver with him which he used to gain entry and used it as a weapon of offence to threaten a young couple at the time of the theft of a video recorder, he was guilty.

For the avoidance of doubt section 10 of the Theft Act of 1968 provides:

> (1) A person is guilty of aggravated burglary if he commits any burglary and at the time has with him any firearm or imitation firearm, any weapon of offence, or any explosive, and for this purpose:
> (a) 'firearm' includes an air gun or air pistol, and 'limitation firearm' means anything which has the appearance of being a firearm, whether capable of being discharged, or not; and
> (b) 'weapon of offence' means any article made or adopted for use for causing injury to or incapacitating a person, or intended by the person having it with him for such use; and
> (c) 'explosive' means any article manufactured for the purpose of producing a practical effect by explosion or intended by the person having it with him for that purpose;
> (2) A person guilty of aggravated burglary shall on conviction on indictment be liable to imprisonment for life.

It should be noted, that the offence of aggravated burglary is not mentioned in the Criminal Code applicable to the southern part of Nigeria. However, what appears similar to section 10 of

---

[10] (1986) 82 Cr App R. 341
[11] (1993) 157 JP 845 (CA)

the English Theft Act[12] is section 417 of the Criminal Code[13] which deals with persons found armed and with intent to commit felony.

Section 417 of the Criminal Code provides that any person who is found in any of the following circumstances:

(a) being armed with any dangerous or offensive weapon or instrument, and being so armed with intent to break or enter a dwelling house and to commit a felony therein;
(b) being armed as aforesaid by night, and being so armed with intent to break or enter any building whatever, and to commit a felony therein;
(c) having in his possession by night without lawful excuse, the proof of which lies on him, any instrument of housebreaking;
(d) having in his possession by day any such instrument with intent to commit a felony;
(e) having his face masked or blackened or being otherwise disguised with intent to commit felony;
(f) being in any building whatever by night with intent to commit a felony therein; or
(g) being in any building whatever by day with intent to commit a felony therein, and having taken precautions to conceal his presence is guilty of a felony, and is liable to imprisonment for three years. If the offender has been previously convicted of a felony relating to property, he is liable to imprisonment for seven years.

It has been argued that an accused is not guilty under section 10 of the English Theft Act if he uses a weapon to gain entry but

[12] The English Theft Act of 1968
[13] Cap C 38, Laws of the Federation of Nigeria 2004

does not take it in with him. In *R.* v. *Klass,*[14] the accused smashed the window of a caravan with a pole, the occupier camc outside and the accused beat him with a pole. These facts do not constitute aggravated burglary. Accordingly, the accused person must know that he has the prohibited article. If a knife is planted on him, he is not guilty. The outcome is the same if he has forgotten that he has a knife on him.

Therefore, for the offence of aggravated burglary to be complete, the accused must be proved to have been armed with dangerous weapons or some explosives intended to be used or used in gaining entry into the dwelling and committing the offence, therein.

ROBBERY AND ARMED ROBBERY

Introduction

The offence of robbery is governed by the provision of sections 401, and 402 of the Criminal Code.

Section 401 provides that any person who steals anything, and, at or immediately before or immediately after the time of stealing it, uses or threatens to use actual violence to any person or property in order to obtain or retain the thing stolen or to prevent or overcome resistance to its being stolen or retained, is said to be guilty of robbery.

The offence of robbery[15] may be seen as a crime against both property and the person. By section 8(1)(a) of the Theft Act,[16] a person is guilty of robbery if he steals, and immediately before or at the time of doing so, and in order to do so, he uses any force on any person or puts or seeks to put any person in fear of being then and there subjected to force. Robbery is essentially an aggravated form of theft. All elements of theft must be proved before a conviction may be secured for this

[14] (1998) 1 CR APP R 453 CA

[15] *Supra* note 1 at 621

[16] The English Theft Act of 1968

offence. An accused is therefore not guilty of robbery if he believes that he has a legal right to deprive the victim of the property. In *R.* v. *Robinson,*[17] the accused person demanded that the victims repay a debt owed by the victim's wife to him. He had a knife to reinforce his demand. The court held that the facts did not constitute robbery because the accused was not dishonest, because he thought he had a legal right to the money. However, in *R.* v. *Forrester,*[18] the accused had no claim of right, he was dishonest. All the elements of theft were present. He used force by knocking off balance his victim, who was also kept under restraint, and the force was used immediately before stealing and in order to do so.

To Okonkwo and Naish,[19] the offence may be committed by a fraudulent conversion provided that the element of violence is present. In *R.* v. *Bekum,*[20] where A and his companions deposited valuable property in B's house and then went out to buy some meat and were attacked and killed on the way by B who intended to, and did in fact steal the property, it was held to be a robbery. But in *Njuguna* v. *Republic,*[21] the accused having burgled a house and stolen therefore was discovered without chase at a distance of about five hundred yards away where he then resisted the owner with violence. It was held that the offence was not robbery but burglary and theft because the element of using violence immediately after the act was lacking.

Meanwhile section 402 of the Criminal Code provides for the punishment of robbery. Section 402(1) provides:

> Any person who commits the offence of robbery shall upon conviction be sentenced to

---

[17] (1977) Crim. L.R. 173

[18] (1992) Crim L.R. 793

[19] *Criminal Law in Nigeria*, 2nd edn (Ibadan, Spectrum Books Ltd, 1980) 303

[20] (1941) 7 WACA 45

[21] (1965) E.A. 583

imprisonment for not less than twenty-one years.

(2). If-

(a) Any offender mentioned in subsection (1) of this section is armed with any firearms or any offensive weapon or any obnoxious chemical materials or is in company with any person so armed; or

(b) At or immediately before or immediately after the time of robbery, the said offender wounds any person, the offender shall upon conviction be sentence to death.

Accordingly, the foundation of the offence of armed robbery is the existence of a clear act that amounts to stealing, that is to convert to one's use or the use of any other person anything other than immovable property with any of the following intent:[22]

(a) An intent permanently to deprive the owner of the thing of it;

(b) An intent permanently to deprive any person who has a special property in the thing of such property;

(c) An intent to use one thing as a pledge or security;

(d) An intent to part with the thing in a condition as to its return which the person taking or converting it may be unable to perform;

(e) An intent to deal with the thing in such a manner that it cannot be returned in the condition in which it was at the time of taking or conversion; or

---

[22] See *Tanko* v. *State* (2009) 4 NWLR (pt 1113) 430 at 439

(f) In the case of money, an intent to use it at the will of the person who takes or coverts it.

In effect, armed robbery means simply stealing plus violence used or threatened.[23]

In *Balogun* v. *Attorney-General, Ogun State*,[24] the court held that by virtue of section 15(1) of the Robbery and Firearms (Special Provisions) Act, robbery means stealing anything and, at or immediately before or after the time of stealing it, using or threatening to use actual violence to any person or property in order to obtain or retain the thing stolen or to prevent or overcome resistance to its being stolen or retained.

The Offence of Armed Robbery

Armed robbery was made a capital offence by the military regime in 1970.[25] While this is emblematic of the regime's preference for the death penalty for serious offences,[26] robbery with violence was a serious menace at the end of the Nigerian Civil War (1967-70), and remains a matter of grave social concern. There has naturally been consistently strong public support for the punishment. Recently, demand for ransom from kidnapping is a fast-growing menace, to be made a capital offence is increasingly voiced. Furthermore, the death penalty is recognised in our statute books,[27] Execution is by hanging

---

[23] *Aruna* v. *The State* (1990) 6 NWLR (pt 155) 125

[24] (2001) 14 NWLR (pt. 7333) 331 (CA)

[25] Ukhuegbe, S. " the Death Penalty in the Supreme Court of Nigeria: A Critical Evaluation of Huri Laws" Constitutional Challenges of the Nineties" (Faculty of Law Seminar Lecture Series 2011) 13

[26] The Inventory of Capital offences under military rule included economic and anti-social crimes/ namely, kidnapping, murder, unauthorized possession or use of firearms, explosive or other offensive weapon during the civil war, disruption of the production and distribution of petroleum products, armed robbery, arson tampering with oil pipelines and counterfeiting of currency. For some of these offences an attempt carries the same penalty as the complete offence.

[27] Smith, D.Z. The Death Penalty in Africa (2004) 4 Africa Human Rights, L.J. 1 (Review of Death Penalty in Africa) for Nigeria. See ILO, U.J. The Rope: Country Report on Death Penalty Application in Nigeria (Lagos, Hurlaws, 2004) report presented at the first African Conference on Death Penalty Application in Commonwealth Africa May 2004. See also Amnesty International Nigeria. The Penal Systems.

and during the military regimes, and execution by firing squad was used for treason and armed robbery.[28]

In a similar vein, the court held in *Bolanle* v. *The State*[29] that any person who commits the offence of robbery with a firearm or any offensive weapon or is in company of any person so armed is liable upon conviction to death sentence. In the instance case, the court further held that the evidence of the case of armed robbery against the appellants was overwhelming and that all the ingredients of the offence were proved against him. In this case, the appellant and others were said to have robbed one Emmanuel Fatundimu and his neighbours, when armed with such dangerous weapons as broken bottles, gun, and matchet and iron rods. At the end of the raid, the robbers took away some money and other valuables belonging to the victims. One of the women was sexually assaulted and the mother of PW4 died from wounds sustained during the robbery incident. The appellant was accordingly found guilty and sentenced to death.

And in the case of *Gabriel* v. *The State,*[30] the appellant and four others were arraigned for robbing one Sunday Omomejoh of the sum of ₦300,000 (Three hundred thousand naira) while armed with offensive weapons, to wit, guns. The court held that the offence of armed robbery is a grave one and attracts death sentence if the person accused of committing the offence is found guilty.

It should be stressed that by a proper construction of the provisions of section 1(3) of the Robbery and Firearms (Special Provisions) Act,[31] it is the Governor that has the power to prescribe the mode of carrying out the death sentence. In *Ikem*

---

[28] See section 1(3) of the Act.

[29] (2005) 7 NWLR (pt. 925) 431. See the case of *Bello* v. *State*. (2007) 10 NWLR (pt 1043) where the court held that failure to prove the fundamental ingredients for the offence of armed robbery is fatal to the prosecution case.

[30] (2010) 6 NWLR Pt (1190) 291

[31] Cap R 11 Laws of the Federation of Nigeria 2004

v. *the State*,[32] the court held that the duty of directing the mode of execution of a death sentence does not lie with the trial court but with the Governor of the state. This would have informed the decision in *Tanko* v. *State supra* where the court held that the trial court's pronouncement that the appellant be hanged, though improper, did not vitiate the whole proceedings nor did it occasion miscarriage of justice.

In *Alor* v. *State*,[33] the appellant was charged with the offence of armed robbery contrary to Section 1(2)(a) of the Robbery and Firearms (Special Provisions) Act, 1970. The allegation against the appellant was that he, on the 13th June, 1981, at Akama Amankwo Ngwo in Enugu Judicial Division, in company of other persons armed with a firearm, to wit, a locally made pistol, robbed one Theresa Okwor of the sum of ₦130.00 in cash and wearing apparels valued at ₦700.00. What could reasonably be inferred from the evidence of the two witnesses mentioned above was that the place in which one of them was living was separate and distinct from the place where the other was living. The allegation was that on the day in question two armed robbery offences were committed and that the appellant was one of the alleged armed robbers who took part in the two separate armed robbery incidents. The P.W. 1 was living in the house in which one of the armed robbery offences was committed and the P.W. 2 was living in the house in which the second armed robbery offence was committed. In order to appreciate the extent and the effect of the confusion which eventually arose, it is necessary to give a brief summary of the evidence of the P.W. 1 and the P.W.2

The P.W.1 told the learned trial Judge that on the day on question (13/6/81), three persons invaded their house. The appellant was one of them. One of the three aforesaid persons had a gun. They took his mother's matchet from under her bed

[32] (1985) 1 NWLR (pt 2) 378
[33] (1998) 1 LRCNCC, 125

and took the sum of ₦60.00 from her by force. With the aid of torchlight, the P.W.1 recognised the appellant who counted the money taken from his mother. One of the alleged armed robbers hit the witness with a matchet and later they went to the premises of the P.W.2

The evidence of the P.W.2 was that while she was sleeping with her children in a room in her house, some strange person outside the house ordered her to open the door and threatened to kill her and her children if they refused to open the door. As a result, she opened the door. Torchlight and a gun were pointed at her. One of them struck her with a mortar three times and she fell down. Before she became unconscious, they forced open her wardrobe and the wardrobe of her husband who was away on night duty. They stole ₦250.00 from her husband's wardrobe and some clothes from her own wardrobe. One of them pointed a torch light at the one who was wrapping the clothes of the witness on himself, and so the witness was able to identify the appellant who was the one who carried the clothes of the witness away. Not long after the incident, she saw some of her clothes taken away and being sold in the open market.

Based on the evidence before the trial court, appellant was convicted and sentenced which conviction, appellant appealed to the Supreme Court, and the court held that the punishment on conviction for robbery with firearms, that is, armed robbery, is sentence of death. It is immaterial whether the offender is found guilty as a principal offender or as a participant or as an aider or abetter or a person who has counselled or procured the commission of the offence or a conspirator who has committed the offence. And if the accused was among the robbery gang that committed the offence, it does not matter that he himself was not armed.[34]

---

[34] See also *Okosun* v. *A.G. Bendel State* (1985) *ILSC and Iyaro* v. *The State* (1988) NWLR (pt 69) 256

In *John Nwachukwu* v. *The State*,[35] the appellant was convicted of armed robbery contrary to section 1(2)(a) of the Robbery and Firearms (Special Provisions) Act 1970 and sentenced to death by hanging or firing squad. The prosecution's case was that on the 19th of October 1975 at night, one Alhaji Mohammed Zil and Mohammed Saleh were returning from the cattle market at Ojo to Amukoko. They alighted from their motorcycle, which they parked at the side of the road and continued, on foot. At a point on the road, the appellant who was accompanied by some other persons brought out a toy-gun and pointed it at Mohammed Saleh who was holding a bag which contained the sum of ₦4,990.00

The appellant there and then demanded from 4th P.W. (Mohammed Saleh) the bag. The appellant snatched the bag at gunpoint. The victims pursued the assailants to a house at No. 82 Cemetery Road Amukoko, and the other persons attracted surrounded the house while the police was called.

The police searched the house and found the accused lying on top of the bag containing the money under a bed at the house. The bag when opened by the police contained the sum of ₦4,900.00 and the toy-gun. At the trial the police gave evidence of how the complaint was made, the details of complaint and how the accused was arrested. The trial Judge convicted the accused for armed robbery and sentenced him to death.

On appeal, counsel for the appellant contended that the toy-gun used by the appellant is not a 'firearms or offensive weapon' within the meaning of the Robbery and Firearms (Special Provisions) Act 1970, and therefore the conviction and sentence for armed robbery was improper. Counsel also contended that the evidence of the police stating the details of the complaint is hearsay and inadmissible and should not have

---

[35] (1985) 2 NWLR 219

been admitted in evidence. It was also contended that the trial judge misdirected himself when he relied on a piece of evidence which was not before him, which was that, P.W 4 said that the accused was identified under an electric light whereas P.W. 4 did not say so. The court held:

1. For an accused to be convicted of robbery under Section 1(1) of the Robbery and Firearms (Special Provisions) Act of 1970, the prosecution must prove robbery as defined in Section 9 of the same Act;
2. For an accused to be convicted of armed robbery under Section 1(2) of the Robbery and Firearms (Special Provisions) Act of 1970, the prosecution must not only prove robbery by the accused but also prove that the accused was armed with 'firearms' or 'offensive weapon' and the weapon employed to commit the robbery must either be a 'firearm' or 'offensive weapon' within the meaning of those words in Section 9 of the same Act;
3. Under Section 401 of the Criminal Code Cap 42 1958 Laws of Nigeria, and Section 1(1) of the Robbery and Firearms Act 1970, robbery is stealing anything and at or immediately before, or immediately after, the stealing, using or threatening actual violence to any person or property in order to obtain or retain the thing stolen or to prevent or overcome resistance to it being stolen or retained;
4. In the instance case, although the accused/appellant threatened violence on the victim at the time of stealing, the offence committed is robbery simpliciter and not armed robbery because the toy-gun he used to threaten the victim is not a 'firearm' or 'offensive weapon' within the meaning of Section 9 of the Robbery and Firearms Act of 1970;
5. In this case, apart from the piece of evidence, which was not before the court that the accused/appellant was identified under an electric light, there is overwhelming evidence that it was the accused/appellant who committed the robbery;

6. The doctrine of recent possession under Section 148(a) of the Evidence Act applies in this case because the appellant was found lying on the bag containing the money, the subject of the robbery, so soon after the act robbery and in the circumstances revealed in the evidence the court could draw the inference that the appellant was in possession of the bag and was one of the robbers;
7. A toy-gun is not normally made or adapted for causing injury to the person and is not capable of being used as an offensive weapon but a plaything for children. Therefore, a toy-gun is neither a firearm nor an offensive weapon.

Accordingly, Per Nnaemeka-Agu J.C.A. held:

> Under the Act "firearms" is defined to include "canon-gun, Rifle, Carbine, Machine-Gun, Cap-Gun, Elirt-Lock gun, Revolver, Pistol, explosive, or Ammunition or other firearms whether whole or in detached pieces." Also 'offensive weapon' is also defined to mean any article apart from firearms made or adapted for use for causing injury to the person or intended by the person having it for such use by him, and it includes an Air-Gun, Air- Pistol, Bow and Arrow, Spear, cutlass, Matchet, Dagger, Cudgel, or any piece of wood, metal glass or stone capable of being used as an offensive weapon.

In the case of *State* v. *Okonkwo,*[36] the court held that armed robbery is committed where at the time of the commission of the robbery the accused is proved to have been armed with *firearms* or offensive *weapons.* Any person in company of a person so armed, or aiding and abetting in the commission of the offence is similarly guilty.[37]

Consequently, it shall be an offence punishable under this Act for any person to knowingly house, shelter, or give quarters

[36] (1998) 1 LRCNCC 37. See also *Nwachukwu* v. *State* (1985) 3 NWLR (Pt 11) 278 and the case of *Okosun* v. *A. G Bendel State* (1985) 3 NWLR (pt 12) 283 at 286

[37] See *Nwachukwu* v. *The State* (1985) 3 NWLR (pt 11) 218

to any person who has committed an offence under section 1(2) of this Act.[38] The Act imposed a duty on any person, hospital or clinic that admits, treats or administers any drug to any person suspected of having bullet wounds to immediately report the matter to the police.[39] Therefore, any person who, or hospital or clinic which fails to report as stipulated in subsection (2) of this section shall be guilty of an offence under this Act.[40] And a person convicted of an offence under subsections (1) and (3) of this section shall be liable:

(a) in the case of an individual, to imprisonment for a term not exceeding five years; and

(b) in the case of a hospital or clinic, to a fine of ten thousand naira and in addition the hospital or clinic shall be closed down.[41]

While section 7 provides to the effect that all the assets, movable or immovable, including motor vehicles, of any person convicted of an offence under this Act shall be forfeited to the government of the state in which the asset or property is situated or found.

REQUIREMENTS TO SUSTAIN A CONVICTION FOR ARMED ROBBERY

In the case of *Musa* v. *The State*,[42] the court held that in order to establish the offence of armed robbery, the prosecution must prove that there was robbery or series of robbery, that each robbery was an armed robbery, and that the accused persons were those who took part in the armed robbery. In the instant case, there was evidence that there was armed robbery, there was also evidence that the robbers were armed and that appellants were involved in the robbery.

---

[38] Section 4(1) of the Robbery and Firearms Act
[39] Section 4(2) of the Act
[40] Section 4(3) (a) and (b) of the Act
[41] See section 4(4) of the Act
[42] (2005) 2 F.W.L.R. 343

Furthermore, in *Abdullahi* v. *The State,*[43] the court held that it is the duty of the prosecution to establish by evidence the following ingredients, beyond reasonable doubt, to wit:

(a) theft by the accused person(s);
(b) the causing of hurt or wrongful restraint on the victim(s) by the accused person(s);
(c) that the acts complained of were done in the process of committing the theft or in order to commit the theft and/or carry away the property obtained by the theft;
(d) that the accused persons did the acts complained of voluntarily; and
(e) that the accused person(s) was/were armed with dangerous weapons while committing the offence in question.

Consequently, the prosecution in a case of armed robbery must establish and prove certain elements against the accused person. In *Dibie & Ors* v. *The State,*[44] the court held that in a charge of armed robbery, the prosecution must prove beyond reasonable doubt, the following in order to succeed. They are:

(a) that there was a robbery;
(b) that the robbery was an armed robbery;
(c) that the accused persons were among those who took part in the armed robbery sufficiently established the offence against the appellant. The court further held that the use of an object and the manner it is made use of is what qualifies it to be an offensive weapon. The appellants were subsequently convicted and sentenced to death.

On proof of "armed robbery" the court held in *Bozim* v. *State,* [45]

1. that there was a robbery;
2. that there was armed robbery;
3. that the accused took part in the armed robbery.

---

[43] (2008) LRCN Vol. 164, 101
[44] (2004) 14 NWLR (pt 893) 257 (CA)
[45] (1985) 2 NWLR (pt. 8) 465

JURISDICTION OVER OFFENCES UNDER THE ROBBERY AND FIREARMS ACT

In Nigeria, jurisdiction is the blood that gives life to the survival of an action in a court of law[46] and without jurisdiction the action will be like an animal that has been drained of its blood. It will cease to have life and any attempt to resuscitate it without infusing blood into it would be an abortive exercise. In *S.P.D. Nig. Ltd* v. *Lalibo*,[47] the court held that the issue of jurisdiction of a court to entertain or try a matter brought before it is terminally fatal to the proceedings conducted therein. This is because jurisdiction is the competence, power and authority that the law vests in a court to entertain, try and determine a matter that is brought before it and any defect in such competence would deprive the court of such authority and power and such matters.

In *Tanko* v. *The State supra*, the court held that by the provisions of section 2(1) and (2) of the Tribunals (Certain Consequential Amendment) Decree No. 62 of 1999, the Federal High Court or the High Court of a State is conferred with the jurisdiction to try the offence of armed robbery. By virtue of section 211 (1) of the 1999 Constitution, not only does a State High Court have the jurisdiction to try cases relating to armed robbery, the officials of the Ministry of Justice of a State are eminently qualified to prosecute the offence of armed robbery in any High Court of a State.

Similarly, in *Emelogun* v. *The State*,[48] the Supreme Court held that the Attorney-General of Imo State armed with the constitutional power under Section 191 of the 1979 Constitution, had the *locus standi* to institute criminal proceedings under the Robbery and Firearms (Special Provisions) Decree or Act No. 47 of 1970 as the offence of

---

[46] Atsegbua, L. *Administrative Law* (Benin City, Ambik Press, 2012) 104

[47] (2009) 14 NNLR (Pt 1162) 569

[48] (1988) 2 NWLR (pt 78) 524

armed robbery under the Act was deemed to be a law of the House of Assembly of the State. Consequently, the question of delegation of authority from the Attorney-General of the Federation did not arise.

On what the Supreme Court decided in *Emelogun* v. *State supra*, the court held, *inter alia*:

a. that by virtue of the provisions of section 274(4)(b) of the 1979 Constitution, the Robbery and Firearms (Special Provisions)(Act No. 47, 1970, became an existing law of a State and "Robbery" *per se* a residual matter, while the Act as amended was deemed to have been made by the State House of Assembly and that in view of this, offences under the Robbery and Firearms (Special Provisions) Act No. 47 of 1970 as amended are not Federal but State offences;

b. that by virtue of section 191 of the 1979 Constitution, the power to institute the prosecution of criminal cases is vested in the State Attorney-General and because the Robbery and Firearms (Special Provisions) Act. No. 47 of 1970 operated as a State Law in so far as armed robbery is concerned, the State Attorney General for Imo State had the *locus standi* to institute criminal proceedings thereunder and the question of delegation of authority does not arise;

c. that even though the provisions of section 6 of the Robbery and Firearms (Special Provisions) Act. No. 47 of 1970 have been repealed by the Federal Republic (Certain Consequential Repeals, Etc.) Decree No. 105 of 1979 by virtue of section 239 of the 1979 Constitution, the Criminal Procedure (Miscellaneous Provision) Edict, 1974 of the East Central State became an existing law of the Imo State on the 1st of October, 1979. Therefore, the provisions of the Criminal Procedure (Miscellaneous Provisions) Edict, 1974, are the applicable law to the trial of offence under the Robbery and Firearms (Special Provisions) Act No. 4 of 1970.

On whether High Court of a State has jurisdiction to try offence of armed robbery, per Rhodes-Vivour, J.C.A. (As he then was) held in *Okafor* v. *State*:[49]

> My Lords, the Tribunals (Certain Consequential Amendments Act) Decree No. 62 of 1999 came into force on the 28th of May 1999 with sweeping amendments for the trial of federal offences such as:
>
> a. Advance fee fraud and other related offences;
> b. Counterfeit and fake drugs;
> c. Money laundering;
> d. Failed banks recovery of debts, etc.
>
> Amendments were also made to section 8 of the Robbery and Firearms (Special Provisions) Decree.
>
> By the amendments offences under the decree shall be triable in the High Court of the State concerned.
>
> Decree No. 62 of 1999 is an existing law, and that explains the trial of robbery cases in State High Courts.
>
> Accordingly, the trial and conviction of the appellant by the Niger State High Court was not a nullity.

In *Eyisi* v. *The State*,[50] it was held that the State High Court has jurisdiction over armed robbery matters by virtue of section 1(2) of the Robbery and firearms (Special Provision) Amendment Decree No. 21 of 1984:

Per Onu, JSC held:

> With the coming back of the Military to the rulership of Nigeria at the end of the year 1983, another Decree - Armed Robbery and Firearms (Special Provisions) Decree No. 5 of 1984 - was promulgated and tribunals were re-established. By section 1(2) of the Robbery and Firearms (Special Provision) Amendment Decree No. 21 of 1984, part-heard matters were allowed to continue and be concluded in the High Courts, while new matters were transferred to the tribunals – see: *Emelogu vs. The State* (*supra*).

---

[49] (2006) 4 NWLR (pt 969) 5
[50] (2001) F.W.L.R. 763

From the records, trial in the present appeal started at the High Court on 10th November 1983, and this was part heard at the time when Decree No. 5 of the 1984 came into force. Therefore, the High Court under section 1(2) of the Amended Decree No. 21 of 1984 had to continue with the trial of the case.

Per Ogundare, JSC has this to say:

> Section 5 of the Act, which prescribed the place of trial of offences under the Act, was amended by replacing the tribunal set up under the original section 5 with "the High Court of the State concerned." The 1979 Constitution came into force on 1st October 1979. From that date, the High Court of a state became seized of offences under the Robbery and Firearms (Special Provisions) Act, 1970. It follows, sitting at Onitsha became seized of the matter on hand by the arraignment of the appellants on 10th November 1983, it had jurisdiction to try them.
>
> According to the record before us, the trial of the appellants did not end in that court until 29th May 1987. The case was, thus, part heard on 31st December 1983 when the constitutional governance of the country was overthrown by the armed forces and military dictatorship was once again introduced. The regime in 1984 promulgated the Robbery and Firearms (Special Provisions) Decree No. 5 of 1984, which repealed the 1970 Act and part of Schedule 3 of Decree No. 105 of 1979 amending the 1970 Act. It reverted to trial of robbery and firearms offences by tribunals. This Decree was soon amended by the Robbery and Firearms (Special Provisions) Amendment Decree No. 21 of 1984 sub section (4) of section 1 of which provided:
>
> 'Any part – heard proceedings before any High Court on the date of the Coming into force of this Decree shall be continued and completed as if the provisions of this Decree had not been made;
>
> This saving clause preserved the trial in the State High Court of offences under the 1970 Act, where the proceedings had commenced and were part- heard on 29th March 1984, the date Decree No. 5 of 1984 came into force.
>
> The trial of the appellants by the High Court of Anambra State was one of such proceedings saved by Decree No. 21 of

> 1984. I, therefore, hold that the trial High Court had jurisdiction to try the appellants.

THE LEGALITY OF DEATH PENALTY IN NIGERIA

The basis of any government, by virtue of section 14(2) (b) of the Constitution, is primarily to provide security and ensure the welfare of the people. By section 318 of the Constitution, government includes the government of the Federation or of any State, or of a Local Government Council, or any person who exercises power and duty. Any social malaise, or act or behaviour of any person or body capable of threatening the wellbeing of the citizenry must be legislated against and in so doing all the three arms of the government must ensure strict compliance with the provisions of the Constitution. Armed robbery is a very serious vice which, when carried out by gangsters, often terminates the lives of the victims. In setting out to battle it or to punish the perpetrators, the government (the three arms) must ensure due compliance with the provisions of the Constitution of the land. By virtue of section 14(2) (b) of the Constitution of the Federal Republic of Nigeria 1999[51] the federal and the state governments can legislate in respect of armed robbery.

By virtue of section 33(1) of the 1999 Constitution, every person has a right to life save in the execution of the sentence of a court in respect of criminal offence of which he has been found guilty.

On whether death penalty is unconstitutional, the Supreme Court held in *Gabriel* v. *State*[52] that:

> A death sentence is an exception to the general rule that no man should be deprived of life. Also, a death sentence does

---

[51] See the 1999 Constitution (as amended)

[52] (2010) 6 NWLR (pt 1190) 280. See also *Kalu* v. *State* (1998) 13 NWLR (pt 583) 531

> not amount to degrading and inhuman treatment, and therefore not inconsistent with the 1999 Constitution.[53]

On legality of death penalty in Nigeria and whether foreign decisions on legality of death penalty binds Nigerian courts, the Supreme Court held in *Gabriel* v. *State supra* that foreign judicial decisions on issue relating to legality of death penalty may be persuasive but they are not applicable in Nigeria. Death sentence is a reality in Nigeria. It is provided for in Nigerian Criminal laws including section 319(1) of the Criminal Code. The Constitution cannot approbate and reprobate.[54]

On whether court has power to commute death penalty stipulated under the Robbery and Firearms (Special Provisions) Act to a term of imprisonment, Per Denton-West, J.C.A. observed:

> On the point that this court should commute the sentence of death to imprisonment not exceeding 10 years, this court is a court of law and it is being guided by the Constitution. This court does not have such powers and rather would exhort that such issue should be taken by way of commencing action vide Fundamental Right (Enforcement) Procedure in the State High Court or Federal High Court. *Abacha* v. *Fawehinmi* (2000) All NLR 35; (2000) 6 NWLR (pt 660) 228. Further, it is the legislature that can effect this change without much ado.[55]

On dissolution of the Robbery and Firearms Tribunal, the Court of Appeal held, in *Ihekwobva* v. *State*[56] that the Robbery and Firearms Tribunal was abolished with effect from 28/5/99 and the tribunal was dissolved by the Tribunals (Certain Consequential Amendments, etc.) Decree No. 62 of 1999. And

---

[53] In *Kalu* v. *State* supra, the Supreme Court held unanimously that the death penalty is not unconstitutional in view of the provisions of section 30 of the 1979 Constitution, which provides for the right to life in qualified and derogable terms. It further held that section 319(1) of the Criminal Code is not inconsistent with section 31 of the same Constitution.

[54] See *Rabiu* v. *State* (1981) 2 NCLR 293

[55] *Abacha* v. *Fawehinmi* (2000) All NLR 35;

[56] (2004) 15 NWLR pt. 303

by virtue of section 2(3) of the Decree, a charge, claim or court process filed before a Tribunal established under any of the enactments specified in the schedule to the Decree shall be deemed to have been duly filed or served before the Federal High Court or a High Court of a State as the case may be and such charge, claim and court process shall be deemed amended as to title, venue and such other matters.

CONCLUSION

Although, it may not be apposite to conclude that an examination of the Robbery and Firearms Act has revealed all the ailments in the Act for proper diagnosis, but it is good to say that a proper platform has been provided for a therapy. Meanwhile, it has been argued, whether section 319(1) of the Criminal Code, which stipulates mandatory death penalty for murder, was contrary to or inconsistent with the Bill of Rights Torture Clauses.[57] The court was unsuccessfully urged to recognise the urgency of the non-derogable character of this norm and its evolving dynamic in the light of international and comparative law rejecting the challenge, the attention of the court instead focused on the capital punishment qualifier in the context of the right to life in the Constitution:

> Every person has a right to life and no one shall be deprived intentionally of his life, save in the execution of the sentence of a court in which he has been found guilty in Nigeria.[58]

In the reasoning of the court, it cannot be seriously argued that section 319 (1) of the Criminal Code is inconsistent with the Torture Clause (or indeed any other section of the

[57] Nigeria Constitution 1979, Section 31 (1). See now, section 34 (1) of the 1999 Constitution section 34. (1). The import of this provision comes directly from Art. 3 of the European Convention on Human Rights.

[58] Nigeria Constitution 1979, section 30 (1). See now 1999 Constitution, section 33(1)

Constitution).[59] In reaching this conclusion, however, the court completely ignores the Torture Clause. It is simply trumped by the Constitution's recognition of capital punishment. The logic of the text is obvious enough in the view of the court:

> The qualifying word, save used in section 33(1) seems to me to be the unmistakable key to the construction of that provision. In my view it is plain that the 1979 Constitution can by no stretch of the imagination be said to have proscribed or outlawed the death penalty. On the contrary, section 33(1) of the Constitution permits it in the clearest possible terms, so long as it is inflicted pursuant to the sentence of a court of law in Nigeria in [sic] a criminal offence.[60]

In this exercise of exaggerated textualism, in the best light of the court's formalist tradition, the absence of an explicit textual warrant for unconstitutionality of the death penalty is fatal to the challenge. "I have," wrote Justice Iguh, "taken great care to go through the entire 1979 Constitution and have been unable to find any single section thereof which abolished or outlawed the death penalty."[61] But the reasoning does not bear close examination.

It is unassailable that the capital punishment clause necessarily excludes any possibility that the Constitution outlaws that punishment *per se*. This much was already well established by the time the Supreme Court considered the question. The European Court of Human Rights affirmed this reading of Article 2 of the European Convention in *R.* v. *Soering*.[62] Two decades earlier, the Privy Council took the same

---

[59] See Ukhuegbe, *supra*, note 11

[60] See Ukhuegbe, ibid.

[61] Ibid.

[62] Ukhuegbe, ibid. "The Convention is to be read as a whole and Article 3 should therefore be construed in harmony with the provisions of Article 2. On this basis Article 3 evidently cannot have been intended by the drafters of the Convention to include a general prohibition of the death penalty since that would nullify the clear wording of Article 2(1). "More recently, however, the European Court has stated without deciding the point that Article 2(1) may now be read more liberally in the light of the abolition of capital punishment throughout Europe. "in the Court's view, it cannot now be excluded, in the light of the developments that have

position with respect to an Article 2-type provision of the Constitution of Southern Rhodesia.[63] In view of this, it is difficult to see how any argument that capital punishment is absolutely unconstitutional in Nigeria is tenable. A closer examination shows that the proper issue before the court in *Kalu* was not constitutionality of capital punishment at large but the limited and highly specific question whether mandatory capital punishment for murder was constitutional.[64] Unfortunately, the unmistakable impression one gets from the arguments, as well as the opinions of the justices, is that the issue was constitutionality of the death penalty at large. Part of the blame for the confusion must rest with appellant's counsel's brief and oral argument.

The reasoning of the Supreme Court seems to suggest that the capital punishment clause of Section 30(1) of the Nigerian Constitution (1979)[65] places this punishment absolutely beyond constitutional challenge. This reasoning is flawed. First, the court confuses the constitutional recognition of capital punishment for constitutional immunity of the punishment. By reading this clause independently of the Torture Clause, it is the court that unwittingly immunises the death penalty from challenge. The result significantly discounts the force of the

taken place in this area, that the state have agreed through their practice to modify the second sentence in Article 2.1 in so far as it permits capital punishment in peacetime" *Ocalan* v. *Turkey (*2003) 37 E.H.R.L.R. 238 at para 198.

[63] *Runyown* v. *R [*1967] AC 26, [1966] 1 All ER 633, [1966] 2 WLR 877; "It was not contended [by the appellant] that it can be said that the death penalty is *per se* or necessarily inhuman or degrading punishment. Such a contention could in any event hardly have been advanced in view of the terms of s. 57. (1) Of the Constitution. That subsection provides that "no person shall be deprived of his life intentionally save in the execution of the sentence of a court in respect of a criminal offence of which he has been convicted. The death sentence as a possible sentence is recognized.

[64] In spite of the general tenor of his opinion, Justice Iguh in fact opened it with a correct statement of the issue. "The first issue relates to the validity or constitutionality of the death penalty as the mandatory punishment in relation to the capital offence of murder as prescribed under section 319(1) of the Criminal Code. The issue, therefore questions the constitutional validity of the death penalty as the mandatory punishment for the offence of armed robbery in Nigeria."

[65] Now section 33(1) of the 1999 Constitution (as amended)

Torture Clause, an unqualified, non-derogable and a dynamically evolving standard restricting the application of the capital punishment or other punishments or treatment in circumstances that may be thought to be torture or inhuman or degrading.

In any event, the assumption that Section 33(1) necessarily excludes the application of the Torture Clause to capital punishment is inconsistent with the historical evolution of the criminal legislations in Nigeria. However, the present law is traceable to the development of our criminal justice system from the English Common Law tradition. It is a tradition in which the state plays a dominant role and have exclusive involvement in and control of criminal justice. [66]

---

[66] Badaiki, A.D. "Signing *Nunc Dimitis* to Death Penalty," *Benin Journal of Public Law*, Vol. 2 No. 1 (Benin City, Ambik Press, 2004) p 1 at 3

Chapter 12

SEXUAL OFFENCES

RAPE

Introduction

Rape is the unlawful carnal knowledge of a woman by a man forcibly and against her will. It is the act of sexual intercourse committed by a man with a woman not his wife and without her consent, committed when the woman's, resistance is overcome by force or fear, or under other prohibitive condition. It is a serious offence and attracts severe penalties under the various Criminal Codes operating in Nigeria. Section 357 of the Criminal Code, provides that any person who has unlawful carnal knowledge of a woman or girl without her consent if her consent is obtained by force or by means of threats or intimidation of any kind or by fear of harm, or by means of false and fraudulent representation as to the nature of the act, or, in the case of a married woman, by personating her husband, is guilty of an offence which is called rape. Also, by virtue of Section 282 of the Penal Code Law of Northern Nigeria, a man is said to commit rape who, save where he had sexual intercourse with his wife, has sexual intercourse with a woman in any of the following circumstances:

a) against her will;
b) without her consent;
c) with her consent when has consent has been obtained by putting her in fear of death or of hurt;
d) with her consent, when the man knows that he is not her husband and that her consent is given because she believes

that he is another man to whom she is or believes herself to be lawfully married;

e) with or without her consent, when she is under 14 (fourteen) years of age or of unsound mind.[1]

The Violence Against Persons (Prohibition) Act 2015 has extended the concept of rape to include intentionally penetrating the vagina, anus or mouth of another person with any other part of his or her body or anything else.

The recognition of anal penetration as rape is an indication that concept of rape is embracive of male victims and has rendered rape gender-neutral unlike the Criminal Code definition which is vagina-based and therefore female specific.[2]

In *Upahar* v. *The State,*[3] the court held that, in a charge of rape or unlawful carnal knowledge of female without her consent, it is the duty of the prosecution to prove the following:

a) that the accused had sexual intercourse with the prosecutrix;
b) that the act of sexual intercourse was done in circumstances falling under any one of the five paragraphs in Section 282 (1) of the Penal Code;
c) that the prosecutrix was not the wife of the accused, or if she was his wife, she had not attained puberty;
d) that the accused had the *mens rea,* that is the intention to have sexual intercourse with the prosecutrix without her consent or that the accused acted recklessly, not caring whether the prosecutrix consented or not and
e) there was penetration.[4]

Furthermore, Section 1 of the English Sexual Offences Act 1956:[5]

---

[1] See also the case of *Obiakor* v. *The State* (2002) 10 NWLR (Pt 925) 493

[2] Section 1(1) of VAPP Act 2015.

[3] (2003) 6 NWLR (Pt 816) 234

[4] See, *Ibo* v. *Zaria N.A* (1962) NNCN 30, *Okoyomon* v. *The State* (1973) NMLR 292, *Jos N.A* v. *Allah Na Gani* (1967) NNLR 107, *State* v. *Ojo* (1980) 2NCLR 391.

Rape of woman or man -

(1) It is an offence for a man to rape a woman or another man.

(2) A man commits rape if -

a) He has sexual intercourse with a person (whether vaginal or anal) who at the time of the intercourse does not consent to it, and

b) At the time he knows that the person does not consent to the intercourse or is reckless as to whether that person consents to it.

(3) A man also commits rape if he induces a married woman to have sexual intercourse with him by impersonating her husband.

In the case of rape, the evidence of the complaint should be corroborated. Similarly, a person cannot be convicted of the rape of a girl under 14 years of age upon the uncorroborated testimony of one witness. Consequently, the proof required to establish the offence of rape is not based on the solitary evidence of the prosecutrix. There must be an independent, credible, corroborative evidence. The nature and content of the corroborative evidence must only corroborate and support the claim of the prosecutrix that the accused raped her by penetrating into her vagina. It must also unequivocally implicate the accused person. It is immaterial that the same evidence corroborates some other portions of the evidence of the prosecutrix. It is therefore the duty of the prosecution when leading evidence in proof of rape to adduce independent evidence to corroborate the complaint made by the prosecutrix.[6] In *Sambo* v. *The State,*[7] it was held that

[5] As amended by Section 142 of the Criminal Justice and Public Order Act 1994. This has replaced the former definition of rape in section 1 of the Sexual Offences (amendment) Act 1976

[6] See the case of *Ekelagu* v. *Queen* (1960) SCNLR 488

[7] (1993) 6 NWLR (pt 300) 399

corroborative evidence with respect to the offence of rape is evidence which shows or tend to show that the story of the prosecutrix that the accused committed the crime is true, not merely that the crime had been committed but that it was committed by the accused.

In *Queen* v. *Omisade,*[8] the court held that in considering whether some evidence is corroborative of some other, the court must take all the little items of the former together and consider whether they all add up to corroboration as a whole. It should be stressed that under section 218 of the Criminal Procedure Code, the High Court has power to convict an accused for attempted rape insofar as the ingredients of the full offence of rape are not satisfactorily established. In *Njovens* v. *The State,*[9] the court held that in a charge of abetment of an offence of rape, the initial element is the instigation or positive act of encouragement to do the act or omission which constitutes the offence.[10]

Meanwhile, it should be acknowledged that by virtue of section 138 of the Evidence Act[11] for a conviction to stand where the accused person is alleged to have committed an offence of rape, the law places the burden of proof on the prosecution and never shifts.[12] In *Rabiu* v. *The States,*[13] the court held that under section 282(1) of the Penal Code Law of Northern Nigeria, the ingredient of the offence of rape, which the prosecution is under a duty to prove, are as follows:

---

[8] (1964) NMLR 64

[9] (1973) NMLR 331

[10] In *Upahar* v. *State, supra*, it was held that the singular act of the 2nd appellant in holding the legs of the prosecutrix astride and pressing them down for the 1st appetent to insert his perish into the vagina of the prosecutrix was a positive act of encouragement to the act of the 1st appellant therefore, the 2nd appellant aided and abetted the 1st appellant in the commission of the offence of attempted rape on the prosecutrix.

[11] Cap E Laws of the federation of Nigeria 2004

[12] *Obiakor* v. *The State* (2002) 10 NWLR (p+776) 612

[13] (2005) 7NWLR (Pt. 925) 495

(a) that a man, the accused had sexual intercourse with a woman, the victim;
(b) that the act of intercourse was unlawful, not being between husband and wife;
(c) that in giving the evidence of intercourse, complete penetration is proved;
(d) that the accused had the requisite *mens rea*, that is, intention to have intercourse with a woman without her consent or that the accused acted recklessly not caring whether the woman consented or not;
(e) also the prosecution must adduce evidence to corroborate the complaint made by the victim and although this is not required as a matter of law, it is required in practices.

Fundamentally, the general principle of the law of rape is that there must be proof of penetration no matter how slight before the offence of rape can be said to be proved. In *Alli* v. *State*, penetration was held to be the entry of the penis or some other part of the body or a foreign object into the vagina or other body orifice.[14] In other words, the essential and most important ingredient of the offence of rape is penetration and unless penetration is proved, the prosecution must fail. But penetration, however slight, is sufficient and it is not necessary to prove any injury or the rupture of hymen to constitute the crime of rape.[15] Emission or ejaculation is not a necessary component neither is resistance, tears, screaming or torn undergarments mandated.

In *Aliyu* v. *State*, the defendant offered the plaintiff a lift in his car and penetrated her vagina without her consent. The Supreme Court held the offence of rape was established. This is more so as the defendant earlier admitted penetrating the defendant with his finger.

---

[14] (2021) 12NWLR (pt. 1789) 159

[15] See the case of *Iko* v. *The State* (2002) 14 NWLR (Pt 732) 221. See also the case of *Igbin* v. *The State* (1997) 9 NWLR (Pt 519) 101

In *State* v. *Masiga,*[16] the Supreme Court stated that unless penetration has been sufficiently proved, the offence of rape cannot be sustained. The depth of the penetration or rupture of the hymen are not a necessity once it has been established by credible evidence that there was penetration.

In *Muhammed* v. *State,*[17] medical evidence of bloodstain in the vagina was adduced to show penetration and unlawful carnal knowledge of a nine-year-old victim who was lured into the house of the Appellant.

Consequently, and by the provisions of section 283 of the Penal Code, the punishment for committing the offence of rape is life imprisonment or any less term and the person shall also be liable to fine. Therefore, the offence of rape is not one punishable with death. While section 358 of the Criminal Code provides that any person who commits the offence of rape is liable to imprisonment for life, with or without caning.[18]

The *Actus Reus* of Rape

The *actus reus* of the offence of rape is the slightest penetration of the male penis into female genitalia. According to Smith and Hogan,[19] the slightest penetration will suffice. In the case of "vaginal" intercourse, any penetration of the female genitalia was enough at Common Law. It was not necessary to prove that the hymen was ruptured[20] or that the vagina in its proper sense was penetrated. Notwithstanding the use of the term "vagina intercourse" in the 1994 Act, it is probable that this rule is unchanged. The purpose of section 44[21] was to remove

---

[16] (2018) 8NWLR (pt 1622) 383

[17] (2020) 17NWLR (pt 1753) 252

[18] But under section 359 of the Criminal Code an attempted rape is punishable with fourteen years imprisonment with or without caning.

[19] Smith and Hogan ,, 9th Edn (London, Bulterworths 1999) 456

[20] Ressen (1777) 4 East PC 438 . In Australia where statute uses the words in penetration of the vagina" it has been held that this means the vagina in its proper anatomical, not its popular sense.

[21] Section 44 of the English Sexual Offences Act 1956

doubts as to the minimum conduct needed to constitute sexual intercourse complete. "Complete" is used in the sense of having come into existence, not in the sense of being at an end. Intercourse continues until the man withdraws. In *R* v. *Kaitamaki,*[22] it was held that D commits rape if, having penetrated with consent or believing he has consent he declines to withdraw on consent being revoked or on realising that P does not consent. So, rape may be committed by omission. It is debatable whether this is right. Is it not penetration without consent an essential part of the *actus reus* which must be accompanied by *mens rea*?[23] It is the sexual intercourse, not the person, which is "vagina or anal", so penetration of the artificial vagina of a man who has undergone "gender reassignment surgery" is rape and indecent assault on a male person.[24]

It should further be noted that until Section 142 of the English Criminal Justice and Public Order Act, 1994 amended section 1 of the Sexual Offences Act 1956, rape was restricted to unlawful non-consensual intercourse performed by a man *per vaginam* upon a woman. The offence has now be extended to cover anal intercourse by a man upon either a woman or another man.[25] Another change was made by the Sexual Offences Act 1993 which removed the presumption that boys under the age of 14 years could not achieve sexual intercourse and could not, therefore by convicted of any offence requiring sexual intercourse. More so, until the decision of the House of Lords in R,[26] there was a presumption that in marrying her husband, a wife gave a general consent to intercourse. This meant that a husband could not be guilty as the principal

---

[22] (1985) AC 147

[23] See the dissent by Woodhouse J. in the New Zealand Court of Appeal (1980) 1NZLR 59

[24] See Smith and Hogan *supra* note 15 at 457

[25] Reed, A and Seago, P. (London, Sweet and Maxwell 1999) 387

[26] (1992) 1 AC 599

offender in the rape of his wife.[27] In *R*, the House of Lords decided that there was no such marital exemption for husbands and although it may be argued that the House was usurping the legislative role of Parliament, the decision was generally welcomed and is confirmed in the amended section 1 of the 1956 *Act.*[28] However, the prosecution must prove that the defendant had sexual intercourse, either *per vaginan* or *per anum* with the victim. For the purpose, section 44 of The Sexual Offences Act makes it clear that the slightest penetration of the vagina or anus by the defendant's penis constitutes sexual intercourse. There is no need for complete penetration nor ejaculation. It would seem that where a transsexual male has had a sex change operation and now has a completely artificial vagina, he can be raped via this organ. But in the words of Philip and Martin,[29] the acts of vagina and anal penetration are too similar to warrant separate legal classification. The motives of the assailant would appear to be similar for the penetrative acts in question, irrespective of the sex of the victim. Indeed, it is argued that male rape is an act of violence committed to assert power, rather than being primarily sexually motivated. The trauma and consequence of rape are similar for both men and women. In addition to any physical injury, victims may suffer serious psychological reactions after rape. It is, therefore, argued that the consequences of either vagina or anal rape are not sufficiently dispersive to justify an exclusionary gender specific approach to rape and that on the evidence the new law is wholly justifiable.

When the term "carnal knowledge" or "carnal connection" is used in defining an offence, it is implied that the offence, so far

---

[27] Exceptions to the marital exemption rule had developed

[28] However, penetration of the vagina or anus with inanimate objects is not rape, similarly, the rubbing of the entrance to the vagina with the penis causing ejaculation is not rape, although all of these may be criminal offences.

[29] Philip Rummey and Martin Morgan – Taylor "Recognizing the male victim" Gender neutrality and the Law of Rape" (1997) 2 Anglo – *American Law Review* 198 at 219-234

as regards that element of it, is complete upon penetration.[30] Unlawful carnal knowledge means carnal connection which takes place otherwise than between husband and wife. In *R.* v. *Mayberry*,[31] it was held that when section 6 is read together with the definition of rape, it does not exclude what takes place after initial penetration from the offence of rape. Skerman J., however, expressed a dissenting opinion which regarded the initial penetration as sacrosanct, leaving one with the impression that all subsequent acts of penetration and even ejaculation would merely amount to a consummation of an illicit sexual intercourse.[32]

In the most recent case of *Ahmed* v. *Nigerian Army*,[33] the Court of Appeal, Abuja division held that the important and essential ingredient of the offence of rape is penetration. Sexual intercourse is deemed complete upon proof of penetration of the penis into the vagina. Emission is not a necessary requirement of the offence of rape. Any or even the slightest penetration will be sufficient to constitute the act of sexual intercourse. Thus, where penetration is proved but not of such a depth as to injure the hymen, it will be sufficient to constitute the crime of rape. Therefore, proof of the rupture of the hymen is unnecessary to establish the offence of rape. In the instant case, the appellant's contention that the girl was not a virgin at the time of medical examination does not change the fact of rape, once the penetration is established.

Consent

Consent is not defined by the Criminal or Penal Code or the Interpretation Act. Section 74 of the British Sexual Offence Act 2003 defines consent as a person agreeing by choice when he has the freedom and capacity to make that choice. Section

---

[30] See section 6 of the Criminal Code

[31] (1973) QD R 229

[32] Akpotaire V., *Criminal Law in Nigeria*, (Benin City Sylva Publications Ltd 1999) 11

[33] (2011) 1 NWLR (pt1227) p. 89 at 95

75(2) qualifies the freedom excluding situations where before sexual intercourse violence was utilised or the victim was placed in a position of fear or was asleep or unconscious at the time of the act or suffering from mental disability.

In *Ahanafule* v. *Imperial Medical Centre*, consent was held to be volition or voluntary agreement, which is the deliberate and free act of the mind not induced by threat, fear, fraud or force.[34]

For the prosecution of the offence of rape to be successful, he must prove that the accused person had the sexual intercourse without her consent, or that her consent was obtained by fraud or by the use of threat. That is, the prosecution must prove that the alleged victim did not consent to the intercourse. It is important to appreciate from the outset that the question is, "did the victim consent?" But to Reed and Seago, the question is not "did the defendant use force, threats or fraud to achieve his end." In some cases, the victim may be incapable of giving a valid consent to the intercourse. There is no statutory age below which a child is deemed to be incapable of giving a valid consent, but where the child is totally unaware of the nature of sexual intercourse his or her consent will be irrelevant. It would be rape for a man to penetrate a woman who is asleep and who has not given consent to such penetration.[35] Where drugs are secretly administered which renders the victim incapable of resistance,[36] or forming the *mens rea* to appreciate the act, this would be clear evidence of a lack of consent. In some jurisdictions, the test has been whether force or threat of force was used to achieve intercourse and here the courts have often required proof that the victim put up

---

[34] (2005) 5NWLR (pt917) 51

[35] Larter and Castleton (1995) Crim. L.R. 75

[36] There are increasing reports of the use of a drug which produces unconsciousness and leaves the system before any medical check can reveal its presence. There is also a separate offence of administering drugs to procure intercourse. See also the provisions of section 4 of the Sexual Offences Act of 1956

strong resistance to the attack. In *R.* v. *Olugboja,*[37] J. who had already been raped by O's friend L, was told by O that he was going to have sexual intercourse with her and that she should take her trousers off. She did so as she said she was frightened. She put up no resistance until sometime after penetration when she thought he was going to ejaculate within her. He withdrew and she got dressed. On a charge of rape, O was convicted and appealed on the basis that rape required that the prosecutor should prove that the girl's submission should have been obtained by force or fear of force. Rejecting this argument, Dunn, L.J. said:

> Accordingly, in so far as the *actus reus* is concerned, the question now is simply at the time of the sexual intercourse did the woman consent to it? It is not necessary for the prosecution to prove that what might otherwise appear to have been consent was in reality merely submission induced by force fear or fraud, although one or more of these factors will no doubt be present in the majority of cases of rape.

It should be noted that the courts have drawn a line between consent and submission, but the dividing line between real consent on the one hand and mere submission on the other may not be easy to draw. Where it is to be drawn in a given case is for the jury to decide, applying their combined good sense, experience and knowledge of human nature and modern behaviour to all the relevant facts of the case. Reed and Seago further noted that the decision which draws a distinction between consent and submission, leaves a rather broad question for the jury. It is quite clear on the facts of *R.* v. *Olugboja supra*, that there was no real consent to intercourse. She behaved as she did because of her fear of what might happen if she refused, taking into account the facts she had already been forcibly raped. Equally, a threat by a boyfriend to

---

[37] (1982) Q.B. 320. See generally, Gardner S. "Appreciating Olugboka" 1996 16 Legal Studies 275

his girlfriend that he would break off their relationship if she would not allow him to have sexual intercourse is not one which should turn any resulting act of intercourse into rape. Should the jury hold that a woman had been raped where she allowed a police officer to have intercourse with her in return for his dropping serious charges against her?

In *R.* v. *Mc Allister,*[38] Brook L.J. observed:

> The focus of the enquiry in all these cases is based on the sexual autonomy of the complainant. The circumstances of a possible reluctant consent may be infinitely varied, and on each occasion the jury has to decide whether an alleged agreement to a sexual act may properly been seen as a real consent or whether it should be regarded as a submission founded on improper pressure which this complaint could not reasonably withstand from this particular defendant.

To Read and Seago,[39] there is a great difference between a partner who submits to sexual intercourse with her husband because she cannot stand his sulky behaviour when he is refused and a wife who submits because she knows that her husband will seriously injure her if she were to offer any resistance; only the latter can claim to have been raped. The first wife may not have enjoyed the experience, but she cannot deny that her husband in reality had consensual sexual intercourse. Where the wife submits because she is in fear of a beating if she objects, the husband may argue that as far as he was concerned, she was consenting to the intercourse. It is suggested that as long as he knows or is aware that fear might lie behind her consent, he will be presumed to have the necessary *mens rea.*[40]

---

[38] (1997) Crim L.R. 233

[39] Supra, note 21

[40] Ibid.

The essential ingredient, the essence of rape is the absence of consent. In *R.* v. *Fletcher*[41] it was held that, there is no need to prove a positive, refusal; it is enough that the victim did not consent. And in *R.* v. *Camplin,*[42] the accused person was convicted for having sexual intercourse with a woman he had rendered insensible through alcohol given to excite her.

To Clarkson and Keating,[43] it is the element of lack of consent that transforms sexual intercourse into rape. Indeed, as majority of victims know their assailant, the issue of consent is in many rape trials the privotal issue. What then needs to be established? The answer in theory is clear; lack of consent is required and not positive dissent.[44] However, in reality there are profound evidential and conceptual difficulties with this rule.

Consent Obtained by Fraud, Threats and Intimidation

Under the Nigerian Criminal Law, it is no consent once it is established that such consent was obtained by fraud, threats or intimidation. And, by the provisions of the Criminal Code,[45] any person who has unlawful carnal knowledge of a woman or girl, without her consent, or with her consent, if the consent is obtained by force or by means of threats or intimidation of any kind, or by fear of harm, or by means of false and fraudulent representation as to the nature of the act, or in the case of a married woman, by personating her husband, is guilty of an offence which is called rape.

It should be noted that in some cases, the victim consents to intercourse because of fraudulent statements made by the accused person.

---

[41] (1859) Bell C.C. 63

[42] (1845) 1 Den 89

[43] *Criminal Law Text and Materials* 4th ed. (London, Sweet and Maxwell 202) 614

[44] See the decision in the case of *R* v. *Lang* (1975) 62 Cr. App. R. 50

[45] Section 357 of the Criminal Code, Cap C 38 Laws of the Federation of Nigeria, 2004

In *R.* v. *Williams,*[46] W, a choirmaster had intercourse with a 16-year-old chorister on the pretence that it was a medical operation to create an air passage to improve her voice projection. The girl, who trusted W, was completely ignorant of sexual matters and so her consent to what occurred was ineffective; she had been raped. Had she been aware that what was happening was sexual intercourse but wrongly believed the sexual intercourse and therefore would not have been rape. And, again, just as consent induced by fear of violence has not been regarded as real consent, neither is consent which is given under certain fundamental mistakes brought about by the deceit of the defendant regarded as real.

In *R.* v. *Clarence,*[47] Stephen J. identified two such kinds of fundamental mistake, the first as to the *identity* of the actor and the second as to the *nature* of the act. As far as the first kind of mistake is concerned, the amended Sexual Offences Act 1956, section 1 (3) states that: "A man also commits rape if he induces a married woman to have sexual intercourse with him by impersonating her husband."

The limitations of such a provision are all too obvious. What of the man who impersonates the victim's boyfriend? In *R* v. *Elbekkay,*[48] the sleepy and drunk victim had intercourse with a man who got into her bed, thinking that it was her boyfriend. The moment she discovered her mistake, she reacted violently, punching the defendant and cutting him with a knife. The Court of Appeal, in confirming that this was rape, stated:

> How could we conscientiously hold that it is not rape to impersonate a husband in the act of sexual intercourse, but not if the person impersonated is merely, say the long-term, live-in lover...the vital point about rape is that it involves the absence of consent. That absence is equally crucial whether

[46] (1920) 1 K.B. 340
[47] (1888) 22 Q.B.D. 23
[48] (1995) Crim L.R. 163

the woman believes that the man she is having sexual intercourse with is her husband or another. Furthermore, a woman is not to be treated as consenting, if she consents because of a threat, express or implied, has been made to use force against her or another. If she does not consent and she believes that if she does not consent, the threat will be carried out immediately or before she can free herself from it.

Therefore, a person submits when he or she yields, or gives in to pressure of some kind. A woman may reluctantly submit to sexual intercourse only because her fiancé threatens that he will break off their engagement if she does not. Such a case is very far removed from rape, but it seems to be one of submission. At the other extreme, a woman may submit because the man is holding a knife at her throat. This is plainly rape. This distinction cannot however be justified by a distinction between consent and submission. In both cases, the woman yields because a threat is made submission may indeed by induced by a promise. The woman gives in only because the man promises that he will marry her if she does so. No one would say that is rape if the man intends to keep the promise (and it is clearly not rape in law if he does not) but is it not a case of submission? In *R.* v. *Day,*[49] Coleridge J, held that every consent involves a submission, but it by no means follows that a mere submission involves consent, seems to be wrong. A woman who joyously embraces her reluctant lover undoubtedly consents to the intercourse which follows, but it would seem inappropriate, to put it mildly, to say that she "submits" to that which she ardently desires and provokes.

Consent when given for sexual intercourse can be withdrawn at any point during the interaction. It constitutes rape when consent is withdrawn and the sexual contact is not terminated within a reasonable time. Reasonableness, it is submitted, has to be dependent on the point of withdrawal of the consent and the intensity of the sexual interaction.

In *Katamaki* v. *R.,*[50] the defendant was convicted of breaking into the victims flat and raping her twice. He admitted that during the first act, he reasonably believed the victim

[49] (1841) 9 C & P 722 at 724
[50] (1985) AC 147

consented. However, during the second act, he did not stop even when he noticed she was no longer consenting. The court held his refusal to stop constituted rape.

The *Mens Rea* of Rape

The *mens rea* of rape is the intention to have sexual intercourse with a woman without her consent.[51] In addition to intending to have sexual intercourse, the defendant must know that the person is not consenting, or be reckless as to whether he or she consents. This is a statutory endorsement of the law as laid down by the House of Lords in *DPP* v. *Morgan*.[52] Prior to *Morgan,* a defendant's belief the woman was consenting had to the based on reasonable grounds. The House of Lords dispensed with this requirement. If the defendant honestly believed the woman was consenting, he lacked *mens rea.*[53] The House of Lords did, however, emphasise that the reasonableness of the defendant's belief would be taken into account by the jury when deciding whether he could possibly have entertained such belief. This evidential proposition was enshrined in the Sexual Offences (Amendment) Act 1976 Section 1 (2) of the Act, namely:

> It is hereby declared that if at a trial for a rape offence the jury has to consider whether a man believed that a woman was consenting to sexual intercourse, the presence or absence of reasonably grounds for such a belief is a matter to which the jury is to have regard in considering whether he so believed.

---

[51] See section 6(a) of the Sexual Offences (Amendment) Act 1976

[52] (1976) AC 182

[53] In *R* v. *Taylor* (1985) 80 Cr. App. R. 327 and *R* v. *Haughian* (1985) 80 Cr. App R. 334, the courts held that it was unnecessary to give detailed guidance on mistaken belief in all cases. Where the conflict of evidence is acute, once the jury decides that the victim's account is truthful; there is no room for such a belief on the part of the defendant.

Where the man knows that the woman is not consenting, he should clearly be guilty of rape. The mental element in rape must, however, go wider than that. It should also be rape if he is aware of a possibility, however slight, that she may not be consenting but he persists. There can be no doubt that it is a major harm for a woman to be subjected to non-consensual intercourse, notwithstanding that the man may believe he has her consent.[54]

Section 1(2) (b) of the Sexual Offences Act 1956 provides that the prosecution must prove that at the time of the intercourse, the man either knew that the woman was not consenting or was reckless as to whether or not she was consenting. In *Kaitamaki* v. *The Queen supra,* the Privy Council held in relation to the New Zealand Law of Rape that if a man realises only after the intercourse has commenced that the woman is not consenting, he will be guilty of rape if he continues after that time.

It should be stressed that in rape, we are dealing not with the kind of mistake that results from the complexity of our endeavours and inevitable human frailty, but with an easily avoided and self-serving mistake produced by the actor's indifference to the separate existence of another. When the harm caused is so great, it seems clear to me that making such a mistake is sufficiently culpable to warrant criminal sanction.

It is, therefore, suggested that the *mens rea* of the offence of rape should cover the following:

i. the defendant has the intention to have sexual intercourse with the victim without consent;
ii. the defendant knew that the victim was not consenting;
iii. the defendant was aware that the victim might not be consenting or did not believe that the victim was not consenting;

---

[54] Pickard T Culpable Mistakes and Rape; Relating *Mens Rea* to the Crime" (1980) 30 *University of Toronto Laws Journal*, 75 at 77

iv. an intention to have intercourse with a woman being indifferent whether she consents or not.

SEXUAL OFFENCES INVOLVING CHILDREN

It is an offence for a man to have unlawful sexual intercourse with a girl under the age of thirteen years.[55] Similarly, it is equally an offence for a man to have unlawful sexual intercourse with a girl under the age of sixteen years.[56] However, it is no crime to have unlawful sexual intercourse with a girl over the age of sixteen years. But, by the provisions of Section 23(4) of Sexual Offences Act 1956, it is an offence for a person to procure a girl under the age of twenty-one to have unlawful sexual intercourse in any part of the world with a third person.

The offence under section 5 is punishable with life imprisonment. Since they were amended by the Criminal Law Act 1967, the offences under sections 5 and 6, which were formerly mutually exclusive, overlap, so that a man who has intercourse with a girl under the age of thirteen years commits both offences. It follows that a belief that the girl is over thirteen years, no matter how reasonable it may be, will not afford a defence to a charge under section 5 and that a belief that the girl is over thirteen years, no matter how reasonable it may be, will not afford a defence to a charge under section 6 only if it is reasonable and held by a man under the age of twenty-four years who has not previously been charged with a like offence. The defence is available only to one who has an actual belief that the girl was over sixteen years. Reasonable cause for such a belief does not afford a defence to one who never directed his mind to the question of the girl's age.[57] Intercourse with a girl under the age of sixteen year is now

---

[55] See section 5 of the English Sexual Offences Act, 1956

[56] Section 6 of the Sexual Offences Act, 1956

[57] *R* v. *Banks* (1916) 2 KB

necessarily unlawful, except in the case of a marriage valid under a foreign law.

Section 30 of the Criminal Code irrebuttably provides that a person under the age of twelve is not criminally responsible for an act or omission (*doli incapax*) unless at the time of the act or omission, he had the capacity to know he ought not to be engaged in it. He is also statutorily disabled from validly consenting to sexual intercourse.

Section 36(c) of the Penal Code unequivocally states that a person under the age of 14 years has no consensual capacity in sexual interactions.

In *Idi* v. *State*,[58] and *Natacha* v. *State*[59] the court held that sexual contact with a child is rape as a child is incapable of giving valid consent.

Section 31 of the VAPP Act criminalises sexual contact between an adult and a child in spite of the willingness of the child to engage in it. It is considered to be sexual violence against the child or rape.

Defilement

Section 218 of the Criminal Code provides that any person who has unlawful carnal knowledge of a girl under the age of thirteen years is guilty of a felony and is liable to imprisonment for life with or without caning. Although an attempt to commit the offence of defilement is punishable with fourteen years imprisonment. However, the prosecution in either offence must commence an action within two months after the commission of the offence.

In a similar vein, section 221 of the Criminal Code provides that any person who:

---

[58] (2018) 4NWLR (Pt1610) 159
[59] (2017) 18NWLR (Pt1596) 108

1. has or attempts to have unlawful carnal knowledge of a girl being of or above thirteen years and under sixteen years of age; or
2. knowing a woman or girl to be an idiot or imbecile has or attempts to have unlawful carnal knowledge of her is guilty of misdemeanour and is liable to imprisonment for two years, with or without canning.

It will be a defence if the accused person reasonably believed that the victim was above the age of sixteen years old. In all these situations, it will equally be a defence, if the testimony of the witness is uncorroborated. In *Upahar* v. *State, supra,* per Obadina, J.C.A. Observed:

> In the instant case, the prosecutrix testified as PW3 to the effect that on the 2nd of August 1994, the prosecutrix went to the village stream to fetch water and on her way back, she met the appellants at the crossroad. The appellants forcibly removed the water she was carrying, pushed her down and dragged her into the bush and while the 1st appellant removed his shorts down his knees, the 2nd appellant held the prosecutrix" legs a stride and pressed them down for the 1st appellant to take out his penis and inserted it into the prosecutrix's vagina. To stifle her cries and protests, the first appellant put sand in her mouth. This was the scenario met by the PW2 who was going to his farm when he came to the cross road and heard someone crying in the bush. PW2 went into the bush in the direction of the cries and to his dismay he met the 1st appellant on top of the prosecutrix copulating with her while the 2nd appellant held the legs of the prosecutrix. The evidence of PW2, to my mind, is an independent evidence and it corroborates in material particulars the prosecutrix's story that the 1st appellant was on top of her but not as corroborating the actual act of penetration.

UNNATURAL OFFENCES

Under the Criminal Code, unnatural offences are classified as offences against morality. Consequently, unnatural offences are governed by the provisions of the Criminal Code. Section 214 of the Nigerian Criminal Code provides:

> Any person who-
> 1. has carnal knowledge of any person against the order of nature or
> 2. has carnal knowledge of an animal, or
> 3. permits a male person to have carnal knowledge of him or her against the order of nature is guilty of a felony, and is liable to fourteen years imprisonment. And an attempt to commit the offences contained in section 214 of the code, is punishable with seven years' imprisonment.[60]

In Nigeria, which remains largely traditional, the recognised sexual intercourse is the interaction between the vagina and penis with heterosexual partners.

The increasing global recognition of lesbian, gay, bisexual and transgender (LGBT) persons has not led to enhanced tolerance. LGBT is stigmatised in Nigeria with dire socio-cultural consequences and death threats. Same Sex Marriage (Prohibition) Act 2013 criminalises all forms of same sex sexual contact with up to 14 years imprisonment for violation of the provisions of the Act.[61]

Patronising gay bars or engaging in same sex amorous relationship is punishable with 10 years' imprisonment.[62]

Unnatural offences may take the form of buggery or sodomy and bestiality. However, buggery has never been defined by statute and its elements are still governed by the Common Law. Section 12(1) of the Sexual Offences Act of 1956 simply enacted the Common Law, that it was an offence for a person to commit buggery with another person or an animal

---

[60] See section 215 of the criminal code

[61] Section 5(1) of the Act

[62] Section 5(2) of the Act

without defining the elements of the offence. The Common Law was first substantially modified by the Sexual Offences Act, 1967 which provided that it should not be an offence for a man to commit buggery or gross indecency with another man provided that the act was done in private, by consenting parties who had attained the age of 21. A more far-reaching reform is made by the 1994 Act. Section 143, which amends Section 12(1) of the 1956 Act, so that it now reads:

> (1) It is an offence for a person to commit buggery with another person otherwise than in circumstances described in subsection (iA) below or with an animal;
> (1A) The circumstances referred to in subsection are that the act of buggery takes place in private and both parties have attained the age of eighteen;
> (IB) An act of buggery by one man with another shall not be treated as taking place in private if it takes place;
> (a) when two or more person take part or are present, or
> (b) In a lavatory to which the public have or are permitted to have access, whether or payment or otherwise;
> (1C) In any proceedings against a person for buggery with another person it shall be for the prosecutor to prove that the act of buggery took place otherwise than in private or that one of the parties to it had not attained the age of eighteen years.

Therefore, in England, consensual buggery between persons aged 18 or above is now lawful provided it takes place in private.

Chapter 13

CORRUPTION

INTRODUCTION

The word "corrupt" connotes the impairment of a public official's duty by bribery. It is an act of gross impropriety. However, corruption is commonly referred to as an economic crime, as it affects all facets of a country's economic growth and development. Corruption is often said to be an act of sabotage. Whatever way corruption is described, it is endemic and therefore should be condemned, if a country must achieve economic sustainability in the new millennium. Corruption is evil and it impacts very adversely on any society or organisation that is plagued by it. The consequences are far-reaching, immediate and long-term. Corruption pollutes and undermines our economy.[1]

In Nigeria, however, several legislations have been enacted to check the menace of corruption. These include the Criminal Code, the Penal Code, the Constitution, Code of Conduct Bureau, the Independent Corruption Practices and other Related Offences Commission Act, the Economic and Financial Crimes Commission Act and the Due Process Unit in the Presidency. These enactments are properly referred to as "Anti-Corruption Legislations" because they are designed to fight against corruption in Nigeria. Nigeria has also equally ratified the United Nations Convention. Against Corruption which was concluded in Mexico City in 2003.

---

[1] Ekpu, A.O. "Curbing Corruption in Nigeria: The Role of the Code of Conduct Bureau," *Benin Journal of Public Law*, Vol. 2 Nol. 1 (Benin City, Ambik Press 2004) 63 at 65

Section 98 of the Criminal Code provides that any person who-

(1) Being employed in the public service and being charged with the performance of any duty by virtue of such employment, not being a duty touching the administration of justice, corruptly asks, receives, or obtains or agrees or attempts to receive or obtains, any property or benefits of any kind for himself or any other person on account of anything already done or omitted to be done or to be afterwards done or omitted to be done by him in the discharge of the duties of his office, or

(2) Corruptly gives, confers or procures or promises or offers to give or confer, or to procure or attempt to procure, to upon, or for, any person employed in the public service, or to upon or for any other person any property or benefits of any kind on account of any such act or omission on the part of the person so employed, is guilty of a felony, and is liable to imprisonment for seven years.

Also, section 419 of the Criminal Code provides that any person who by any false pretence and with intent to defraud obtains from and other person anything capable of being stolen, or induces any other person to deliver to any person anything capable of being stolen or induces any other person to deliver to any person anything capable of being stolen is guilty of a felony and is liable to imprisonment for 3 years.

Under the Penal Code, the offence is referred to as cheating.[2] Section 321 of the code provides that whoever by deceiving any person:

[2] Okogbule, N.S., "The Regulation of Economic Crimes in Nigeria: Old Problem, New Challenges and Responses," *University of Benin Law Journal* Vol. 9 No 1 (Benin City, Ambik Press 2006) 18 at 23

(a) fraudulently or dishonestly induces the person so deceived to deliver any property to any person or to consent that any person shall retain any property; or
(b) intentionally induces the person so deceived to do or omit to do anything which he would not do or omit to do if he were so deceived and which act or omission causes or is likely to cause damage or harm to that person in body, mind, reputation or property is said to cheat.

ECONOMIC CRIMES AND ANTI-CORRUPTION LEGISLATION IN NIGERIA

Today, it can rightly be posited that the Independent Corrupt Practices and Other Related Offence Commission Act (ICPC) 2000 and the Economic and Financial Crimes Commission (EFCC) Act, 2004 are the principal anti-corruption legislations in Nigeria. Consequently, section 9(1) of the Independent Corrupt Practices and Other Related Offences Commission (ICPC) Act, 2000 provides:

9(1) Any person who corruptly-
(a) Gives, confers or procures any property or benefit of any kind to, on or for a public officer or to, on or for any other person, or
(b) Promises or offer to give, confer, procure or attempt to procure any property or benefit of any kind to on or for a public officer or any other person on favour to be done or shown by the public officer is guilty of an offence of official corruption and shall on conviction be liable to imprisonment for seven (7) years.

Similarly, section 6 of the ICPC Act provides: that it shall be the duty of the commission to-

(a) Where reasonable grounds exist for suspecting that any person has conspired to commit or has attempted to commit or has committed an offence under this Act or any other law prohibiting corruption, to receive and investigate any report of the conspiracy to corrupt, attempt to commit or the commission of such offence and in appropriate cases, to prosecute the offenders;

(b) To examine the practices, systems and procedures of public bodies and where in the opinion of the commission, such practices, systems or procedure aid or facilitate fraud or corruption, to direct and supervise a review of them.

Again, section 22(5) of the same Act provides that any public officer who transfers or spends any sum allocated for a particular project or service, shall be guilty of an offence under this Act and on conviction be liable to a one (1) year imprisonment or a fine of fifty thousand naira. Therefore, the combined effect of the aforementioned provisions, is that the Act vest in the commission the power to investigate and prosecute offenders. Consequently, the commission can investigate and inquiry into a matter systematically or to make a suspect the subject of criminal inquiry. In other words, the commission is vested with investigatory powers, among other function thereto.

In *Yakubu* v. *The Federal Republic of Nigeria*,[3] the appellants and one other person were arraigned before the High Court of

---

[3] (2009) 14 NWLR (Pt 1160) 154

Kaduna State on a charge of conspiracy to transfer various sums of money from the salary account to the overhead account of Ahmadu Bello University Teaching Hospital (ABUTH). At the conclusion of the trial, the learned trial Judge found the appellants guilty and fined them subsequently. Being dissatisfied, they appealed to the Court of Appeal which held, *inter alia*, that investigatory power is the authority to inspect and compel disclosure of facts germane to an investigation. The Court of Appeal further held that, in the instant case, the Independent Corrupt Practices and Other Related Offences Commission is empowered by the Corrupt Practices and Other Related Offences Act to investigate allegations of corruption made against any person based on the reports made to them, but if in the process of investigation of an allegation, they uncover any breach of finance or other regulation that is prohibited by the Act, nothing whatsoever should stop them from proceeding to act on it.

It should be noted that the offences created under section 22(5) of the ICPC Act, are offences of unlawful acts. The elements of the offence do not contain the need for criminal intent or *mens rea*. It is enough for conviction for prosecution to prove the *actus reus*, that is, the act of transfer itself. However, the transfer has to be a sum of money allocated for a particular project or service. In *Ojo* v. *Federal Republic of Nigeria*,[4] it was held that an accused person can only be charged with an offence created by a penal statute. This can either be in the Criminal Code, Penal Code or any other penal statute such as the Corrupt Practices and Other Related Offences Act 2000 which is the relevant law under which the charges were preferred in the instant case. Furthermore, each count, which is an indictment on the conduct of an accused person, must be specific and precise. It must be tied to the offending section of

---

[4] (2008) 11 NWLR (pt. 1099) 470

the penal statute in order to enable the court deal with the specific criminal conduct. In the instant case, the appellants were arraigned on a two-count charge contrary to section 26 (1)(c) and punishable under section 9(1) of the Corruption Practices and Other Related Offences Act, 2000.

And to prove the offence committed under section 22 (5) of the Corrupt Practices and Other Related Offences Act, 2000 the prosecution must show:

a. evidence of allocation of money;
b. the particular project or service;
c. the evidence of transfer of money from one particular project or service to another.[5]

On its part, section 6 of the Economic and Financial Crimes Commission (EFCC) Act provides,

> 6 The commission shall be responsible for:
> (a) The enforcement and the due administration of the provisions of this Act;
> (b) The investigation of all financial crimes including advanced fee fraud, money laundering, counterfeiting, illegal charge transfers, futures market fraud, fraudulent enhancement of negotiable instruments, computer credit card fraud, contract scam, etc.;
> (c) The co-ordination and enforcement of all economic and financial crimes laws and enforcement functions conferred on any other person or authority;
> (d) The adoption of measures to identify, trace, freeze, confiscate or seize proceed derived from

[5] Mandatorily, the ingredients of the offence charged must be proved beyond reasonable doubt by the prosecution. This age-long principle of law cannot be whittled down, not even by the proviso to section 36 of the 1999 constitution (as amended) and the provisions of section 141 of the Evidence Act and sections 11(C) and 53(1) of the ICPC Act, 2000.

terrorist activities, economic and financial crime related offences or the properties the value of which corresponds to such proceeds;

(e) The adoption of measures to eradicate the commission of economic and financial crimes, etc.

And by virtue of the provision of the same Act[6] the Commission has the power to cause investigation to be conducted as to whether any person, corporate body or organisation has committed on offence under this Act or other law relating to economic and financial crimes. The Agency can equally cause investigations to be conducted into the properties of any person if it appears to the Commission that the person's life style and extent of the properties are not justified by his sources of income.[7] In *Almed* v. *The Federal Republic of Nigeria,*[8] the appellant was arraigned at the High Court of Kaduna State on a nine-count charge relating to fraud and forgery by the Economic and Financial Crimes Commission (EFCC). The appellant raised an objection to the jurisdiction of the trial court to try him on counts two to nine as contained in the charge sheet. The ground of objection was that the EFCC lacked the *locus standi* to prosecute him for the offences alleged in the said counts two to nine as the counts did not contain the requisite *mens rea* of any economic and financial crime because it was not stated in the counts of the charge that the alleged forgery by the appellant was done with the aim of earning wealth illegally. The respondent opposed the application. After hearing the objection, the trial court held that the EFCC has power to prosecute the appellant for the offences charged in counts two to nine in charge sheet.

---

[6] The Economic and Financial Crimes Commission Act, 2004

[7] Section 7(1)(b) of the EFCC Act, 2004

[8] (2009) 13 NWLR (Pt. 1148) 538

The appellant was dissatisfied with the ruling of the trial court. He appealed to the Court of Appeal and contended that counts two to nine of the charge disclosed only facts of forgery simpliciter against the appellant, and that the EFCC lacked the statutory power to prosecute him for the same. The Court of Appeal held (unanimously dismissing the appeal) that by virtue of section 7(1)(a) and (2)(f) of the Economic and Financial Crimes Commission Act, 2004, the Commission has the power to cause investigations to be conducted as to whether any person, corporate body or organisation has committed an offence under the Act or other law relating to economic and financial crimes. The Commission shall be the coordinating agency for the enforcement of the provisions of any other law or regulation relating to economic and financial crimes, including the Criminal Code and Penal Code. Consequently, the Economic and Financial Crimes Commission has power under section 13 (2) of the Act to prosecute offences so long as they are financial crimes. The Court of Appeal further held that section 13(2) (a) of the Economic and Financial Crimes Commission Act, 2004 charged the Legal and Prosecution Unit of the Economic and Financial Crimes Commission with the responsibility of prosecuting apprehended offenders under the Act.[9]

It should be noted that the Economic and Financial Crimes Commission is an agency of the federal government. But it has been stated that both the state and the federal government have the joint responsibility to fight corruption and abuse of office which have been the bane of Nigerian society.[10]

---

[9] It should be acknowledged that by virtue of section 10(1) and (2) of the Interpretation Act, where an enactment confers a power or imposes a duty, the power may be exercised and the duty shall be performed from time to time as the occasion requires. An enactment which confers power to do any act shall be construed as also conferring all such other powers as one reasonably necessary to enable that act to be done or are incidental to the doing of it

[10] See *A.G, Abia State* v. *A.G, Federation* (2006) 16 NWLR (Pt. 1005) 265

Nigeria, as a sovereign state, has a duty to maintain a crime - free society within its territory in conjunction with the rest of the world, hence it has maintained virile criminal sanctions through its agencies. Although, it is argued that the prevention of crimes is still substantially a *federal government* affair,[11] hence organisations like the Nigeria Police, the Economic and Financial Crimes Commission (EFCC) and all other related agencies.[12] In *Amaech* v. *INEC,*[13] the court held that the Economic and Financial Crimes Commission (EFCC) is a statutory body created under the laws of Nigeria. Its duties include the investigation and prosecution of a class of criminal offences. In essence, once its investigation has shown, *prima facie,* that a person has committed a criminal offence, the duty of EFCC is to have such offender prosecuted in a court of law.

Furthermore, section 15(5) of the 1999 Constitution (as amended) provides that the state shall abolish all corrupt practices and abuse of office. In recognition of this provision, Ogwuegbu JSC observed in the case of *Attorney-General of Ondo State* v. *Attorney-General of Federation 7 Ors*:

> Corrupt practices and abuse of power can if not checked, threaten the peace, order and good government of the Federation or any part thereof.

In *Ibori* v. *Federal Republic of Nigeria,*[14] the Court of Appeal, Kaduna Division held that the Economic and Financial Crimes Commission Act established the Economic and Financial Crimes Commission which is charged with the responsibility of co-ordinating the various institutions involved in the fight against money laundering and enforcement of all laws dealing

---

[11] The Federal Government created the Economic and Financial Crimes Commission by an Act of the National Assembly 2004

[12] See *Nyame v. F.R.N.* (2010) 7 NWLR (pt 1193) 368

[13] (2008) 5 NWLR (Pt 7080) 252

[14] (2009) 3 NWLR part 1128 pg. 283

with economic and financial crimes in Nigeria. The court further held that the Economic and Financial Crimes Commission is a statutory body created and established by an Act of the National Assembly. It is saddled with the duties of investigating and prosecuting a class or category of criminal offences. Thus, once it, *prima facie,* establishes that a person who is under investigation has committed any of the specified offences, it has the bounden duty to prosecute such an accused person in court and in accordance with established norms and principles of criminal jurisprudence, which include respect and recognition for territorial jurisdiction or venue of trial with regards to criminal prosecution.

EFFECTS OF CORRUPTION ON THE NIGERIAN ECONOMY

According to the EFCC Act,[15] economic and financial crimes mean the non-violent criminal and illicit activity committed with the objectives of earning wealth illegally, either individually or in a group or organised manner, thereby violating existing legislation governing the economic activities of government and its administration and include any form of fraud, narcotics drug trafficking, money laundering, embezzlement, bribery, looting and any form of corrupt malpractices, illegal arms deal smuggling, bunkering and illegal mining, tax evasion, foreign exchange, malpractice including counterfeiting of currency, theft of intellectual property and piracy, open market abuse, dumping of toxic wastes and prohibited goods, etc.

What then are the effects of these ugly activities on the Nigerian economy? Such effects may be succinctly itemised as follows:

i. corruption distorts the composition of government expenditure;

[15] See section 46 of the EFCC Act, 2004.

ii. it reduces real expenditure on operations and maintenance;
iii. it lowers the quality of public infrastructure and services;
iv. it reduces government revenue;
v. it increases the cost of doing business in Nigeria and thereby lowers incentives to private investment;
vi. it influences and undermines the outcome of legal, regulatory and electoral process;
vii. it violates the social economic rights of the poor and the vulnerable;
viii. it displaces merit and excellence and ensures the enthronement of mediocrity in government;
ix. it discourages richer nations from extending aids to less developed nations; and
x. it equally erodes the moral fabric of the society.

More so, corruption also breeds inefficiency, diminishes productivity, discourages investments, fuels inflation and capital flight, and institutes a regime of poverty and unemployment. Corruption is an affront on human dignity, an assault on the human conscience and a negation of the Christian vocation to build here on earth a kingdom of truth and justice.[16]

It has equally been posited that corruption is the greatest threat to democracy and good governance.[17] Accordingly, it is submitted that corruption hinders economic development, exacerbates inequality, and desecrates the rule of law and stability of democratic regimes. To this writer, corruption killed the Second Republic and the subsequent military regimes.

---

[16] Adamolekun, L. "The National Assembly and the Fight Against Corruption" *Vanguard*, Friday 29/10/2004 P. 17

[17] Owasanoye, B "Transparency, Accountability and Good Governance" in *Nigeria: Issues in the 1999 Constitution Ayua*, I. A. *et al.* (eds") (Nigerian Institute of Advance Legal Studies 2000) 235 at 246

THE CHALLENGES OF COMBATING CORRUPTION IN NIGERIA

The major challenges facing the control and regulation of corrupt practices in Nigeria today is the marked change in the socio-economic conditions of the country. Not only has the economy witnessed a serious downturn in recent times with the attendant consequences, the rate of unemployment has grown to patently unacceptable levels.[18] The result is that a large crop of young men and women who are qualified, capable and ready to work are not gainfully engaged in productive economic activities. This is said to be largely responsible for most of the social vices to which these abled body men and women have been forced into. Today, it is a common feature to celebrate wealthy people in the society without bothering about the sources of their wealth. Rather, they are quickly rewarded and awarded with several honours.[19] It is, however, a truism that a large number of people in this category are either money launderers or those engaged in advanced fee fraud.[20]

Reference must equally be made to the increased complexity and sophistication introduced into economic crimes in recent times. The availability and use of high technology, computer and Internet have brought with them fundamental advances in strategies and mechanism of committing crimes. This explains the growing concern for and calls for a concerted fight against corruption, computer and Internet facilitated crimes.[21] Closely related to this is the effect of globalisation of economic relations with the attendant internationalisation of

---

[18] Amale, S. The Impact of the Structural Adjustment Programme on Nigeria Worker" in OLukoshi, A. (ed) *Crisis and Adjustment in the Nigeria Economy*, Lagos, 123, 133 -134. The Economic Reform Programme of the Federal Government is also having adverse effects on the employment situation in the country. *The Guardian*, Sunday August 31, 2005

[19] Some are awarded prestigious University Honorary Doctorate Degrees, Honoris Causa. While others may be decorated with National Honours awards.

[20] These are high flier economic crimes that give quick money to the perpetrators

[21] Sal, A.O. "Cyber Laws- Its Application and Enforcement in Nigeria," *Modern Practice Journal of Finance and Investment Law*, Vol. 2 No. 4 (1998) at pp. 10, 30 - 34

economic crimes. In this category must be placed money laundering, drug and human trafficking and economic terrorism that have assumed a frightening dimension in recent times.[22]

Again, the complexity in these economic crimes has equally led to an overwhelming need for effective enforcement machinery to scrupulously monitor and control the incidence of economic crimes in Nigeria. This is because the ordinary machinery of the Nigeria Police Force has sadly proved to be incapable of handling some of these economic crimes. The fundamental question that arises is, what has been the response of the government to the challenges posed by the complexity and sophistication of economic crimes? This, however, may have informed the various anti-corruption regulations enacted towards curbing these challenges. Again, how effective these legislations have been in combating corruption may be another question that demands an urgent answer. However, it can be said that since the inception of this current democratic system, frantic efforts have been made by the government to tackle the menace of corruption in Nigeria. It is only hoped that with time, every patriotic citizen of Nigeria will see corruption as not only evil but also an immoral conduct capable of bastardising the country's image.

But can laws in themselves ensure a corruption-free society without an effective enforcement mechanism? It has been argued that law would become ineffective when it is out of alignment with social and political forces.[23] It was posited that any substantial divergence between the intended effects of a law and the relevant social and political forces will result in the

---

[22] Osinbajo, Y. and Ajayi, K. Money Laundering in Nigeria in Kalu A.U. and Osinbajo, Y. (eds) *Perspectives on Corruption and Other Economic Crimes in Nigeria*" (Lagos, FMJ 1991) 58

[23] Ocheje, P.D. "When Law Fails: A Theory of Self -Enforcing Anti- Corruption Legislation in Africa" being the 12th Justice Idigbe Memorial Lecture Series of the Faculty of Law University of Benin, held in Benin City Tuesday 26th July 2011 at p. 16

law being ineffective, at least in terms of its announced goals.[24] This probably begins to explain why despite frequent proclamations of a desire to eradicate corruption, Nigeria leaders have demonstrated a lack of political will in that direction. Some have explained this divergence by the personal and informal nature of politics in Nigeria. Citizens demonstrate a wide margin of tolerance for corruption and are often ambivalent about it.[25]

Corruption in Nigeria rests on a complex of social and cultural logics which citizens are often powerless to resist. From the perspective of consumers of administrative services, for example, corruption provides a way to manage and overcome uncertainty. As far as the relationship between the public service and the citizen is concerned, the uncertainty is permanent, and it derives from many factors, principal among which is the impenetrability of administrative regulations and the almost endless possibilities for manipulation of same by the official.

Another important factor is the ever-present pressure on individuals to meet social obligations, referred to in some of the literature as "over-monetisation" of social relations. This pressure makes the need for money a constant reality for everyone in position of authority or leadership. Some writers have described the hold of corruption on the Nigeria society as a "vicious cycle". Again, the fact that everyone believes that they must protect themselves against the dysfunction of their public services using favours or corruption, means that everyone exploits personal relationship or indulges in corrupt practices all the times. Thus, the more widespread and common corrupt practices become, the greater the dysfunction

---

[24] Bogart, W.A., *Consequences: The Impact of Law and its complexity* (Toronto: University of Toronto Press Inc 2002) 120, cited in Ocheje, Ibid note 24.

[25] Bratton, Formal V. "Information Institution in Africa," *Journal of Democracy*, vol. 18 no. 3 (July 2007).

and uncertainty that prevails with respect to the outcome of administrative procedures and the greater the reach of corruption.[26]

Another challenge to conformity in the fight against corruption is the pronounced social and economic inequality. Entrenched inequality militates against a social consensus about corruption and the evils commonly associated with it. For example, research findings indicate that the average citizen views petty corruption as a morally acceptable adaptive response to inequality. On the other hand, grand corruption is considered a cause of inequality and it is therefore morally unacceptable.[27] The common understanding seems to be that petty corruption - the theft or extortion of a few dollars from the populace by public officials in return for services - does not have the capacity to retard the economic progress of the country. Rather, it is the theft or misappropriation of billions of dollars, which are then cached in offshore banks, that threatens the economies of African countries.

Furthermore, a lack of capacity for the implementation of anti-corruption laws has been put forward as a reason for the persistence of corruption in Nigeria. For some time, persistent corruption in Nigeria has been characterised as a principal-agent problem, requiring monitoring systems and punishment regimes for its effective control. However, the argument goes in contexts of pervasive corruption, that these systems of control are ineffective simply because the benefits of corruption to its perpetrators far outweigh its costs. As a result, there are no "principals" willing to enforce control measures.[28]

---

[26] Bundo, G and Oliver de Sardan, J.P., *Everyday Corruption in West Africa: Citizens and Public Officials in Africa* (London & New York Zed Books, 2006) 69 at p.106

[27] Uslaner, E. Corruption, Inequality and the Rule of Law," *The Bulging Pocket Makes the Easy Life* (New York: Cambridge University Press, 2008)

[28] Persson, A. *et al.*, "The Failure of Anti-Corruption Policies: A Theoretical Mischaracterization of the Problem, QOG working paper series (2010) 19, ISSN 1653 - 8919, the QOA Institute, University of Gothenburg (June 2010).

CONCLUSION

In Nigeria, corruption remains endemic. Although it has been institutionalised in Nigeria and in most developing countries of the world, consequently, the fight against corruption has yielded little or no result. Not even the enactment of anti-corruption legislations could serve enough deterrent to its perpetrators. Accordingly, it is observed that legal sanctions alone cannot effectively address the now entrenched social, economic and political foundations of corruption. In acknowledgement of the limitations of law for the containment of corruption, most anti-corruption regimes concentrate their resources on catching "the big fish" so as to deter all others; but deterrence is a doubtful efficacy against institutionally entrenched corruption.[29]

Consequently, it is recommended that the fight against corruption requires determined, sustained and concerted efforts of individuals, organisations, groups, institutions and the government. The government at all levels must put in place an effective enforcement mechanism against corruption. It is equally opined that special courts should be created to deal with corruption cases. The anti-corruption bodies should equally ensure that the fight against corruption is total. This is imperative because it is only an all-involving fight against this menace that can bring about a corruption-free society and ensure sustained economic growth and development in Nigeria.

Finally, according to Ocheje, "let's put off our old nature which belongs to our former manner of life and is corrupt through deceitful lusts, and be renewed in the spirit of our minds, after the likeness of God, in true righteousness and holiness."[30]

---

[29] Supra, note 24

[30] See Ephesians Chapter 4 verses 22-24

Chapter 14

TERRORISM

INTRODUCTION

Terrorism implies any use of terror in the form of violence or threats meant to coerce an individual, group or entity in a manner in which any person could not otherwise lawfully force them to act.[1]

Terrorism is not new and even though it has been used since the beginning of recorded history, it can be relatively hard to define. Terrorism has been described variously as both a tactic and strategy, a crime and a holy duty, a justified reaction to oppression and an inexcusable abomination. Despite its popularity, terrorism can be a nebulous concept.[2]

The United States Department of Defence defines terrorism as, 'the calculated use of unlawful violence or threat of unlawful violence to inculcate fear; intended to coerce or to intimidate governments or societies in the pursuit of goals that are generally political, religious or ideological.'[3]

Terrorism has also been defined as the use or threat of violence to intimidate or cause panic especially as a means of affecting political conduct.[4]

In Nigeria, the Anti-Terrorism (Prevention) Act 2011 defined acts of terrorism to include, "attacks upon a person's life which may cause bodily harm or death, kidnapping as well as

---

[1] http://www.wisegeek.com/what-is-terrorismhtm (accessed August 30,2011)

[2] http:/ /wwwterrorisrn-cesearclicorn.(accessed August 30, 2011)

[3] Ibid.

[4] *Black Law Dictionary* (9th edn.) 2009

destruction of government facilities or private properties in a manner likely to endanger human life or result in economic loss."[5]

The Federal Bureau of Investigation (FBI) defines "terrorism" as the unlawful use of force and violence against persons or property to intimidate or coerce a government, civilian population or any segment of thereof, in furtherance of political or social objectives.[6]

Despite legal definitions, terrorism means different things to different people. The threat to the modern world appears to involve more religious extremists than any other type of terrorist and Muslims have been accused of playing dominant roles in exporting terrorism. It should be clearly acknowledged that not all Muslims are terrorists and not all terrorists are Muslims. Terrorist bombs, explosives and other devices are in most cases detonated without distinguishing the religious affiliations of the human targets.

African Union, in its Convention on the Prevention and Combating Terrorism, defines terrorism as

> any acts of which a violation of the criminal laws of a state party and which may endanger the life, physical integrity or freedom of, or cause serious injury or death to any person, any number of group of persons or cause or causes damage to public or private property, natural resources, environmental or cultural heritage and is calculated or intend to.[7]

TYPES OF TERRORISM

There is no uniform perception of the concept of terrorism among nations. Terrorism means different things to different

---

[5] Section 2 (c) of the Anti-Terrorism Act, 2011

[6] http://www.economist.com/node/2 1528307 (accessed September 7, 2011

[7] Article 3 of African Union Convention on the prevent and combating Terrorism

people. Thus, there are various typologies, some of them are now discussed.

State Terrorism

This form of terrorism is used by radical states or countries as foreign policy tools. Its origin is rooted in the World War I, when Germany launched over 110,000 chemical shells filled with phosgene in their final onslaught against French in Verdum in 1916. It is estimated, by historians, that the German's use of chemical weaponry resulted in death of between 300,000 and 900,000 people during this war. In essence, terrorism can be employed in the context of both, as a violent resistance to a state, as well as in the services of state interest.[8]

National Terrorism

This type of terrorism is employed by groups seeking to form a separate state for their own national group by engaging in armed conflict for liberation from a state. Such separatist groups are the Palestine Liberation Organisation, Irish Republican Army, Basque Fatherland and Liberty, Hamas, etc.[9]

Religious Terrorism

Of all the factors that promote terrorism, religion is the most potent and volatile and poses the greatest threat to humanity. Religious terrorists usually engage in extreme violent activities to propagate their causes and confront the status quo of secular states. The doctrinal foundations and religious sentiments undergirding their formations and operations make them a menace to the society.[10]

---

[8] http: // members.tripod.com/Brain-Blodgett/ chemical.htp. (accessed August 30, 2011)
[9] Ibid.
[10] Ibid.

Transnational and Domestic Terrorism or Insurgent Terrorism

In this category, terrorist groups carry out terrorist activities within a State, sometimes with transborder connivance. The 1995 truck bombing of a nine-storey building in Oklahoma in USA[11] and various terrorist activities carried out by separatist groups in Nigeria, such as MEND and BOKO HARAM, are examples of this type of terrorism.

Right-wing Terrorism

These groups seek to abolish liberal democratic governments and create fascist States in their place.[12]

Left-wing Terrorism

This developed following the contradictions of capitalism. The major aim of this group is outright elimination of capitalism and subsequent replacement with a communist or socialist regime such as the Japanese Red Army, the Weatherman, the Red Brigades, the Baader Mainhef Group, etc.[13]

Revolutionary Terrorism

This type of terrorism is targeted at enthroning political revolution.[14]

Sub-Revolutionary Terrorism

Under this, terrorism is employed for political motives other than revolution.[15]

Repressive Terrorism

This refers to government-directed terror aimed at "restraining certain groups, individual, or forms of behaviours deemed to be undesirable."[16]

---

[11] Ibid.

[12] Ibid.

[13] Ibid.

[14] Shultz, R, "Conceptualising Political Terrorism: A typology," in *Journal of International Affairs* (1978), Vol. 32 (1): 7-15.

[15] Ibid.

Other types of terrorism are Cyber terrorism, Anarchist terrorism, Narco-terrorism, etc. Cyber terrorism or computer terrorism is becoming common place. It is the utilisation of computers as tool for illegal purposes, such as fraud, intellectual property theft, identity theft, phishing, child pornography and other activities which target virtual information.

The Nigerian Cybercrime (Prohibition, Prevention, etc.) Act 2015 attempts to provide a comprehensive platform for the prohibition, prevention, prosecution and punishment of illegal cyber activity.

The Economic and Financial Crimes Commission (EFCC) has revealed that 80 per cent of its convictions are related to illegal cyber activity.[17]

MODES OF TERRORISM

Terrorist acts are perpetrated in diverse forms or modes. Some of which are:

Bio-chemical Terrorism

This is one of the deadliest forms of terrorism. Under this, terrorists employ the use of toxic chemicals that are harmful to humans and the environment on their targets. In 1994 and 1995, a group, Aum Shinrikyo (supreme truth) religious sect led by Shako Sham (otherwise called the "pope") executed chemical attacks on Japanese citizens in Tokyo and other cities. Also, chemicals and biological weapons were also used on the U.S. troops during the Persian war.[18]

---

[16] Ibid.

[17] Abdulrasheed Bawa, at a conference organized by the Cyber Security Experts Association of Nigeria (CSEAN) "Cyber secure Nigeria Conference 2021", October 6, 2021.

[18] http: //www.nye.gov/html(accessedAugust13,2011)

Suicide Terrorism

This is one of the most popular modes of carrying out deadly attacks by terrorists, especially terrorism based on religious sentiments.

For example, the modern-day *Jihad* propagates the concept that suicide attacks purify the perpetrators and cleans the world of the evils of liberalism and capitalism. They believe that suicide strengthens the Muslims brotherhood and serves the goal of eliminating the opponents of Islam.[19]

This mode is widely embraced due to its simplicity and the fact that it is not capital-intensive. Also, it usually has a maximum impact on targets by guaranteeing total devastation and mass casualties. Suicide terrorists, most often than not, succeed and there is no fear of them divulging information.[20]

Nuclear Terrorism

This involves the use of nuclear weapon on specific targets by terrorists. Its effects on humans and the environment are devastating. Under this, shock waves disperse radioactive fallout over a wide area, poisoning wildlife and groundwater and the heat (thermal radiation) destroys vegetation. Its effects on human are severe.[21]

Bio-Terrorism

Under this mode, the environment is used as a conduit for terrorism. Usually, biological elements, such as disease-causing bacteria and viruses, when taken out of their natural habitats, can become potent weapons. For example, following the WTC attacks in the United States in 2001, several mails tested positive to biocontaminant anthrax in Washington D.C. and New York City. Antrax is a bacterium that, in its most potent

---

[19] Ibid.

[20] Ibid.

[21] Makhijan Harvard and others, eds. *Nuclear Wastelands. A Global Guide to Nuclear Weapons Production and Its Health and Environmental Effects* (Cambridge: MIT Press. 2000)

form, when inhaled has a fatality rate of over 90 per cent. Over ten thousand people were exposed while five people died of inhalational anthrax before the contaminated mails were quarantined.[22]

IMPACT OF TERRORISM ON SOCIETY

Amidst the shock and outrage that reverberate as a result of terrorist violent activities in respect of their "effects on human lives and human rights, structural damage and economic loss, there is one voice that is silent...Mother earth." Few will choose to focus on the negative impact of these terrorist attacks on the environment because it is nearly as visible an effect. The damage caused by terrorist attacks on the environment might possibly be the most fatal outcome of all.[23]

The destruction inherent in any act of mass terrorism inevitably causes secondary environment pollution effects, many of them serious. Acts of terrorism can be directed against the environment itself, or specific natural resources such as freshwater, oil, or agricultural products.[24]

The secondary environmental effects of terrorism can often be as significant as its primary effects These secondary environmental consequences go beyond the staggering loss of life (in most instances) but also the collapse of structures and the subsequent fires which spew forth enormous cloud of dust and toxins into the air. The drifting winds facilitate the slow movement of these cloud of dusts for miles, depositing an unknown cocktail of gases and airborne particulates all over everything. Oil spill arising from terrorist attack on oil

---

[22] Gulgiha Guy and Matsumoto Oa.y: FBI Theory on Anthrax is Doubted," *Washington Post*, October 28, 2002 Al.

[23] htpp:/www.care2.com/causes/the impact of terrorism-on-the-environment html (accessed August 2,2011)

[24] htpp://www.pollutionissues.com/Te-un/Terrorism. Html (accessed on August 2,2011).

installations result in devastating consequences for the environment.[25]

In Nigeria, the Martyrs Brigade blew up oil pipelines belonging to the Nigerian National Petroleum Corp (NNPC) at Ehor in Edo State. Apart from damaging production facilities, the resultant spill had serious environmental consequences.[26] Also in May 2008, the Shell Petroleum Development (SPDC) Diebu Creek flow station was blown up by militants operating along the Creeks of Southern Ijaw Local Government Area of Bayelsa State, causing massive oil spillage along the waterways.[27]

The pollution or environmental fallouts of bombed structures include asbestos and fibrous glass from such buildings, mercury, dioxins, furans and other toxins and cancer-causing agents. Burning of fluorescent light bulbs and computer screens produce heavy metals such as cadmium and lead and volatile organic compounds like benzene. And, also these secondary pollution concerns include possible contamination of waterways.

For example, in the September 11, 2001 terrorist attacks on the World Trade Centre in the US, the simultaneous collapse of the Twin Tower caused a serious and acute environmental disaster. As the plane hit the Twin Tower, more than 90,000 litres of jet fuel burned at a temperature above 1,000 °C. An atmospheric plume formed, consisting of toxic materials such as metals, furans, asbestos, dioxin, PAH, PCB and hydrochloric acid; asbestos level rose above 0.83% of the total mass; PAH comprised more than 0.1/0 of the total mass and PCBs less than 0.001% of total mass.

---

[25] Ibid.

[26] Aigbokhaevo V.,. 'Environmental Terrorism in the Niger Delta: Implication for Nigeria's Developing Economic'. *IELR* (2009) 40

[27] Ibid.

At the site, now called Ground Zero, a large pile of smoking nibbles burned intermittently for more than three months. Gaseous and particulates kept forming long after the Towers had collapsed.[28]

In Nigeria, on the 1 October, 2010, two cars rigged with bombs exploded in front of the Federal High Court Abuja leaving three people dead. A militant group behind the spate of unrest in Niger Delta, MEND, claimed responsibility for the attacks. The damaged that occurred in the bombardment of the Nigeria Police Headquarters in Abuja, where a powerful bomb ripped through the car park causing a huge fire that wrecked 77 vehicles parked there is unquantifiable volume of toxic smokes from burning metals and fuel billowed from the burning cars into the atmosphere releasing deadly toxins into the air and chunks of human flesh splattered all over the scene of explosion.[29]

Also on the 26 August 2011, a car laden with explosive was driven through the gates of the United Nations House, Abuja by a Boko Haram suicide bomber, into the reception where it was detonated, killing scores of people and resulting in massive damage to the building.[30]

Dust particles of various sizes containing deadly toxins are dispersed into the atmosphere during terrorist attacks. *In vivo* inhalation and epidemiological studies pointed out the impact of these dust clouds on the environment and humans are extremely severe due to the high alkalinity of particles.[31]

TERRORISTS ACTIVITIES IN NIGERIA

With over 250 ethnic groups, 5,000 dialects, adherents of two dominant religions that view each other with suspicion, political

---

[28] http:/ /www.lcnnlcch.com/environrnental-clfccts-war.htm(accessed September 14, 2011

[29]http://www.tribunecom.ng/indexphp/frontpagenews/africa (accessed July 27, 2011)

[30] Ibid.

[31] Lenntech, *supra*

contestation for power that sometimes engender acrimony;[32] Nigeria is a country perpetually under siege. During the military era, the blockaders operated in uniform from the corridors of power. Democracy only succeeded in accomplishing a reshuffling of the prime characters in that siege scenario, replacing the military with militias and militant groups such as the Oodua People's Congress (OPC), Movement for the Actualization of the Sovereign State of Biafra (MASSOB), Arewa, People's Congress (APC), BAKASSI BOYS Egbesu and a flurry of shadowy group in the Niger Delta (NDPVF, MEND etc.).[33]

However, most of the ethnic tensions fizzled out but the Niger Delta militias have justified their actions as years of criminal neglect and oppression by successive governments and upgraded themselves into full-scale terrorist organisation and in effect began to wage war against the Nigerian state. Their agenda was not only to pressurise the government for their fair share of the country's oil money or for the development of the Niger Delta region, but to enforce their demand through armed rebellion.[34] They resorted to kidnapping expatriate staff of oil companies, sabotaging oil pipelines, blowing up of oil installation, engaging in confrontation with Nigerian security forces (especially the navy and army) etc. Their armed resistance and sabotage cut down Nigeria's oil production by 20%, leading to loss of much revenue and environmental degradation. In 2009, President Umaru Yar'Adua launched an amnesty programme that aimed to disarm, reintegrate and employ militants in the Niger Delta

---

[32] No to Terrorism: Sunday comment" *ThisDay* newspaper, 28 August, 2011

[33] Tolu Ogunlesi: "Ongoing Concern: Boko Haram and the Nigeria's wars on terror,' *Next Newspaper*, September 18, 2011

[34] Ibid.

and this helped tamp down the conflict and ushered in relative peace in the Niger Delta.[35]

Nigeria's security problem has been worsened by the infusion of religion as a motivation and rationale for the activities of criminal thugs. A new aspect of this security problem is the role of the Boko Haram Islamic state movement (BHISM). The activities of this group are frightening. Despite the death of its leader, Mohammed Yusuf, and several hundreds of his supporters by security forces, Boko Haram is still strong and resorting to terrorist acts in pursuit of its goal, i.e., fighting for a separate, independent and sovereign state whose legal system will be based on Islamic "sharia" and the total eradication of Western education in Nigeria.[36]

On April 14, 2014, 276 female students aged 16 to 18 were kidnapped by Boko Haram from Government Girls Secondary School, Chibok in Borno State. As at 2021, over 100 of the girls remain missing.[37]

In December 2020, approximately 300 school boys were kidnapped from the Government Science Secondary School, Kankara, Katsina State with over 18 million dollars paid as ransom.[38]

Many schools have been closed in northern Nigeria due to incessant attacks by Boko Haram and other bandits masquerading as Islamic Crusaders.

Religious conflict is a huge leadership challenge and a major threat to the security, unity and national progress of Nigeria. Religious ignorance and intolerance breed violence. Religious violence and war have decimated more lives in Nigeria in the

---

[35] http://www.modernghana.com/news/337342/1/boko-haramterroristhirn (accessed 28 August2011)

[36] Ibid.

[37] Amnesty International "Nigeria: Seven years since Chibok, the government fails to protect children" April 17, 2021.

[38] Lionel Rawlins "ANALYSIS: Kidnappings and School closures: What the Nigerian government must do" Premium Times, December 1st, 2021.

last forty years than hunger, disease, and accidents combined. Northern Nigeria especially has been a battleground between Islam and Christianity. Since 1960, Nigeria has had countless incidents of religious extremism and Islamic fundamentalism in an attempt to islamise the nation. Islamic fundamentalism, fanaticism, terrorism and jihads are big threats and enormous challenges. Fanatical uprisings have mostly originated in the northern parts of Nigeria, arguably the poorest part of the country. Indeed, out of the 178 clashes that have taken place in northern Nigeria between 1980 and 2004, 104 were related to religion.[39]

The social effect on northern Nigeria and, indeed, Nigeria at large is the disposition and vulnerability to an ideology of terror which has been ignored. This poses a great danger to the future of the country. Terrorism is not a tool used at the international level alone. The use of terror for religious and political purposes in northern Nigeria is a reality.

Violent fundamentalism and extremism, especially in the name of religion, has grown in northern Nigeria. From the 1980s after the Maitasine sect unleashed terror on innocent citizens and were eventually routed by the superior firepower of the federal military government, northern Nigeria has become a festering ground for a remarkable number of radical Islamic sects that have demonstrated their readiness to inflict violence and mayhem to pursue their agenda. Over time, in some parts of the north, religion-inspired violence has become more and more vicious and better organised. The instruments of violence have also grown in sophistication, just as intellectual capacity of the leadership of these extremist groups has improved with the recruitment of university graduates, top government officials and important elements from the upper rung of the society in the north.[40]

---

[39] http://nigeria.com/opirflon/9642-Nigeria-Boko-Haram htm (accessed September 2, 2011)

[40] Ibid.

For all practical purposes, it must be recognised that religious extremism and terrorism have become obvious by the frequency and the systematic occurrence of these events, that they are planned to intimidate or cause terror in pursuit of religious, political and other goals. This is certainly the perception of victims of these crimes. This conclusion is further justified by the fact that perpetrators of these crimes usually go scot-free; they are hardly punished. Where the government overwhelms the perpetrators of the acts, the leaders of the sect involved are usually eliminated in action, extra-judicially killed or set free. That is why since the 1980s, no leader of these terror groups has had the opportunity to make a case in the law court, fuelling rumours that people in high places have something to hide concerning state sponsorship of such groups.[41] The Commissioner for Information, Lai Muhammed, had at a press conference stated that financiers to terrorism had been uncovered and that Nigerian government officials were compromising the prosecution of terrorist offenders.[42]

The Anti-Terrorism (Prevention) Act 2010[43]

Before now, it can be said that Nigeria did not have a comprehensive anti-terrorism law and for this reason failed to meet the requirements of the Financial Action Task Force (FATF) established by the G7 summit held in Paris in 1937.[44] The FATF recommendations and requirements are to detect, prevent and suppress the financing of terrorism and terrorist acts. However, out of the Task Force's 9 special recommendations, Nigeria was rated "non-compliant" in 7 and "partially compliant" in only 2.[45]

---

[41] Ibid.

[42] Ameh Ejekwonyilo, "Nigerian Officials have comprised prosecution of suspected terrorism sponsors-Ex-police Commissioner," *Premium Times*. February 3rd, 2022.

[43] This Act was passed into law on February, 17 2011

[44] supra

[45] http://www234net,com/CSP/senate-Okays-Nig-terrorism-bill.htmon august 2,2011)

The Anti-Terrorism (Prevention) Act was passed into law on 17 February, 2011, by President Goodluck Jonathan. It provides a legal framework for the prevention, prohibition and combating terrorism in Nigeria. The law empowers the president to declare any group as a terrorist organisation and security agencies to tackle terrorist activities within the country and mete out appropriate sanctions on offenders of its provisions. The Act provides for a maximum of 20 years imprisonments for anyone who commits an offence under the Act, and where death results, the penalty is death sentence.[46]

The Act has five essential parts covering acts of terrorism and related offences, terrorism funding and terrorist properties, mutual assistance and extradition, investigation and prosecution.[47]

The Act also addressed the hijacking of aircrafts, ships or other means of public transport, as well as the manufacture, possession or acquisition or transport, supply or use of weapons and exp1osives.[48]

The propagation and dissemination of information of any form calculated to cause panic, evoke violence, or intimidate a government, person or groups of persons, also fall within ambit of the Act which it seeks to deal with or prevent.

Harbouring or concealing a person suspected of terrorism activities constitutes an offence punishable with 10 years' imprisonment.[49]

The Act empowers the police and security officials the right to access post, e-mails, phone calls or other data if they believe it is in the interest of national security to do so. Also, they are empowered to seal off a property or vehicle without a warrant

---

[46] Section 4 of the Anti Terrorism Act 2011

[47] Ibid.

[48] Ibid.

[49] Section 5 of the Act

and allow judges to order the detention of suspect for up to 30 days if it is in the interest of public safety to do so.[50]

The Act prohibits the possession or use of explosives as well as research into the development of explosives including biological or chemical types without lawful authority.

By enacting this Act, Nigeria has joined the band of countries that have passed strong legislation against terrorism such as United Kingdom, France, Italy, USA, Canada, India, Pakistan, etc.[51]

On its part, the Money Laundering (Prohibition) Act 2010 established a legal framework for the prevention, prohibition and combating of acts of terrorism, including the financing of terrorism in Nigeria. It also promotes the effective implementation of the International Convention On the Prevention and Combating of Terrorism, as well as the suppression of the financing of terrorism.[52]

Under the provisions of this Act, many organised crimes such as oil bunkering, hostage taking and kidnapping will attract stiff penalties. It defined acts of terrorism as "causing an attack on transport system and infrastructural facility including information system, a fixed platform located on the continental shelf, life or results in major economic loss."[53]

And under the Economic and Financial Crimes Commission Act,[54] "terrorism" means -

(a) any act which is a violation of the Criminal Code or the Penal Code and which may endanger the life, physical integrity or freedom of, or cause serious injury or death to, any person, any

---

[50] http://wwwin.fromafrica.com/polities-africa/first-anti-terrorismact(accessed August 22, 2011)

[51] 77 http://wwwthe Nigeria dily.com/201 1/06/15/the new-anti-terrorlsni1aws (accessed August 20, 2011

[52] Ogunlesi *supra*

[53] Ibid.

[54] Section 46 of the EFCC Act

number or group of persons or cause or may cause damage to public or property, natural resources, environmental or cultural heritage and is calculated or intended to:

(i) intimidate, put in fear, force, coerce or induce any government, body institution, the general public or any segment thereof, to do or abstain from doing any act or to adopt or abandon a particular standpoint, or to act according to certain principles; or

(ii) disrupt any public service, the delivery of any essential service to the public or to create a public emergency; or

(iii) create general insurrection in a state;

All these laws complement each other in the fight against terrorism in Nigeria.

Causes of Terrorism in Nigeria

Terrorism is a phenomenon linked to multiple circumstances whose origins go beyond ideological concepts. It is necessary to analyse its causes in order to address the myriad of issues associated with it. It has been suggested that terrorism[55] is motivated mostly by certain factors, some of which we now examine.

Social and Political Injustices

It is believed that people choose terrorism when they are trying to fight what they perceive to be a social or political or historical wrong, when they have been stripped of their land or rights, or denied.[56]

---

[55] http://terrorism.about-com/od/causes/a/causes/htni(accessed 17 September, 2011

[56] The Niger Delta militants resorted to armed conflict as a result of years of neglect and deprivation, despite the fact that their communities generate the hulk of Nigeria's wealth.

Manipulation of Religion

Of all the factors that promote the activities of terror groups, religion is the most potent. Many people, especially youths, fall prey to religious radicalisation. No religion is evil, or justifies the killing of innocent people but any religion can become a deadly weapon if utilised and manipulated where communities are struck by poverty, disease, illiteracy and hopelessness.

Significantly, there has been an invasion of moderate Islam in the past three decades by militant Islamic ideologists around the world. Militant Islam, originating from Sudan, Libya, Somalia, Yemen, Syria and Iran, has found its way into northern Nigeria from the country's borders with Niger Republic, Chad and Cameroon.[57] There has been a new wave of Islamic sermons in northern parts of Nigeria that tend to be targeted at spreading hatred, disunity and violence. Such preachers openly refer to anyone or group with a different religious view as a pagan or unbeliever and try to enforce their ideologies through intimidation and violence.[58] This is festering religious intolerance and societal schism.

Poverty

The prevalence of deprivation, misery, starvation and extreme poverty provide breeding grounds for extremism and terrorism. Mass poverty is one of the conditions that creates a favourable climate for terrorism to thrive. Poor economic circumstances of people make them vulnerable to manipulation by mischievous people. The growing disenchantments, disillusionment and impoverishment swell the army of vulnerable people and make them easy prey in the hands of terrorist groups who capitalise on their vulnerability by indoctrinating them with pervasive views.

---

[57] John Shiklam, "Violence in North, Failure of Regional Leadership," *ThisDay* newspaper 20, October, 2011

[58] Ibid.

Globalisation

Terrorism is greatly facilitated by globalisation. Due to the integration of the world markets, tools of terrorism such as explosives, weapon, gadgets and basic information on how to assemble and detonate explosives are readily available at the touch of a button.

Globalisation is largely viewed as a permissive cause of terrorism as it increases complexities at various levels of the society and economy, thereby creating opportunities and vulnerabilities, sophistication of network of communication, transportation, scientific inventions, urbanisation which makes a city the arena of terrorism due to anonymity, modality and accessibility of target.[59]

Marginalisation and Misuse of Resources

Before the commencement of oil exploration and production in the Niger Delta, the communities in this region utilised their resources in a sustainable manner. There were no cases of environmental degradation as harmony existed between man and environment. The commencement of oil exploration and production in the region, however, led to the pollution and marginalisation of the inhabitants. As a result of the above, some inhabitants in these communities resorted to militancy, by engaging the state in armed conflict and blowing up oil installations, to press home their demands for control, management and development of their region.[60]

Partisan Politics and Political Patronage

These factors played a major role in the incursion of terrorism in Nigeria. Politicians, in a bid to actualise their political aspirations, patronise and arm youths to attain their interest. They also patronise various groups, militias or religious sects,

---

[59] Crenshaw M, The Causes of Terrorism, *Comparative Politics Journal*, Vol 13.4, 379-399

[60] Atsegbua L. *et al*, *Environmental Law in Nigeria, Theory and Practice* (Benin City, Ambik Press 2010), 245-246

either for support or protection, use them as tools and later discard them or unleash them on innocent people after having been trained to handle guns.

Most politicians encourage violent and revolutionary groups by financing their activities because they utilise their violent disposition to achieve their political and selfish economic ends.

In *SSS* v. *Senator Mohammed Ali Ndume and Alli Sanda Umar Konduga (aka Al Zawahiri)*[61] the Chief Magistrate Court, Zone 2 Abuja convicted the second accused person (Al Zawahiri) on terrorism charges. Al Zawahiri was charged with terrorist activities, to wit, terrorist communication, threat messages to prominent Nigerians and the likes in Bornu State and other parts of Nigeria. At his trial he pleaded guilty. He was tried summarily, convicted of the charges and sentenced to three years' imprisonment.

Senator Ndume who has been accused of facilitating terrorist activities in Bornu State and other parts of the North, however pleaded not guilty and his no case submission was upheld.

CONCLUSION

The escalating problem of terrorism in Nigeria, especially Islamic fundamentalism, appears to be more deeply rooted than the feeble approaches adopted by the Nigerian governments to address it and engage in more monitoring of sects activities in volatile areas.

Given the danger terrorism poses to the country and global security, and responses by nations around the world to tackle terrorism-related events, it is recommended that comprehensive and drastic measures, aimed at preventing and combating the root causes of terrorism be fashioned. Wishing

---

[61] See the *Vanguard* of Sunday, November 27, 2011 vol. 24, No. 10691007 front page at page 5. It was titled, Boko Haram: How SSS established case against Senator Ndume.

the problem away, pretending it is not there, or that it is not as serious as it is, is akin to sitting on a time bomb.[62]

Government must adopt a holistic, systematic and coordinated intelligence-based approach to fighting the menace posed by terrorism. What is being witnessed today in Nigeria are the consequences of a national intelligence and security system that fails to recognise that contemporary crimes demand more reliable and timely intelligence than guns and armoured personnel carriers which will only bring a temporary halt to the crisis.[63]

Government should make concerted efforts, devoid of rhetoric and grandstanding, to promote social justice and equity to put an end to the conditions that breed terrorism, such as poverty, unemployment, marginalisation and corruption. Instead of continuous use of repressive state policies that can never fully address the problem of terrorism, attempts should be made to isolate and address grievances of all interest groups as fairly as possible. Government should regulate preaching in religious gathering and ensure that only people with the requisite qualifications are allowed to preach and engage in religious evangelism, especially in the northern part of Nigeria. Particularly, the *Almajiri* organisation is seen as a ready outfit for the spreading of militant Islamic ideology; a large number of the children, who end up uneducated and unemployed, are given all forms of negative indoctrinations.

Thus, government should keep a close watch and investigate various religious sects and radicals that hold the potential of unleashing terror. Proactive and pre-emptive measures must be the focus of intelligence.

---

[62] Abimbola, *supra*

[63] In 2009, the military routed the Boko Haram sect, killing several hundred of them and executing their leader, Yusuf Mohammed. This approach incensed the other sect members and they are currently on a revenge mission to atone for the death of its members

It is further recommended that government should take proactive measures to implement effective poverty alleviation policies to stem the tide of chronic deprivation through job creation and sustainability. Consequently, government at all levels - the federal, states and local government - should co-operate to address social, political and economic conditions that fuel fundamentalism and intolerance typified by widespread deprivation and hunger, lack of access to quality education, marginalisation, unemployment, political manipulation of religion by the elite class and struggle over control of state resources.

There must also be cooperation and intelligence sharing by different intelligence agencies. The federal government should diversify and strengthen its means of creating avenues for international intelligence sharing and inter-agency co-operation through diplomatic channels.

Also, there should be enhanced border patrol and regulations to stem the influx of immigrants and aliens into the country, through porous and unmanned borders.

There should be an effective mechanism for conflict mediation and resolution through the establishment of alternative dispute resolution mechanism or agencies.

The government should put in place good policies to promote effective and efficient leadership, good governance, transparency and a mechanism to check, prevent and totally eliminate corruption in Nigeria.

Terrorism is a global menace. It is indeed a scourge which needs to be confronted frontally. It is a violation of our fundamental human rights, especially the right to life and that of peaceful coexistence. The terror and tragedies that terrorists unleash on innocent and suspecting citizens pose a serious threat to the stability of all societies. Thus, terrorism has become a global phenomenon that cannot be fought in isolation.

There is no justification for resorting to terrorism because it undermines everything it claims to fight. Terrorists' acts whenever and by whoever committed, are criminal and unjustifiable by political, religious or philosophical considerations.

Terrorism may grow out of inequality and oppression, but such circumstances do not justify terrorist acts. There is no "just" terrorism whatever the causes. Terrorism is a menace that must be curbed collectively by all, no matter what it takes.

Chapter 15

DEFENCES

ACCIDENT

Generally, accident means a fortuitous circumstance, event or happening without any human agency, or it happening wholly or partly through human agency, an event which under the circumstances is unusual and unexpected by the person to whom it happens. The word may be employed as denoting a calamity, casualty, catastrophe, disaster, an undesirable or unfortunate happening, any unexpected personal injury resulting from any unlooked-for mishap or occurrence, any unpleasant or unfortunate occurrence that causes injury, loss, suffering or death. An event that takes place without one's foresight or expectation, an undersigned, sudden and unsuspected event.[1] An event which occurs by accident connotes an act totally unexpected, unwilled, unintentional and without any fault as against an act which is deliberative, willed or intentional.[2]

Section 24 of the Criminal Code provides for the defence of accident. It states that subject to the express provisions of the Criminal Code relating to negligent acts and omissions, a person is not criminally responsible for an act or omission which occurs independently of the exercise of his will or for an event which occurs by accident. The test for the defence of accident under section 24 of the Criminal Code is whether the prohibited act was or was not done accidentally or

---

[1] See the case of *Agwu* v. *The State* (1998) 4 NWLR (pt 544) 93

[2] *Thomas* v. *The State* (1994) 4 NWLR (pt. 337) 129

independently of the exercise of the will of the accused person.[3] As pointed out earlier, an event is said to be accidental when the act by which it was caused was not done with the intention of causing it and its occurrence as a consequence of such act is not probable that a person of ordinary prudence ought under the circumstances in which it was done, to take reasonable precaution against it. In *Amaremor* v. *The State*,[4] it was held that, for an event to qualify as an accident, such event must be the result of an unwilled act or an event which occurred without the fault of the person alleged to have caused it or an event totally unexpected in the ordinary course of events.[5]

Furthermore, it should be noted that the defence of accident, like all other defences, presupposes that the accused physically committed the offence but should be acquitted because it was an accidental act. In *Amaremor* v. *the State, supra* it was further held that when an accused person pleads the defence of accident, he admits the *actus reus,* but denies only the necessary *mens rea*. It is, therefore, contradictory for an accused to plead accident in one breadth and deny the *actus reus* in another, as the appellant did in the instant case. If an accused person admits the *actus reus* by pleading accident, he is merely denying that he is mentally responsible for the *actus reus*. In other words, he is saying that the event happened independently of the exercise of his will or accidentally. This is the essence of the plea of accident as a defence. It has been observed by a learned Justice of the Court of Appeal, when he said:

> The prisoner cannot plead accident and at the same time assert that the fatal bullet did not come out of the gun he had on the fateful day. If the appellant pleaded accident as he did

---

[3] *Oguonzee* v. *The State* (1998) 5 NWLR (pt. 551) 521

[4] (2010) 7 NWLR (pt 1193) 322

[5] *Adelumola* v. *The State* (1988) 1 NWLR (pt. 73) 683

> in exhibit 'A' it no longer matters whether the pistol is Baretta or Browning. That is why I find the totality of the defence of the appellant ridiculous and incredible. I think they are skilful manoeuvres to mesmerize the trial court. These are tactics in guerrilla warfare purposely to cause distractions. They are not permitted in adjudication.[6]

Section 24 of the Criminal Code does not deal with an 'act' but an 'event' and the event within the meaning of the section is what apparently follows from the act.[7] The act leading to an accident must be a lawful act done in a lawful manner. Thus, for an event to qualify as accidental under section 24 of the Criminal Code, it must be a surprise to the ordinary man of prudence, that is, a surprise to all sober and reasonable people. The test of the plea or defence of accident is always that if the act, even though unlawful, is not such that would from the view of a reasonable man, cause death or grievous bodily harm though death resulted therefrom, the person charged can only at most be convicted of manslaughter. But in *Oghor* v. *The State*,[8] it was held, that an accused person cannot take refuge on a defence of accident for a deliberate act even if he did not intend the eventual result.

Where an accused person seeking to rely on the defence of accident does not testify to explain how the accident occurred, and to be open to cross-examination, the defence is not given in evidence. Consequently, the defence of accident is bound to be rejected.[9] In *Adekunle* v. *The State*[10] the accused/appellant was charged with murder contrary to section 319(1) of the Criminal Code Law of Ogun State at the High Court of Ogun State, Ijebu Ode. The court was among others to determine whether the defence of accident under section 24 of the

---

[6] Per Eko, J.C.A. in *Amaremor* v. *The State* (2010) 7 NWLR (pt 193) 323

[7] *Umoru* v. *The State* (1990) 3 NWLR (pt 138) 363

[8] (1990) 3 NWLR (pt 139) 484

[9] *R* v. *Akerele* (1941) 7 WACA, 56

[10] (2006) 14 NWLR (pt. 1000) 923

Criminal Code Law, Cap 29 Laws of Ogun State 1978 was available to the appellant having regard to the evidence on trial. At the conclusion of trial, the trial court in its judgment held that the prosecution proved its case of murder against the appellant and convicted him. The appellant was sentenced to death. The appellant's appeal to the Court of Appeal was dismissed. Dissatisfied, the appellant appealed to the Supreme Court contending that his conduct was accidental. The Supreme Court held that, where a person discharges a firearm unintentionally and without attendant criminal malice or negligence, he will be exempted from criminal responsibility both for the firing and for its consequences. In the instant case, what the appellant raised in his written statement, exhibit 'A' was not a defence of accidental discharge but something else entirely that arose from his own imagination as the defence was not raised instantly until much later in the appellant's exhibits 'A'.[11] And in *Sholuade* v. *The Republic*,[12] it was held that when an accused person raised the defence of accidental discharged in a criminal trial, it was the duty of the prosecution to disprove the defence of the accidental discharge raised by the accused person.

By virtue of section 48 of the Penal Code, nothing is an offence if it was done by accident or misfortune and without any criminal intention or knowledge in the course of doing a lawful act in a lawful manner by lawful means and with proper care and caution. Consequently, the provision of section 48 of the Penal Code and section 24 of the Criminal Code are in line with the rules of English law relating to *mens rea* which stipulates that a person should not be convicted of an offence unless he has a guilty mind. However, under section 48 of the Penal Code, the act leading to the accident must be a lawful act done in a lawful manner. But there is no such restriction under

[11] See *Iromantu* v. *The State* (1964) All NLR 311

[12] (1966) 1 All NLR 134

section 24 of the Criminal Code. Rather, for an event to qualify as accidental under section 24 of the Criminal Code, it must be a surprise to the ordinary man of prudence. That is, a surprise to all sober and reasonable people. It should further be noted that by the words of section 48 of the Penal Code, the defence of accident presupposes that the accused physically committed the offence he is charged with but that having regard to the facts which he admits, he should be acquitted because his conduct in the commission of the offence was an accident, for an accident is generally regarded as the result of an unwilled act and is understood to be an event without the fault of the person alleged to have caused it. Thus, where the defence of accident is successfully set up by an accused person, it relieves the accused person of criminal responsibility as it constitutes a negation of any deliberate act or omission on the part of the accused person.[13]

In *Maiyaki* v. *The State*,[14] the appellant was arraigned before the High Court of Yobe State on a charge of culpable homicide, punishable with death under section 221(a) of the Penal Code, on the ground that he caused the death of one Habu Usman by shooting him on the head with a rifle with the knowledge that the death of deceased would be the probable consequence of his act. The defence of the appellant was that his colleague, DW2, and some of the passengers who alighted from the bus were attacked by a crowd of the ten men holding sticks and iron bars who started beating the passengers. That five of the men attacked DW2 and tried to disarm him, that he went to the rescue of DW2, and that in the course of the struggle with the men, his finger touched the trigger of the gun of DW2 and the shot hit somebody. The appellant claimed he did not intentionally shoot the deceased. He stated that his finger accidentally pulled the trigger of the gun held by DW2.

---

[13] See the case of *Chukwu* v. *The State* (1992) 1 NWLR (pt. 217) 255

[14] (2008) 15 NWLR (pt. 1109) 177

In judgment, the trial court found that the defence of accident did not avail the appellant. It found the appellant guilty as charged, it convicted him of culpable homicide punishable with death and sentenced him to death. Dissatisfied with the judgment of the trial court, the appellant appealed to the Court of Appeal, which upheld the findings of the trial court and affirmed its judgment. Still dissatisfied, the appellant appealed to the Supreme Court. In determining the appeal, the Supreme Court considered section 48 of the Penal Code which reads thus:

> 48. Nothing is an offence which is done by accident or misfortune and without any criminal intention or knowledge in the course of doing a lawful act in a lawful manner by lawful means and with proper care and caution.

The Supreme Court held that for an accused person to avail himself of the defence provided by section 48 of the Penal Code, the absence of *mens rea* must be clearly established by the accused person. In other words, the act of the accused person must have been accidental not intentional or premeditated. Accordingly, an accused person cannot take refuge under the defence of accident for a deliberate act, even if he did not intend the eventual result. In the instant case, the accused person had the *mens rea* and the intention to deal with, maim or kill the deceased. In the circumstances, the Court of Appeal was right when it upheld the judgment of the trial court that the defence of accident was not made out by the appellant.[15]

But in *Dangai* v. *The State*,[16] the court held that where an accused person raises the defence of an accident, the onus

[15] See the case of *Stephen* v. *The State* (1986) 5 NWLR (pt. 46) 680

[16] (1968) 1 All NLR 246

remains on the prosecution to prove its case beyond reasonable doubt by leading credible and admissible evidence to negate the defence and to convince the trial court that the defence does not avail the accused person. Where the prosecution fails to discharge that onus, the accused person is entitled to an acquittal.

While commenting, per Chukwuma-Eneh, J.S.C in *Maiyaki* v. *The State* (*supra*) noted:

> in summary, therefore, to raise the defence of accidental discharge here is quite incomprehensible to me in the scenario in which the death of the deceased has occurred, having considered the circumstances of this case particularly taking into account the nature of the weapon used in causing it, that is a gun - a dangerous weapon any day for that matter, the apparent excessive force used in silencing the deceased over a simple innocuous direction by the accused to the deceased and the other passengers to move to another spot to urinate as urinating at a certain spot near Texaco Petrol Filling Station (in Potiskum) is prohibited. This is the singular act that has led to this unfortunate incident and even then the part of the deceased's body (that is the deceased's head) hit by the bullet discharged from the accused's gun resulting instantaneously in his death speak for themselves. It would be stretching the defence indeed to a breaking point to suggest that the death of the deceased in the circumstances is accidental and that the act by which it is caused is not done with the intention to kill the deceased instantly or cause him grievous bodily harm. Again, it would be hard if not naïve to suggest on the evidence before the trial court that shooting the deceased on the head would not cause his death nor grievous harm. Therefore, the conviction of the appellant has met the justice of the case on the prosecution having proved its case beyond reasonable doubt.

Further commenting on the need for Nigerian police officers to stop reckless killing of persons under the guise of accidental discharge of firearms, Justice Chukwuma-Eneh of the Supreme Court, again observed:

> I must however admonish here that enough of the type of raw killing which the police have timidly termed as deaths from accidental discharges. Our law reports are replete with such cases. Even then, who otherwise is being fooled, as it were, by such warped defence to obvious cases of culpable homicide? Certainly not the courts nor any longer the public they are paid to protect. It is time the police did a *volte–face* to this type of crimes if they have to start the process of salvaging their steadily waning image in this country.

ALIBI

The term "Alibi" originated from Latin. It stemmed from the combination of two words: "*Alus*" and "*Ibi*", meaning "other" and "there" respectively. Put together under English usage, it means "elsewhere".[17] As stated earlier, the Latin expression, *alibi*, in its adverbial content and part of speech simply means "elsewhere". It is a defence when an accused person stated that he was not at the scene of the crime alleged against him. In raising the defence, the accused person is saying that he was somewhere other than the place where the offence was committed or simply that he was not at the scene of the crime. Therefore, it is a defence that places the accused person at the relevant time when the crime was committed in a different place - in view of that fact that it is humanly impossible for a human being to be in two places at a point in time. Consequently, a successful defence of alibi totally exonerates or exculpates the accused person of criminal responsibility.[18] Meanwhile, where an accused person has put up a defence of

[17] See *Alani* v. *The State* (1993) 7 NWLR (pt 303) 112. See also the case of *Gachi* v. *The State* (1965) NMLR 333.

[18] Thus, alibi is a defence by which an accused person alleges that at the time when the offence with which he was charged was committed, he was elsewhere. See also the decision of the court in the case of *Peter* v. *The State* (1994) 5 NWLR (pt. 342) 45.

alibi, what the law requires him to do is to introduce evidence of the alibi. The onus is on him to prove where he was at the time of the incident and he has to call evidence to support his defence of alibi. Once the defence of alibi is raised, it is for the prosecution to investigate it properly as failure to do so could raise reasonable doubt in the mind of the court and will lead to quashing the conviction. In *Ani* v. *The State*,[19] the appellants were charged with armed robbery contrary to section 1(2) (e) of the Robbery and Firearms (Special Provisions) Act Cap. 398 Laws of the Federation of Nigeria 1990. The appellants put up a defence of alibi. The 1st appellant in giving an account of his whereabouts to establish his defence of alibi stated that on 28/6/1997, he left to load sand at Nyeme at about *noon* and did not return home until he closed at 6pm. He was seen by his parents and he slept with his sister and left their house around 10am on 29/6/1997. The 2nd appellant on his own gave a detailed account of his whereabouts wherein he left for a specific place at 8a.m on 28/6/1997 only to return home at 7pm and eventually to a marketplace where he ate some food, returned home and slept. He stated that he did not see the 1st appellant on 28/6/1997 or 29/6/1997, that his mother knew he slept in the house and was the person who woke him up at about 9am. At the conclusion of the trial, the trial court convicted the appellants of armed robbery and sentenced them to death by hanging. Dissatisfied, the appellants appealed to the Court of Appeal contending that the trial court failed to consider their defence of alibi. The appeal was dismissed. In addition, the court held that it is the duty of the prosecution to disprove the defence of alibi set up by an accused person and to this end to investigate the alibi. However, where there is an eyewitness evidence of participation by an accused person in the crime, it is an issue of credibility and if the evidence of the

---

[19] (2003) 11 NWLR (pt 830) 144

witness is believed by the court, it displaces the defence of alibi. Once an accused is fixed at the scene of crime, his defence of alibi must fail. The court further held that in the instant case, the trial court believed the evidence of the prosecution that the appellants whom he knew very well before the date of the robbery were the two persons who robbed him. That the evidence of the prosecution displaced the appellant's defence of alibi and it was immaterial that the police did not investigate the alibi.

But in *Nunukwe* v. *The State,*[20] it was held that, once a defence of alibi is put up by an accused person, it is the duty of the police to investigate it properly because failure to do so raises reasonable doubt in the mind of the trial court and would lead to the quashing of the conviction of the accused person. In the instant case, the police failed to investigate the alibi out up by the 1st appellant. In the circumstances, his conviction ought to be quashed.

It should be noted that the evidence led by a trial court by the prosecution may be direct or circumstantial. However, whether the evidence is direct or circumstantial, it must establish the guilt of the accused person beyond reasonable doubt. The onus is always on the prosecution as a general rule and it never shifts. The obligation on the prosecution is to prove the whole crime, including the negative of defences which are in issue, such as alibi. Accordingly, an accused who pleads not guilty to a criminal charge casts upon the prosecution the burden of proving the facts in issue and if, when the totality of the evidence has been heard and considered, the court is not satisfied beyond reasonable doubt, it must acquit the accused person. A reasonable doubt may be created in the mind of the trial court, either by the evidence given by the defence or by the prosecution. All it means is that the prosecution must

---

[20] (2003) 14 NWLR (pt 840) 219

adduce such evidence which if believed, and if let uncontradicted, it could be accepted as proof. In *State* v. *Azeez,*[21] it was held that where the prosecution calls evidence, strong and cogent enough, to convince the court that an accused person had been seen at the scene of crime committing an offence, the defence of alibi crumbles because the acceptance of the evidence of prosecution witnesses necessarily implies that the accused could not have been anywhere else than as stated by witnesses whose evidence have been accepted by the court.[22]

However, it should be pointed out that the defence of alibi is complete once the accused person discloses to the police his whereabouts without more at the time of the commission of the crime. Furthermore, once an accused person sets up a defence of alibi, the burden of disproving it rests on the prosecution. In other words, where an accused person sets up alibi in answer to a charge, he does not thereby assume responsibility of proving the answer. The onus still lies on the prosecution to prove beyond reasonable doubt that the accused person was not only at the scene of the crime but that he committed the offence. There is no burden of proof on an accused person who puts forward an alibi as his defence. Therefore, it will be a misdirection to refer to any burden as resting on an accused person in a case where he raises the plea of alibi. Meanwhile the standard of proof required to establish the defence of alibi is one based on the balance of probabilities.[23]

---

[21] (2003) 14 NWLR (pt) 439 at 448

[22] Where the defence of alibi succeeds, there is no need for the court to consider other elements involved in the offence charged as the accused is taken not at the scene of the crime and the presumption will be raised that he did not, *ipso facto,* commit the crime.

[23] In *Almu* v. *The State* (2009) 10 NWLR (pt) 38, it has held that for a plea of alibi raised by an accused person to be destroyed, the prosecution must adduce sufficient evidence to fix the appellant at the scene of the crime.

In *Archibong* v. *The State,*[24] the court held that even though it is the duty of the prosecution to check on a statement of alibi by an accused person and disprove the alibi or attempt to do so, there is no inflexible and or invariable way of doing this. If the prosecution adduces sufficient and accepted evidence to fix a person or an accused person at the scene of crime at the material time, his alibi is thereby logically and physically demolished and that would be enough to render such plea ineffective as a defence. In the instant cases, the court further held that when the appellant gave an undisclosed address of his said native doctor brother/relation at Aba, the police were not expected to go on a wild goose chase in order to disprove the said alibi.[25]

Per Ogbuagu, J.S.C. observed:

> However, the appellant had thought, foolishly I may say, that the defence of alibi would conclusively avail him. But the said alibi was not only watery but was bogus in the extreme...The trial court rightly, in my view, rejected the said plea or defence of alibi.

AUTOMATISM

Automatism means a behaviour performed in a state of mental unconsciousness or dissociation without full awareness. The term is applied to actions or conduct of an individual apparently occurring without will, purpose, or reasoned intention on his part, a condition sometimes observed in persons who without being actually insane, suffer from an obscuration of the mental faculties, loss of volition or of memory, or kindred affections. Automatism may be asserted as a defence to negate the requisite mental state of voluntariness for commission of a crime. Again, "Ambulatory automatism" describes the

---

[24] (2006) 15 NWLR (pt 1000) 352

[25] See also the decision in *Queen* v. *Turner* (1957) WRNLR 34 and *Yanor* v. *The State* (1965) NMLR 337.

pathological impulse to purposeless and irresponsible wandering from place to place often characteristic of patient suffering from loss of memory with dissociation of personality.[26]

As earlier noted, by virtue of section 24 of the Criminal Code, a person is not criminally responsible for an act or omission which occurs independently of the exercise of his will or for an event which occurs by accident. Fundamentally, there are two arms in the above section. These are:

(a) a person is not criminally responsible for an act or omission which occurs independently of the exercise of his will; and
(b) a person is not criminally responsible for an event which occurs by accident.

It is plain that section 24 provides for two types of defences. In the one labelled (a) above, the accused person would have acted or omitted to act under a condition which is involuntary. In other words, it is independent of the exercise of his will. Such a defence has hardly been raised in any criminal trial. However, it must not be ruled out that it can be raised or that it is available under that arm of section 24 when an appropriate condition arises. After all, what gives rise to it is a human condition which does not discriminate between race and colour to affect a person. It is separate from the defence of accident and should, therefore, be treated as such. One has no will to accompany an act which is essentially involuntary, the other generally is not a matter of absence of will, but an event which was unexpected.

In England, the generic term of automatism occurs without a person's will or consciousness, and it is involuntary, such as somnambulism, blackout, convulse, spasm, etc. The second arm of section 24, labelled (b) above, concerns the defence of accident. This has been appreciated and well-articulated.

---

[26] *Blacks Law Dictionary* 9th edition, 2009

Furthermore, it may be helpful to illustrate the two arms of section 24. However, what seems to be very close facts shall be used in order that the difference may be drawn to mind and appreciated. For example, a man is working with a matchet in a field in the company of other workers. He is suddenly stung by a bee in the back. In a quick reaction he tried to use the flat side of the matchet to hit that part of the body to get rid of the bee. The matchet lands on the head of a co-worker, either by slipping from the man's hand or because of the swift manner he swung round. That would be an accident even though he had the will to swing round to make use of the matchet. But the result of what he did was an event which occurred suddenly and unexpected. Now, suppose the same man suddenly had a spasm which swung him round unconsciously resulting in the matchet landing on the head of the co-worker. The act of swinging round by the man occurred independently of the exercise of his will. Although the result in both situations may be the same for which there is no criminal responsibility, the second situation just illustrated cannot be described as an accident for the purpose of raising the defence of accident. It is an unwilled act negating any mental state of voluntariness. It is lower than an unintended act, which itself has an element of voluntariness in the sense that it is coupled with a mental state to do something as in the first illustration. In the second illustration, there was no will at all to do something. The man's defective human condition propelled him.

In *Agwu* v. *the State* (*supra*), per Uwaifo, J.C.A. (as he then was) held that no act is punishable if it is done involuntarily. An involuntary act is an act which is done by the muscles without any control by the mind, such as a spasm, a reflex action or a convulsion or an act done by a person who is not conscious of what he is doing, such as an act done whilst suffering from concussion or whilst sleepwalking. Thus, a man who thought he might be perfectly sane, committed what would otherwise be a crime in a state of somnambulism, would be entitled to an acquittal on the ground that he was not conscious of what he was doing. However, the court further held that the defence of automatism as contained in the first arm of section 24 of the Criminal Code must be considered with great circumspection and the evidence must invariably be supported by medical evidence in order to eliminate simulation by the accused person. There are genuine cases of automatism. However, a layman cannot safely attempt without the help of some medical or scientific evidence to distinguish the genuine from the fraudulent.

Somnambulism is a general automatism occurring in the course of and interrupting normal sleep.[27] In this condition, the patient rises from sleep, disregards the ordinary significance of his environment and those in it, and behaves as if he were living in an environment conjured up by himself. Patients in somnambulism states have sometimes met with unfortunate accidents, e.g., scalding, or even death from drowning. Although they are still comparatively rare, pleas of non-insane automatism are becoming increasingly frequent, and questions may legitimately be raised concerning the sufficiency of the court's powers. Is it right that someone who has been acquitted on the ground of non-insane automatism should inevitably go free?[28] In *R* v. *Charlson,*[29] the accused person was acquitted on various charges of causing bodily harm to his son because he acted in a state of automation which may have been due to a cerebral tumour. It is only natural to feel the deepest sympathy for the accused in such a case, but it is equally natural to question the propriety of an unqualified acquittal. One way of dealing with such problems would be to give the judge powers in all cases of a successful plea of automatism, insane or non-

---

[27] Henderson, D. and Gillespie, R.D. ,*A Textbook of Psychiatry* (7th ed, 1950) pp. 125 and 191
[28] Cross, R. Reflections on Bratty's case" (1962) 78 L.Q.R. 236 at 238 - 239
[29] (1955) 29, Cr. App. R. 37

insane to order the detention of the accused pending a medical inquiry, after which the appropriate order could be made. Lord Denning was decisive when he properly put it in perspective, a situation in which an accused person could be said to be acting under automatism in the case of *Bratty* v. *the Attorney-General for Northern Ireland.*[30] Lord Denning made it clear that an act is not involuntary simply because the accused does not remember it, nor simply because he could not control it, nor simply because it is unintentional or its consequences are unforeseen. And, if the accused person could reasonably have taken steps to prevent the conduct which he claims as automatism, then obviously he has no defence.

BONA FIDE CLAIM OF RIGHT

The defence of *bona fide* claim of right is governed by the provisions of section 23 of Criminal Code. The defence is usually raised by accused person in a charge relating to ownership of property. It should be noted that the most important question in relation to this defence is whether it applies only to cases where the accused person has, in fact, a right to the property in question or whether it extends also to those cases where the accused believes he has a right to the property, but, in fact, has not.[31] In *Commissioner of Police* v. *Otosi & Ors,*[32] the respondents were arraigned on a two-count charge of conspiracy to steal contrary to section 516(A) of the Criminal Code as amended by section 3(a) of the Imo State Edict No 5 of 1971 and stealing of palm fruits valued at ₦200.00 property of Ibina Igbere community. The trial magistrate found the 1st and 3rd respondents guilty and sentenced them to 9 months imprisonment with hard labour.

---

[30] (1961) 3 All ER. 523

[31] See Okonkwo and Naish at pg 109

[32] (1998) 1 NWLR (pt 532) 166

The respondents were dissatisfied with the judgement and they appealed against their convictions to the Imo State High Court sitting at Umuahia. The High Court allowed their appeal, set aside their convictions and sentence and acquitted and discharged them. Being dissatisfied with the judgment of the High Court, the appellant appealed to the Court of Appeal which in determining the appeal considered the provisions of section 23 of the Criminal Code Laws of Eastern Nigeria, 1963, which provides:

> 23. A person is not criminally responsible, as for an offence relating to property, for an act done or omitted to be done by him with respect to any property in the exercise of an honest claim or right and without intention to defraud.

The Court of Appeal, Port Harcourt Division held that, under section 23 of the Criminal Code, where the owner of the land on which the property allegedly stolen is situated is not ascertainable or ascertained or there are rival claims to the land, one of the claimants cannot be validly prosecuted for stealing property situate on the disputed land. The court held further that in such a case, the defence of *bona fide* claim of right will avail any of the claimants charged with stealing on the land. Per Katsina-Alu, J.C.A. (as he then was) who presided and delivered the lead judgment stated:

> in effect, the learned trial Chief Magistrate held that the rest of the area not verged yellow was no man's land. Although the Supreme Court did not award this area to either party, it is manifest from the record both parties still laid claim to it. It is also in evidence that both parties had a palm plantation in the area...it is for this reason that I agree with the learned counsel for the respondents and the learned judge that a defence of *bona fide* claim of right under section 23 of the Criminal Code availed the respondents.

Similarly, in *Uzoka* v. *The Federal Republic of Nigeria*,[33] it was held that by virtue of section 23 of the Criminal Code, a claim of right made in good faith is a defence to all offences relating to property. An accused will not be held criminally liable so long as he asserts that he honestly believed he had a lawful claim of right even though it might be unfounded in law or in fact. Once it is shown that an accused has a *bona fide* claim of right, the required *mens rea* is negatived.[34]

It is here asserted that although the right need not actually exist, but the mistaken belief must be that a right exists at the time of the act or omission in question. It is not enough that an accused person believes at the time that he may acquire a right in future. Most importantly, it should be stressed that the provision of section 23 of the Criminal Code which affords a defence of *bona fide* claim of right only applies to a person who acted or omitted to act in respect of the property if he has done so or omitted to do so in good faith. Consequently, the defence can only assist an innocent person. However, the innocent person must satisfy the following for him to be entitled or enjoy the defence:

i. the claim must be a lawful one; and
ii. the person must have acted honestly and innocently without any malice or ulterior motive.

In *Apamadari & Anor* v. *The State*,[35] it was held that when a person merely acted as a thug or supported in the damaging of a property at the request of another claiming ownership of the property, the defence of *bona fide* claim of right will not avail the thug or supporter since he is not claiming ownership or right over the damaged property. But in *Adegoju* v. *Lemono*,[36] the appellant was charged with stealing a talking-drum used by his

---

[33] (2010) 2 NWLR (pt. 1177) 123
[34] See also the decision in *Nwakire* v. *Commissioner of Police* (1992) 5 NWLR (pt 24) 289
[35] (1997) 3 NWLR (pt. 493) 289
[36] (1959) WRNLR 138

opponent in a chieftaincy dispute. The court held that the appellant was entitled to the defence of *bona fide* claim of right under section 23 of the Criminal Code because at the time he took the talking drum, he believed that he had an honest right to it. But in *State* v. *Okolo,*[37] the accused person was convicted of robbery because during the civil war he had used the services of armed soldiers to demand from a chief money due to the accused from an oil company which had been paid to the chief. The court held that the accused may be legally entitled to the property and he may also feel satisfied that his demand is honest but when the demand is accompanied by the use of some violence or threat to life, the law negatives the legality of what may be a legitimate right in the property claimed.

The submissions of Okonkwo appear to be right when he stated that such decisions are wrong. He contended that section 23 does not require that the conduct of the claimant should be lawful.

A person who under false pretence makes a claim of right to a property would not be availed of the defence of *bona fide* claim of right. In *Uzoka* v. *FRN (supra)* it was held that false pretence is the crime of knowingly obtaining title to another's personal property by misrepresenting a fact with intent to deceive. And by the express provisions of section 23 of the Advance Fee Fraud and Other Fraud Related Offences Decree No. 13 of 1995,[38] false pretence is a representation, whether deliberate or reckless, made by word, in writing or by conduct of matter of fact or law either past or present which representation is false in fact or law and which the person making it knows to be false or does not believe to be true.

---

[37] Unreported case No. UHC/15C/70, cited in Okonkwo & Naish at 111
[38] Now Cap. A6. Laws of the Federation of Nigeria 2004

IMMATURITY

The defence of immaturity is governed by the provisions of section 30 of the Criminal Code.[39] However, under section 30 of the Criminal Code, three categories of persons are classified as immature for the purpose of criminal responsibility: The section which contains three paragraphs provides thus:

> 30. A person under the age of seven years is not criminally responsible for any act or omission.

A person under the age of twelve is not criminally responsible for an act or omission, unless it is proved that at the time of doing the act or making the omission he had capacity to know that he ought not to do the act or make the omission.

A male person under the age of twelve years is presumed to be incapable of having carnal knowledge.[40]

However, section 2 of the Children and Young Persons Act, defines young persons to mean a person who has attained the age of fourteen years and is under the age of seventeen years. This position of the law has been given judicial approval in the case of *Ugheneyovwe* v. *The State,*[41] where the court held that by virtue of section 2(1) of the Criminal Procedure Laws of Bendel State, a child is any person who has not attained the age of fourteen years.

In England, the law absolves infants under the age of 10 years from responsibility for what would otherwise be criminal acts or omissions. What is being argued is that a child under the age of ten years is irrebuttably presumed incapable of criminal fault, irrespective of whether or not the *actus reus* was committed under the relevant *mens rea*. A child is said to be

---

[39] It should stated that similar provisions can be found in section 5 of the Penal Code applicable to the northern part of Nigeria.

[40] Section 50 of the Penal Code is not much different from the provisions of section 30 of the Criminal Code.

[41] (2004) 12 NWLR (pt 888) at 631

doli incapax. Although, a child under the age of ten years will be absolved of all criminal responsibility for his actions, however civil proceedings may be commenced by the Local Authority under section 31 of the Children Act (CA), 1989, if as a result of his behaviour, the relevant sections of the CA 1989 are satisfied. The defence of immaturity is not based on the *absence* of the *mental capacity* to commit an offence. The policy appears to be that children *cannot distinguish* between (moral) rights and wrong.

In Scotland, however, normal criminal liability starts from the age of eight years, and while commenting in the case of *C* v. *DPP*,[42] Lord Jauncey of Tullichettle said:

> I do not understand that injustice is considered to have resulted from this situation.

And in *Watters* v. *Lunt*,[43] a seven-year-old boy passed on to his parents a tricycle which he had stolen. It was held that they could not be found guilty of handling stolen goods as the goods could not in law be regarded as being stolen. Consequently, under the English Children and Young Persons Act of 1933,[44] a child cannot be convicted of any offence. However, under section 16 of the same Act, such person may be subject to care proceedings in the youth court. Again, if an adult encourages a child to commit a crime and the child does perform the *actus reus*, the child is the innocent agent and the adult is deemed to be the principal offender.

CHILDREN ABOVE THE AGE OF TEN YEARS

The presumption that a child cannot form the requisite *mens rea* of an offence in order to attract criminal sanction has been

---

[42] (1995) 2 All ER 43, p. 45

[43] (1951) 2 AL ER 645

[44] See section 50, as amended by the Act of 1963

rebutted.[45] Today, the laws in England and Wales impose criminal liability on children aged ten years and above in the same manner it imposes criminal liability on adults. Accordingly, in the English statute on children above ten years, "the rebuttable presumption of criminal law that a child aged 10 or over is incapable of committing an offence is hereby abolished."[46] Consequently, the presumption is rebutted by the prosecution showing that the accused had a mischievous discretion. That is, the child knew that what he was doing was morally or seriously wrong.[47]

Furthermore, the move towards criminalisation of younger defendants can also be found in section 1 of the Criminal Justice Act of 1993 which abolished the longstanding presumption that a boy under 14 years of age could not be convicted of serious offence of rape.

In addition, the English Home Office's consultation paper[48] proposed to abolish the presumption, citing the following reasons:

a. a child over ten years can distinguish right from wrong in an age of universal compulsory education;
b. such a child no longer needs protection from state punishment because the court has many sentencing options;
c. the presumption was illogical in that it could be rebutted by showing that the accused was of normal mental development for a child of that age, yet it was presumed that the accuse did not know right from wrong;
d. the interests of justice and the victim are not served by not convicting children;

---

[45] The English Law on Crime and Disorder Act 1998
[46] Section 34 of the Crime and Disorder Act 1998
[47] See the White Paper on Crime Justice and Protecting the Public, CM 965 1990
[48] Tackling Youth Crime, 1997

e. discontinuance of prosecution is not in the young offender's interest if it means that the opportunity is missed to take appropriate action to prevent re-offending; and
f. justice is best served by allowing courts to take account of the child's age and maturity at the point of sentence, not by binding them to presume that normal children are incapable of the most basic moral judgments.

The Nigerian courts appear to have supported this abolition when it was held in *Audu* v. *the State*[49] that by the combined provisions of sections 272(1) and 303(1) of the Criminal Procedure Code, where a person is convicted of an offence punishable with death and it appears to the court by which he is convicted that he was under the age of seventeen when he committed the offence, the court shall order that he be detained during the Governor's pleasure and if the court so orders, he shall be detained in such place and under such conditions as the Governor may direct and whilst so detained, shall be deemed to be in legal custody.

Now, the general view is that the criminal liability of children aged 10 years and above is now assimilated with that of older people. But Walker N[50] sees things differently. He argued that while the presumption is abolished, children can still have a defence if they can show that they do not know that what they did was serious wrong.[51] However, in *T's case,*[52] the court rejected *CPS* v. *P,* holding that section 34 of the Crime and Disorder Act, 1998 abolished not just the rebuttable presumption of incapacity but the whole concept that a child aged 10-13 inclusive could not be guilty of any crime. In *T* v. *UK,*[53] the applicant sought to argue that the imposition of

---

[49] (2003) 7 NWLR (pt. 820) at 533
[50] See Walker, N. "The End of an Old Song" (1999) 149 NLJ 64
[51] Ibid.
[52] See the case of *Crown Prosecution Service* v. *P* (2007) EWHC 946
[53] (2000) Crim LR 187

liability for murder on defendants as young as 10 years or 11 years of age amounted to a violation of Article 3 of the European Convention on Human Rights. This argument was rejected by the court. The court further held that there was no common standard amongst the member states of the Council of Europe as to the minimum age of criminal responsibility. It is therefore opined that any child charged with any criminal offence should be dealt with in a manner which takes full account of his age, level of maturity and intellectual and emotional capacities, and that steps should equally be taken to promote and enhance his ability to understand and participate in the proceedings

INSANITY

Insanity is a defence to criminal liability. However, it must be proved that at the time of the commission of the alleged offence, the accused person was, in fact, insane, a condition which deprives him of knowing what he was doing. This is necessary because, under the law, every person is presumed to be sane, until the contrary is proved.[54]

The defence of insanity is provided for under the provisions of section 28 of the Criminal Code thus:

> 28. A person is not criminally responsible for an act or omission if at the time of doing the act or making the omission he is in such a state of mental disease or natural mental infirmity as to deprive him of capacity to understand what he is doing, or of capacity to control his actions, or of capacity to know that he ought not to do the act or make the omission.[55]

---

[54] See section 27 of the Criminal Code.

[55] Similar provisions can be found in section 51 of the Penal Code.

In *Ejinima* v. *The State*,[56] the Supreme Court held that by virtue of the provisions of section 27 of the Criminal Code, there is a presumption that every person is of sound mind and to have been of sound mind at any time which covers the period in question until the contrary is proved. The defence of insanity can only avail the accused person if he can show that he was insane at the time he committed the act. Consequently, the onus to overcome the presumption that every man is sane and accountable for his action rests on the accused person. It is not for the prosecution to disprove insanity where the accused has not adduced evidence of insanity. It should only prove sanity in reply to evidence of insanity proffered by the defence and not as part of its case. Meanwhile, proof of insanity can, however, be established from compelling evidence of eye witnesses, particularly relatives of the accused relating to his general behaviour before, during and after the incident.

Under the provisions of section 28 of the Criminal Code, proof of either mental disease or natural mental infirmity and not both will suffice as precondition for the requisite mental state. This is because the word 'or' separating either mental disease or natural mental infirmity puts the two requirements in the alternative. However, the best way of establishing the defence of insanity is by medical evidence. The problem of relying on the evidence of relatives only without medical report or evidence is that there are certain traits in human beings, to varying degrees, which are sometimes mistaken for insanity. Some of them are irascibility, irritability, eccentricity and quarrelsomeness. It should, therefore, be pointed out that persons afflicted with any of these traits to a high degree are easily spurred to violence and wrongly regarded as being insane by the uniformed.

---

[56] (1991) 6 NWLR (pt 200) 627.

In *R* v. *Podola*,[57] the accused had been indicted for murder. He claimed that he was unfit to plead owing to loss of memory of events prior to and at the time of the alleged homicide. The jury found that his memory loss was not genuine and he was eventually found guilty of murder.

Section 2 of the English Criminal Lunatics Act (CLA) 1800 provides to the effect that:

> ...if any person indicted for any offence shall be insane and shall upon arraignment be found so to be by a jury lawfully empanelled for that purpose so that such person cannot be tried upon such indictment...

It should, however, be noted that the principle governing insanity was laid down in *R* v. *M'Naghten*.[58] In that case, the accused believing he was being persecuted by the Tories, fired his gun at the Prime Minister, Peel, but killed Peel's secretary, Edward Drumond. Medical report showed that M'Naghten was suffering from morbid delusions which might have affected his perceptions of right and wrong. He was found not guilty by reason of insanity. And when the case came up at the House of Lords, Tindal CJ had this to say:

> the Jurors ought to be told in all cases that every man is presumed to be sane and to possess a sufficient degree of reason to be responsible for his crimes, until the contrary is proved to their satisfaction, and that to establish a defence on the grounds of insanity, it must clearly be proved that accused was labouring under such a defect of reason from disease of the mind as not to know the nature and quality of the act he was doing, or if he did know it, he did not know he was doing what was wrong.

---

[57] (1960) 1 QB 325.
[58] (1843) All ER Rep. 229.

In *Guobadia* v. *The State*,[59] it was held that it is not every form of mental disorder that can relieve an accused person from criminal responsibility. Before a mental disorder can avail an accused person as a defence, it must fall within the statutory provision of the Criminal Law. In *R* v. *Windle*,[60] the accused person had killed his wife by giving her a fatal dose of aspirin tablets. The report indicates that his wife was some 18 years older than her husband and that she was probably certifiably insane and constantly talked about committing suicide. Her husband endured a miserable existence until he decided to kill her. The statement indicated that he knew his actions were contrary to law. He raised insanity as a defence, but Delvin J at Birmingham Assizes had withdrawn it from the jury. The Court of Criminal Appeal held that he was correct to do so. Lord Goddard CJ puts it succinctly thus:

> the question...in all cases is one of responsibility. A man may be suffering from a defect of reason, but, if he knows that what is doing is wrong and by 'wrong' I mean contrary to law he is responsible.

INSANE DELUSION

The *Black's Law Dictionary* defines insane delusion to mean a conception of a disordered mind which imagines facts to exist of which there is no evidence and belief in which is adhered to against all evidence and arguments to the contrary and which cannot be accounted for on any reasonable hypothesis. The second paragraph of section 28 of the Criminal Code gives credence to the situation of insane delusion, provides in part:

> A person whose mind, at the time of doing or omitting to do an act, is affected by delusions on some specific matter or matters, but who is not

[59] (2004) 6 NWLR (Pt. 869) 360.
[60] (1952) 2 QB 826.

> otherwise entitled to the benefit of the foregoing provisions of this section, is criminally responsible for the act or omission to the same extent as if the real state of things had been such as he was induced by the delusions to believe to exist.

This was carefully examined in the case of *Akhidime* v. *The State.*[61] In that case, the appellant killed his brother stating that he had acted in a dream state, in the belief that he was defending himself from people beating him around and asking him to leave the house. It was held that an insane delusion is a belief based on the figment of the accused person's imagination for which there is no reasonable foundation and which is ordinarily incredible to a sane person. In a defence based on delusions, the court is not dealing with reality. It is dealing with an imaginary state, a state of fantasy, a state of mistaken belief.

The American Model Penal Code provides:

> A person is not responsible for criminal conduct if at the time of such conduct, as a result of mental disease or defect, he lacks substantial capacity either to appreciate the criminality of his conducts or to conform his conducts to requirements of laws.

And in *R* v. *Kemp,*[62] Devlin J held that the law is not concerned with the brain, but with the mind in the sense that the mind is ordinarily used. In my judgement, the condition of the brain is irrelevant and so is the question whether the condition of the mind is curable or incurable, transitory or permanent.

---

[61] (1984) NSCC 588.

[62] (1957) 1 Q.B. 399.

DISEASE OF THE MIND

The disease of the mind has been said to be any mental disorder which has manifested itself in violence and is prone to recur.[63] It would, however, be strange that insanity should be restricted to violence and the courts have not restricted it. In *R* v. *Falconer,*[64] the High Court of Australia held that a temporary mental disorder had to be prone to recur if it was to be classified as a disease of the mind. The likelihood of recurrence showed an underlying pathological infirmity. The law on insanity was laid down in 1843 by the House of Lords. According to the House of Lords in *R* v. *Sullivan,*[65] it is not necessary to go further back. Lord Diplock in that case said that the law on insanity was to protect society against recurrence of the dangerous conduct. It was said in *DPP* v. *H*[66] by the Divisional Court that insanity is available in magistrate court only if the offence is one of *mens rea*.

Lord Diplock noted that it might seem harsh to call epilepsy insane, but to him, any reform was for Parliament. But in *Sullivan supra*, the accused kicked a friend's head and body while he was recovering from an epileptic fit. The House of Lords held that despite his state of mind being temporary, he was insane. His defence was not automatism because the cause of his mental aberration was not external, but internal.

INTOXICATION

The term 'intoxication' means a situation where by reason of taking intoxicants, an individual does not have the normal use of his physical or mental faculties, thus rendering him incapable of acting in the manner in which an ordinary prudent and cautious man, in full possession of his faculties using

---

63 See *Bratty* v. *Attorney-General for Northern Ireland* (1963) AC 386.
64 (1990) 65 ALJR 20.
65 (1984) AC 156.
66 (1997) 1 WLR 1406.

reasonable care, would act under like conditions.[67] Intoxication could also mean the disturbance of mental or physical capacities results from the introduction of substance into the body.[68] An intoxicant is a substance, such as alcohol, that produces false feelings of pleasure and a lack of control.

The law governing intoxication can be found in section 29(1)-(5) of the Criminal Code and section 52 of the Penal Code. It is an area of the law where legal scholars and judges have expressed divergent views over the years, as to whether or not intoxication should avail an accused person as a defence to criminal responsibility. Intoxication could be said to be both illegal as well as immoral dilemma. In the case of *Reniger* v. *Fogossa*,[69] the Exchequer Chamber stated that if a person that is drunk kills another, this shall be felony and he shall be hanged for it and yet he did it through ignorance, for when he was drunk, he had no understanding or memory. But in as much as that ignorance was occasioned by his own act and failing, and he might have avoided it, he shall not be privileged thereby.

Aristotle and Coke were of the opinion that an intoxicated offender should serve a double punishment because he has committed two offences. First, for being drunk to the evil examples to others. And second, for committing the actual crime in question. Under the Common Law, intoxication was not generally accepted as a defence to a criminal charge. Intoxication shall not be a defence to any criminal charge save as provided by law.[70] What is said in a court of law to prove that a person did not commit a crime, it is the act of presenting this argument in a court of law.[71] It could also mean the evidence offered by an accused to defeat a criminal charge.

---

[67] *Black Law Dictionary* 9th edn.

[68] Model Penal Code Section 208.

[69] (1551) 75 E.R I.

[70] Section 29(1) of the Criminal Code.

[71] *Oxford Advanced Learners Dictionary* 6th edn.

Intoxication is not an excuse because a drunken man is legally not better that a sober man and he is also not worse off. Intoxication may include the state of mind induced by narcotics and drugs.[72] The defence of intoxication poses something of a problem for the law. While looking at intoxication as no excuse to the law, it could be argued, on the other hand, that intoxicated people are not in full control of themselves, and do not think rationally and as such should not be held liable for their actions as when they know exactly what they are doing.

Moreover, there are obvious reasons for not allowing people to use intoxication as an excuse for their criminal behaviour or conducts, particularly crimes of violence against the person of another, as a result of intoxication. It has been noted that intoxication will provide a defence only when it negatives the required *mens rea*, and even here the defence is severally restricted. We can say that where the effect of intoxication is simply to remove the inhibitions, it will be no defence, an intoxicated or drugged intent is still an intent. The defendant will have a defence in the circumstance only if he can bring himself within a defence such as diminished responsibility.[73] If the defendant actually had the *mens rea* of the crime, then intoxication would not be a defence. This was made very clear by the House of Lords in the case of *R* v. *Kingston,*[74] overturning an unexpected decision in the case by the Court of Appeal. The defendant was attracted to young boys, but normally managed to control these tendencies and prevent himself from acting on them. Unfortunately, his business associates decided to set him up so that he could be photographed in a compromising situation with a young boy, which could then be used to blackmail him. The defendant was invited with a 15-year-old boy to a flat, where their drinks were laced with drugs. When

---

[72] Section 29 (5) Criminal Code.

[73] This defence may be open a drug addict or alcohol, but not to someone who is simply drunk.

[74] (1995) 2 A C 355.

they were both intoxicated, the defendant indecently assaulted the child. Kingston admitted that at the time of committing the assault he intended it, but argued he would not have committed the offence if he had been sober. The House of Lords held that an intoxicated intent was still an intent, and the fact that the intoxication was not voluntary made no difference to that. He had the *mens rea*, and so intoxication was no defence and he was liable.

It has also been stated that even where intoxication means that the accused lacks the *mens rea* of a crime, in some circumstances they can still be found liable, forming an exception to the rule that both *mens rea* and *actus reus* are required. In this respect, the court distinguishes between crime of basic intent and crimes of specific intent. Intoxication will usually be a defence to crimes of specific intents where by the defendant lacked *mens rea*, but not usually to crimes of basic intent.[75]

Intoxication is divided into two. They are voluntary and involuntary intoxication this division would enable us look at those cases in which the defendant has been held responsible and situations where the defendant cannot be blamed for his state of intoxication.

Voluntary Intoxication

This type of intoxication is self-induced. Voluntary intoxication, whether under the Criminal Code, Penal Code or the Common Law, is not a defence. Section 44 of the Penal Code provides that who does an act in a state of intoxication is presumed to have the same knowledge as he would have had if he had not been intoxicated. In the case of *Chukuwa* v. *the Queen*,[76] the appellant murdered his wife by stabbing. Before the incident, he had been drinking for nearly one and half days. Shortly

---

[75] (1977) Act 433

[76] See the case of *DPP* v. *Majewisk* (1977) AC, 433

before he started drinking, he had a dispute with his wife because he suspected her of having committed adultery. The court rejected his defence that excessive alcohol made him insane and convicted him of murder.

However, under the Criminal Code, voluntary intoxication is a defence to any criminal charge if by reason thereof the person charged at the time of the act or omission complained of did not know that such act or omission was wrong or did not know what he was doing[77] and the person charged was by reason of intoxication insane temporarily or otherwise, at the time of such act or omission.[78] For this defence to be available to an accused person, therefore, the state of intoxication must be proved to amount to temporary insanity and the burden of proof is on the accused person. In *D.P.P* v. *Beard*,[79] the court held that evidence of drunkenness which renders the accused incapable of forming the specific intention essential to constitute the crime should be taken into consideration with other facts proved in order to determine whether or not he has this intention. In that case, the accused was charged with the murder of a thirteen-year-old girl. His defence was that he was drunk. He was convicted of murder.

Similarly, in the case of *R.* v. *Hansen Owarey,*[80] the appellant and the deceased were co-workers in a mining company in Sokoto. They had minor misunderstanding while in their manager's office, the manager intervened and settled the matter. Now, the appellant said he was going to rest at home and he came back and shot the deceased to death and pleaded intoxication and provocation. His defence were rejected. Also, in *R.* v. *Chapman*[81] the man who stole boots in a shop after having an intelligent discussion with the shop owner was

[77] See Section 29 (2) of the Criminal Code.
[78] See Section 29 (2)(b) of the Criminal Code.
[79] (1920) AC 479.
[80] (1939) 5 W.A C. A 66.
[81] (1910) 4 Cr App. R. 276.

refused the defence of intoxication. It has also been stated that if evidence showed that a theft was not due to intoxication, being drunk will not avail as a defence.

Voluntary intoxication results from the intentional taking of drink or a drunk knowing that it is capable in sufficient quantity of having an intoxicating effect. Voluntary intoxication can at best afford a defence only if it negatives the *mens rea* required of the offence. It can be no defence if it causes the accused to form the necessary *mens rea* nor if it simply removes his inhibitions. In *R.* v. *Prince,*[82] the court held that the accused's honest and reasonable belief that the girl he abducted was 19 years of age was no defence.

Also, if a person, while sane and sober, forms an intention to kill, and then gets himself intoxicated so as to give himself 'Dutch courage' to do the killing, and while drunk carries out his intention, he cannot rely on his self-induced drunkenness as a defence to a charge of murder. This was the position of the court in the case of *Attorney-General for Northern Ireland* v. *Gallagher.*[83] In that case, a man was charged with the murder of his wife. The man, after forming the intention to kill his wife, went and bought a knife and a bottle of whisky. On the same day, he killed his wife with the knife and consumed a considerable quantity of the whisky. He pleaded insanity and drunkenness of such a degree that he was incapable of forming the intent necessary for murder. The court, however, did not accept his defence as he was convicted.

From all said and done, it could rightly be inferred that voluntary intoxication is not a defence to any criminal responsibility or charge. And would not avail an accused as a defence. Judges and juries have in a number cases examined the word "voluntary" as an intention to bring about an act and therefore should not be taken as an excuse to any criminal

---

[82] (1875) L.R 2 CC 154.
[83] (1961) 3 All ER 299.

liability. This was the view expressed in the case of *Kofi Mensah* v. *The Queen.*[84] In that case, the appellant was co-habiting with the deceased and anxious to marry her but disappointed in his hopes, took a gin and later that day invited her to go with him to a place to gather mushrooms. On the way, he drank some palm wine at her uncle's farm. His evidence was that at the place where the mushrooms were, the drink began to affect him and thereafter he had no recollection of what happened until the moment he found himself beside her covered in blood. The deceased died of gunshot wounds. The court held that the appellant took the woman out in order to kill her and that the defence of drunkenness could not be considered and the appellant was convicted of murder.

Therefore, the position of the court seems clear that voluntary intoxication is not a defence to a criminal charge.

Involuntary Intoxication

This is an area of intoxication where the courts have taken a very sympathetic view of the accused who has become involuntarily intoxicated. That is, where the accused state of intoxication was not caused by him (the accused himself) but by the tricks of another.

The law governing involuntary intoxication can be found in section 29 (2) (a) of the Criminal Code and section 52 Penal Code.

Section 29 (2) (a) of the Criminal Code provides that:

> The state of intoxication is caused without his consent by the malicious or negligent act of another person.

---

[84] (1952) WACA 174 (March 31) Vol. viv

For the defence of involuntary intoxication to avail an accused under the Criminal Code, therefore, he must prove disability and to show that:

i. the state of intoxication was caused without his consent; and
ii. that it was caused by the malicious or negligent act of another person.

It therefore means that for intoxication to be regarded as involuntary, the intoxicant must be given or administered by another person. The above have to be proved because the general rule in Nigeria is that it is not a defence for an accused person to plead that he acted in the state of intoxication.

Section 52 of the Penal Code on its part provides that:

> Nothing is an offence which is done by a person who at the time of doing it is by reason of intoxication caused by something administered to him without his knowledge or against his will, incapable of knowing the nature of the act or that he is doing what is either wrong or contrary to law.

It must be emphasised, therefore, that for the defence of involuntary intoxication to stand as a defence, which an accused person could rely on for any criminal charge or responsibility under the Penal Code, he must prove that:

i. he did not know what he was doing;
ii. he could not differentiate right from wrong (whether morally wrong or contrary to law);
iii. the intoxication must have been administered to him by another person.

However, the burden of proving intoxication under the law is on the accused person and not prosecution.

The position of the law is that if the drunken state of an accused is occasioned by the tricks of another, he will have a defence to any criminal charge. This view was expressed in *Pearson" case*[85] where Park B. said, "if a person is made drunk by the stratagem or the fraud of another, he is not responsible." It has also been argued that if the state of intoxication of an accused person was occasioned by the prescription from a doctor who has failed to warn him of the side effects, especially the effect of consuming any alcohol in conjunction with the drugs,[86] he would be treated as being involuntarily intoxicated and as such he would have a defence to any criminal charge. In the case of *R.* v. *Quick & Paddision,*[87] it was stated intoxication is a defence where the substance is taken in pursuance of medical treatment.

If, on the other hand, a person who thought he was drinking only orange juice but which had, in fact, been spiked with quantities of vodka (alcoholic drink), would not be regarded as being voluntarily intoxicated and would have a defence that his resultant state of intoxication or mind warranted, on ordinary principles, that he lacked the *mens rea.*

The state of intoxication of an accused person could be caused by alcohol or drugs or a combination of both where the accused has taken drugs that normally have a soporific (producing sleep) effect, making the user relaxed or sleepy, he will be treated as involuntarily intoxicated. In *Hardie* (1985), the accused had been living with a woman at her flat, but the relationship broke down and she wanted him to leave. Very upset, the accused tried to calm his nerves by taking valium, a tranquilliser which had been prescribed for the woman. He then started a fire in a bedroom, while the woman and her daughter were in the living-room. He was prosecuted for damaging with

---

[85] (18.35) 168 E.R 1108.

[86] See *R* .v. *Bailey* (1983) I.W.LR 760.

[87] (1973) 3. W.L.R.26.

intent to endanger life of another or being reckless whether life would be endangered, contrary to Section 1(2) of the Criminal Damage Act 1971. On an appeal, the Court of Appeal confirmed that, as a general rule, self-induced intoxication from alcohol or a dangerous drug would not be a defence to ordinary crimes involving recklessness, since the taking of the alcohol or drug was itself reckless behaviour. However, the court stated that where the normal effect of a drug was merely sedative (tending to calm the nerves and reduce stress) different rules apply. The issue, according to the court, was whether the taking of valium had itself been reckless, taking into account the fact that the drug was not unlawful in prescribed quantities, that the accused did not know the drug was likely to make him behave as he did, that he had been told it would do him no harm, and that the normal effect of the drug was soporific or sedative. It was held that Hardie had a defence. That is, he was found not guilty.

Suffice it to note that if the state of intoxication is treated as involuntary, it would avail the accused person as a defence to any criminal responsibility.

MISTAKE

Mistake may be raised as a possible defence by an accused person. However, mistake is divided into two. These are mistake of law and mistake of facts. The general rule is that if the accused person makes a mistake of law, he is guilty, whereas, he may not be so guilty if he makes a mistake of facts.

The above argument is well articulated in section 25 of the Criminal Code thus:

> 25. A person who does or omits to do an act under an honest and reasonable, but mistaken belief in the existence of any state of things, is not criminally responsible for the act or omission to any greater

extent than if the real state of things had been such as he believed to exist.

The operation of this rule may be excluded by the express or implied provisions of the law relating to the subject.

What is being stressed is that, for a mistake to avail an accused person as a defence, the mistake must be a mistaken belief in the existence of any state of things. Noting that mistakes of law are irrelevant because ignorance of the law does not afford any excuse for any act or omission which would otherwise constitute an offence, unless knowledge of the law by the offender is expressly declared to be an element of the offence.[88]

In *Aiguokhian* v. *The State,*[89] it was held that where an accused person acted under an honest and reasonable belief in a given state of situation which, if true, would have justified the act, he may set up such credible defence of mistake. But the story must be true or capable of being believed and not an insult to intelligence. Also, there may be a relief from criminal liability or guilt unless the mistake arose from lack of proper care expected from a reasonable man of average intelligence.

Mistake of Law

Mistake of law is generally thought not to provide a defence to a criminal charge. This is often expressed in terms that an individual is always presumed to know the law. In reality, it means that no individual can be excused liability for his criminal act on the basis of his ignorance of the law. As with all such truisms, there are exceptions. A defendant may be found to be criminally insane because he does not realise that his actions are unlawful. Furthermore, a defendant might escape criminal liability because he makes a mIstake of civil law, typically in the

---

[88] See section 22 of the Criminal Code.

[89] (2004) 7 NWLR (Pt. 873) 565.

areas of theft or criminal damage, where the defendant honestly believed that the property he appropriated or damaged was actually his own. Beyond such exceptions, however, the courts are understandably reluctant to recognise errors of law as providing any form of defence to a criminal charge. In *R* v. *Lee,*[90] the defendant was convicted of assault with intent to resist lawful apprehension contrary to section 38 of the Offences Against the Person Act (OAPA) 1861. He appealed on the basis that the trial judge should have directed the jury that they should acquit, if the defendant had honestly albeit mistakenly believed that there were no lawful grounds for his arrest. The Court of Appeal refused to imply any requirement into section 38 to the effect that the prosecution had to prove the defendant knew or believed the apprehension to be lawful. The result was that a defendant could rely on a mistake of fact but could not rely on a mistake of law.

As stated earlier, the rule is that ignorance of the law is no defence is supported by the arguments that if it were a defence, the floodgates would open and the courts would be swamped by bogus claims of ignorance, people would not try and find out what the law is. Floodgates is a weak argument against justice and it would be impossible for the prosecution to show that the accused was truly ignorant of the law. However, it has be said that no person could know all possible offences, and it may well be unjust to convict a person when only a few people would know of the crime. There is no defence if the accused consulted a lawyer who stated that their activity was not a crime, where in fact, it was. In *Shaw* v. *DPP,*[91] the defendants wanted to know whether publishing a list of prostitutes and their services, the Ladies Directory, was lawful. The House of Lords held that they were guilty of conspiracy despite the legal advice that they had been given.

---

[90] (2000) NLJ 1491.
[91] (1962) AC 22 (HL).

Again, it has been held that reliance on local authority, or policy advice is also no defence to the criminal responsibility resulting from mistake. In *Cambridgeshire & Isle of Ely CC* v. *Rust,*[92] the English Divisional Court directed magistrate to convict the accused on the crime of setting up a stall on a highway without lawful excuse, even though he had sought advice and had paid rates on the stall to the local council.

However, it can be argued that mistake of law should be a defence, if the accused person tried to find out the law or relied on official advice. He attempted to comply with the law, but failed. It is doubtful whether convicting him serves any purpose other than preventing bogus defences. At present, reliance on official advice does not exculpate, but only mitigates the sentence.[93] And in *Survey CC* v. *Battersby,*[94] the case involved a crime of undertaking childcare without informing the council that the children were to spend more than a month in the house. She had taken advice that she was not guilty of the offence because no one period extended beyond a month because the parents took the children away at certain weekends. She was held to be guilty. In the Maryland case of *Hopkins* v. *The State,*[95] reliance on the state attorney's advice was no defence. A writer has once observed:

> if we are seeking to achieve respect for law, it is surely unwise to tell citizens that they must disregard the considered advice of the public officials whose duty it is to administer the law and who may therefore be expected to tell the citizens in effect that the advice which they received *bona fide* from qualified lawyers is to be treated as worthless.[96]

---

[92] (1972) 2 QB 426.

[93] See the case of *Howell* v. *Falmouth Boat. Construction Co* (1951) AC 837.

[94] (1965) 2 QB 194 (DC).

[95] (1950) 69 a 2D 456.

[96] Brett P "Mistake of Law as a Criminal Defence (1966) 5 Melb ULR 179 t 203.

Mistake of Fact

In England, the law draws a sharp difference between mistake of law and mistake of act. It is postulated that mistake of fact is a defence because, as with some other defences, punishing the accused would not deter him.[97] In Ogbu v. *R.*,[98] one of the accused said at his trial that he did not know that it was contrary to law to pay a bribe in order to induce the other accused to appoint him as village headman and therefore tax-collector. The trial judge accepted this story and acquitted him. On appeal by the other accused person, although the Federal Supreme Court had no power to convict the first accused person, they remarked (*obiter*):

> ...we are not at present satisfied that the learned judge was right in law in acquitting Utachia Okobi on those findings, and that if the matter ever fell to be decided by this court, we should require cogent arguments to convince us that on a charge involving doing some act 'corruptly', ignorance of the law is no defence to a person who had an intent of a kind which the law regards as corrupt.

What is the existence of any state of things for the purpose of section 25 of the Criminal Code? Presumably, it means that at the time he committed the unlawful act, the accused person was mistaken as to certain material fact or facts then existing, e.g., mistake as to time.

SELF-DEFENCE

Self-defence is a defence of oneself or other persons whom one is under a duty to defend, against a wrongdoer in prevention of a forcible and violent felony.[99] A man is justified in using against an assailant, a proportionate amount of force in

---

[97] Bentham J., *An Introduction to the Principles of Morals and Legislation* (Methuen, 1982).
[98] (1959) N.R.N.L.R. 22.
[99] *Queen* v. *Adelodun* (1959) WRNLR 144.

defence of himself or other persons who he is under a duty to defend where he considers his life or such persons' lives to be in danger.[100]

Under section 32(3) of the Criminal Code, a defence is provided where the act committed by an accused person is reasonably necessary in order to resist actual and unlawful violence threatened to him or to another person in his presence. Consequently, when a person does or omits to do an act in order to save himself from immediate death or grievous harm threatened to be inflicted upon him by some persons actually present and in a position to execute the threats, and believing himself to be unable otherwise to escape the carrying of the threats into execution.[101] However, the harm threatened must be death or grievous harm, and it must be immediate. But, presumably, if it is not immediate, the person threatened has time to seek the protection of the authorities.

Again, section 33 of the 1999 Constitution of the Federal Republic of Nigeria allows a person to use such force as is reasonably necessary for the defence of any person from unlawful violence or for the defence of property.[102]

Therefore, a person is entitled to kill in the defence of his property provided the force used is reasonably necessary in the circumstances. The essence of this is that, self-defence is only available to an accused person if there is a reasonable apprehension of death or grievous harm and if the person who claims to have exercised that right had reasonable grounds for believing that the only way to protect himself from death or grievous harm was to kill his assailant.[103]

In *Okonkwo* v. *The State*,[104] the appellant and 3 others were charged with murder contrary to section 274 of the Criminal

---

[100] *State* v. *Agbo* (1973) 3 ESCLR (pt.1) 4.
[101] See section 32 (4) of the Criminal Code.
[102] *State* v. *Musa* (1993) 2 NWLR (pt. 277) 550.
[103] *Stephen* v. *The State* (1986) 5 NWLR (pt. 46) 978.
[104] (1998) 4 NWLR (pt. 544) 142.

Code of Anambra State. The case of the appellant was on the day in question he had been in the house of his in-laws where he was paying his dowry to take a wife home. He later left the in-laws' place and came home to take snuff to his in-laws. It was when he got home that he met the 1st accused fighting the deceased to recover a matchet from him. He asked what the matter was and he was told. He denied rushing headlong into the conflict to fight on the side if the 1st accused, his brother. At the end of the trial, the trial court found the appellant and the 1st accused guilty of murder and sentenced them to death by hanging. The appellant being dissatisfied appealed against the decision. In considering the appeal, the Court of Appeal considered the provision of section 45 of Anambra State Criminal Code which provides thus:

> 45. It is lawful for any person who is in peaceable possession of a dwelling house, and for any person to use such force as he believes, on reasonable grounds to be necessary in order to prevent the forcible breaking and entering of the dwelling house, either by night or day, by any person whom he believes, on reasonable grounds, to be attempting to break and enter the dwelling house with intent to commit a felony or misdemeanour therein.

It was held that a person will not be criminally responsible for the use of such force as is reasonably necessary for his preservation even though such force may result in death or grievous harm. Commenting on the case per Akpabio, J.C.A. stated as follows:

> In the instant case, it is undisputed that the deceased was found in the premises of the appellant and his brother at such an unholy hour as midnight or near it, with a dagger in his

> hand. He was reasonably suspected to have been there for an illegal purpose, and therefore apprehended and beaten up. From the medical report, nobody used a matchet or other weapon on the deceased, only fist blows were meted out to him. I therefore consider that the force used against the deceased was reasonably necessary in the circumstances...

Similarly, in *Akpobosa* v. *The State,*[105] it was held that a person who in the night finds another person in the act of committing a felony, is entitled to use such force as may be necessary to apprehend the felon, even to the extent of killing him in order to prevent his escape, but the force used must be justifiable in the particular circumstance of each case.

While disagreeing with the decision of the trial court in the case of *Okonkwo* v. *The State (supra),* the Court of Appeal held that a court of law must consider all the defences raised by an accused person, no matter how stupid they may appear. The court further held, while citing *Njoku* v. *The State,*[106] that in the instant case,[107] the statutory defences of "aiding in self-defence" and "aiding in defence of dwelling house" provided under sections 45 and 51 of the Criminal Code Law of Anambra State were not properly considered for the appellant by the trial court. Per Akpabio J.C.A. also, maintained this position in *Okonkwo* v. *The State* (*supra*) when he stated:

> It is my respectful view that it was natural and in fact commendable for the appellant to have gone in aid of his Junior brother (Gregory Okonkwo) immediately he came back, and was told (whether rightly or wrongly) that armed robbers invaded their house and that one of them was engaging in combat with his junior brother with a dagger. Under the circumstances the appellant was entitled to an acquittal and a discharge, and not to conviction and sentence.

---

[105] (1969) 1 All NLR 104.
[106] (1993) 6 NWLR (pt. 299) 272.
[107] *Okonkwo* v. *The State supra* note 43.

However, in *Audu* v. *The State*,[108] the court held that where a person who was attacked used a greater degree of force than was necessary in the circumstances and thereby caused the death of his assailant, the trial court is entitled, after considering all the evidence adduced, to reject the issue of self-defence raised by the accused and convict him of murder. In the instant case, the deceased was fighting with the appellant unarmed when the appellant drew his army jackknife and stabbed the deceased twice in the abdomen. In the circumstance, the defence of self-defence was not open to the appellant.[109] It should further be stressed that the plea of self-defence is not open to an abnormally nervous or excitable person because the defence is predicated on the reasonableness of the apprehension of death or grievous harm.[110]

In *Baridam* v. *The State*,[111] it was held that self-defence is a complete answer to a charge of murder or manslaughter. However, an accused can only rely on self-defence where he shows that his life was so much endangered by the act of the deceased and that the only option open to him to save his life was to kill the deceased. The accused must also show that he did not want to fight and that he was at all material times prepared to withdraw.

---

[108] (2003) 7 NWLR (Pt. 820) 530.

[109] See *Duru* v. *The State* (1993) 3 NWLR (pt 281) 283.

[110] See *Ahmed* v. *The State* (1999) 7 NWLR (pt. 612) 641.

[111] (1994-) 1 NWLR (pt 320) 250.

INDEX

www.ingramcontent.com/pod-product-compliance
Lightning Source LLC
Chambersburg PA
CBHW061353240926
51846CB00007B/1389
* 9 7 8 9 7 8 5 8 9 7 9 9 9 *